-2595-
$15
Travel
3/11

TIBETAN MARCHES

The Author

ANDRÉ MIGOT

TIBETAN MARCHES

TRANSLATED FROM THE FRENCH BY
PETER FLEMING

RUPERT HART-DAVIS
36 SOHO SQUARE LONDON WI
1955

Printed in Great Britain by Richard Clay and Co. Ltd.
Bungay, Suffolk

Contents

CONTENTS

Illustrations

7

Maps

(Drawn by K. C. Jordan)   *between pages 8–9*

Maps

✻

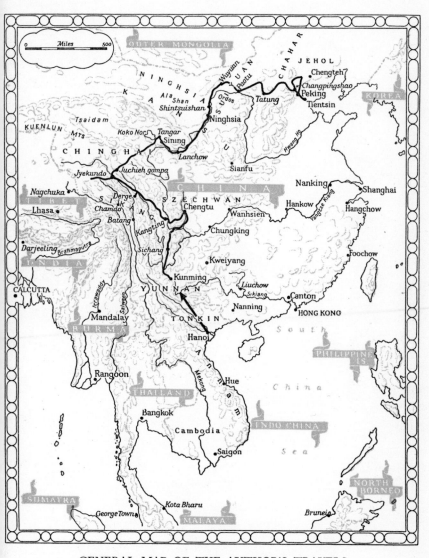

GENERAL MAP OF THE AUTHOR'S TRAVELS

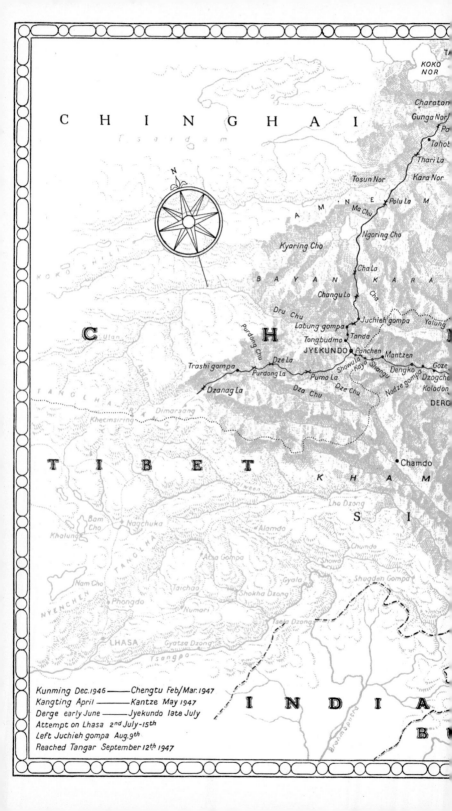

Introduction

IT is unlikely (but only because it is scarcely possible) that the Western traveller will ever be denied access to wider areas of the continent of Asia than he is today. By "traveller" I mean what the word means; I do not mean the fraternal delegate or the official guest who is privileged to spend an afternoon in a cotton-mill outside Tashkent or is given, from the aircraft which bears him from one cultural *gabfest* to the next, a glimpse of the Great Wall of China. These, though they may be classed as passengers, are really freight: as little masters of their destinies, as little able to see what is really going on, as little (almost) exposed to any risk as the dormice which country-bred children still occasionally transport in boxes with perforated lids and which are at intervals extracted, bemused and somnolent, to be admired and touched with a gingerly forefinger by their masters' comrades before being put back in their conveyances.

By the end of the nineteenth century man's questing spirit, backed by the knowledge and resources it had led him to acquire, had conquered almost all the physical obstacles and barriers which his planet had to offer. It was left to the twentieth century to throw up more artificial but more insurmountable barricades which quickly rendered obsolete and irrelevant such formerly useful items of equipment as curiosity, and courage, and the determination to go somewhere because you have a strong but not always completely explicable wish to go there.

It follows that contemporary accounts of journeys in remote parts of Asia, or anyhow of East and Central Asia, have virtually ceased to appear; and it will certainly be many years, perhaps even many decades, before a citizen of the

9

Free World penetrates the regions which Dr. Migot describes, vividly but with great fidelity, in this book.

He travelled, alone, the whole way up the mountainous border-land where Western China marches with Eastern Tibet. He had been charged, by the Ecole Française d'Extrème-Orient in Hanoï, with the task of carrying out research into various archæological and other aspects of the Buddhist religion, and during his journey was initiated with the prescribed rites into one of its sects. At one stage he was stripped by bandits of everything he possessed; at another, disguised as a mendicant lama, he attempted a clandestine digression to Lhasa and got a long way towards his objective before being arrested—apologetically, for they respected his piety—by the Tibetans. The northward limit of his journey was the great lake of Kokonor, and thence he travelled east, through Inner Mongolia, to Peking; in the environs of this city he and a female companion were arrested by the Communists, in whose custody they spent several arduous but instructive weeks among the Manchurian hills.

It would ill become a translator to praise a narrative in whose shaping he has had a hand; but it cannot be presumptuous to call attention to Dr. Migot's qualities as a traveller. The reader will not have gone very far before he realises that he is dealing with a man whose extraordinary powers of endurance are matched by his powers of observation. Like Heinrich Harrer, he became very fond of the Tibetans (whose language he both speaks and writes) and a streak of mysticism in his character enabled him to enter into the spiritual side of their life more fully, perhaps, than any Westerner has done before. The result is an unusually intimate and detailed picture of a society outwardly primitive and outlandish but based on values and traditions from which the West has much to learn.

Dr. Migot has had—and, I suspect, will continue to have—a varied life. He served in the First World War as medical officer to a battalion of infantry, being awarded the Croix de

Guerre. For ten years thereafter he carried out researches, both in the laboratory and at sea, into marine biology, in his spare time making a reputation as a mountaineer in the Alps and the Pyrenees. From 1925 to 1938 he practised medicine in France and then bicycled to India, where he continued the studies of Oriental religions which have always engrossed him. When war broke out he was posted to a military hospital at Dijon, and during the German occupation of France worked as a doctor in Paris. After the war he went to Indo-China, where the story of *Tibetan Marches* begins.

From Peking, where it ends in 1948, he travelled back across China to Eastern Tibet (the Communist armies were now completing the overthrow of the Nationalists, and his return journey was scarcely less exciting than that described in the pages which follow), and thence went back to his post in Indo-China. Returning to France for some leave, he incontinently signed on as doctor to a French scientific expedition to the Kerguelen Islands, spent two years in this uninhabited archipelago and early in 1954 was attached by the French Government to an Australian expedition in the same general region.

This brief summary suggests that Dr. Migot is a remarkable man; and I should be doing the reader a disservice if I delayed any further his opportunity of getting better acquainted with a traveller whose company I think he is almost bound to enjoy.

                                        PETER FLEMING

PART ONE

Into China

1. HANOI TO KUNMING

In Hanoi, on December 5th, 1946, you could smell the war which was to break out two weeks later: the atmosphere was charged with tension. The big town, once so gay and so serene with its miniature lakes, its parks, its broad, shady avenues, seemed to crouch under the threat of a catastrophe. There were few people in the streets, but much military activity, oddly unobtrusive in its manifestations. Though you could feel that the garrison's heart was beating faster than usual, you saw very few French soldiers. Barbed wire had gone up round the Vietnamese strong-points—little blockhouses where smart, well-equipped sentries stood on guard, rigid, motionless, alert. Every morning fresh trenches appeared, partitioning the town, cutting across the streets which led to the Annamite quarters. People watched each other, appraised each other. The flags of the opposing camps billowed in an impartial wind. But, apart from small local incidents, everything was calm; it was the lull before the storm.

I wanted to get to China before the storm broke—the great storm which had already claimed victims at Langson and Haiphong. Was I going to be able to? I had looked forward so long and so anxiously to the start of my journey to Tibet; was I now going to fall at the first fence? In 1939 I had made a solitary journey, lasting ten months, through France, Italy, Greece, Turkey, Irak, Persia, Afghanistan and India; and when I reached Calcutta I felt the irresistible attraction of Tibet, lying just ahead. It was only the steady approach of war which diverted me to Saigon. Duty called me back to France, and there my dreams of Tibet helped to keep me going through the tragic days of collapse and the dark years of the Occupation. In Paris, joyless and crushed

15

under the weight of defeat, the magic name had been for
me the glimmer of light glimpsed at the end of a sombre
tunnel which would one day lead to the great plains of
liberty. Asia kept a small flame alight in my soul. The
pervasive brutality and the stresses under which one lived
made me long all the more ardently to return to the calm,
gentle, scented territories of Buddhism.

In October 1945 I had, and took, the chance of going
back to Cambodia as a doctor attached to the Assistance
Médicale Indochinoise, and there, in the intervals of looking
after the lovable people of the province I was responsible
for, I was able to continue my studies of Buddhism. There
were plenty of stresses in Cambodia, too; but I managed—
and it took a bit of managing—to stick to my doctoring and
not to be caught up in the ubiquitous cross-currents of
hatred and the atmosphere of war. The call of Tibet was
as strong as ever; thinking of its high frozen plateaux, I
found the stifling heat of a Cambodian summer less
oppressive. At last, in December 1946, I found myself
entrusted with a mission of research into various aspects of
Buddhism in China and Tibet. I was overjoyed; but would
I, now, be able to get there? After endless palaver, I
managed to get a place on the plane from Hanoi to Kunming
(it was one of the last for a long time); and a few hours later,
after flying over the extraordinarily picturesque but at
present inaccessible highlands of Tonking, I was in the
capital of Yunnan.

It was delightful to be, at last, in China, to be surrounded
by friendly or, at worst, indifferent faces; in Hanoi they had
all been secretive and sulky, barely concealing their hostility.
It was delightful, too, to renew one's acquaintance with a
Chinese crowd, all dressed in dark blue cloth, animated,
noisy, packed, bustling—always the same crowd, whether it
happens to be in Cholon or Colombo or Singapore, in the
smallest Chinese village or the biggest Chinese city: a
totally different crowd from the Indian crowd, which may—

at Benares, for instance—comprise an even denser mass of humanity, but which is so extraordinarily quiet, so—almost—introspective. I was amazed by the innumerable tiny shops, their counters groaning under merchandise: piles of fruit and vegetables, cuts of fat pork, open-air kitchens, brightly coloured blinds, heaps of rich silks, of linen, of cloth, pyramids of shoes, of things to wear, of tinned milk, of patent medicines, of military uniforms, and other flotsam and jetsam from American army depots or UNRRA supply centres.

After a year in the sultry heat of Cambodia, I was agreeably surprised by the climate of Kunming. The nights were cold (the town stands some six thousand feet above sea-level); but by day the sun shone brightly in an impeccably blue sky. My journey as far as Kiating was to be blessed by this unforgettable Yunnanese sun, hot without being oppressive and never once masked by a cloud. The French consul, M. Bouffanais, showed me the sights of Kunming, a picturesque city whose mediæval walls, furnished with huge gates, enclose much that is old and curious; with him I explored the hilly countryside, where ancient, serene pagodas are hidden under groves of trees clinging to rocky cliffs above a great blue lake.

But it was time to tear myself away from this sheltered existence and to press on towards Sikang. The quickest way of getting there was obviously by the air-line to Chengtu; but I intensely dislike this method of locomotion, which would have allowed me to see none of the things I had come to look at. I was moreover in no particular hurry, and my purpose was, after all, to get to know China, to soak myself in her civilisation, her life, her religion, in all her infinite variety. There was only one way to do that—to take the road. Not the boring main road along which buses run to Kweiyang and Chungking, but the old, disused highway which goes through Lolo territory by way of Sichang and Fulin. I particularly wanted to have a look at the great

B

mountain bastion to the north of Kunming; it is very little known. Since no motorable road serves this region, I should have to follow the old caravan trail. Thanks to the good offices of the Catholic Mission, a party of Chinese merchants bound for Hweili agreed to take me with them. They hired me two ponies—one for my kit, the other to ride—and accepted responsibility for my bed and board in return for an extortionate price. Since I spoke only a few words of Chinese and knew absolutely nothing about the country through which we were to travel, these arrangements struck me at the time as being in the highest degree convenient and auspicious.

2. THE FIRST STAGE

WE left Kunming at dawn on December 18th and made our way through the dreary suburbs; in the little grey hovels the people were still asleep. I had looked forward for years to this moment—to the sharp joy which the start of a long journey, in the twilight before a perfect sunrise, can bring you. It was a moment which had always seemed unattainable.

As soon as we were clear of the city we took to the hills. The track, after surmounting the foothills, began to scale a succession of steep ridges; it became a sort of staircase cut out of the hard, bare, reddish earth. I was by now having trouble with my horse. The animal was equipped neither with a riding-saddle nor with stirrups. He had on his back a plain wooden pack-saddle, which—in order to soften its impact on my person if the horse stopped suddenly—I had padded with my bedding roll; my feet found some sort of toe-hold in the animal's neck-strap. To keep one's seat on top of this oscillating superstructure was far from easy; to take one's seat on it was even harder. At the start of the journey my efforts to mount were a constant source of delight to the men; but in the end I adapted myself fairly successfully to what was, for me, an unfamiliar style of equitation.

We passed innumerable strings of coolies, bowed under a diversity of burdens: timber, charcoal, salt, tobacco, huge panniers crammed with highly articulate hens or ducks, or fat black pigs, lashed to their bearers' backs and uttering shrill lamentations. These caravans of coolies are an integral element of the Chinese scene. You see them everywhere, each endless convoy jogging along the road through the valley or the path over the mountain; their mouths intone a sort of dirge-like rhythm which helps them to keep in step. Some carry the load on their backs, in huge wickerwork containers; but most use a pliable bamboo pole, from either end of which the burden, divided in half, hangs in perfect equipoise. The pole rests on one shoulder, but at regular intervals the coolie adroitly and unobtrusively performs the feat of shifting the whole load on to the other shoulder without slackening his pace.

Chair-coolies (who transport men, not merchandise, upon their backs) no longer use the obsolete litter with side-curtains tightly drawn, but the more practical *hua kan*, which is a kind of *chaise-longue* suspended like a stretcher between two shafts. The coolies move ahead swiftly, taking short, quick steps; the rhythm of their progress is delicately adjusted to the displacement of their passenger; when he (or she) is very heavy, a relief team jogs along behind them, ready to take over the shafts so smoothly that the rhythm of their passenger's progress is not interrupted or even disturbed. Where motor-roads do not exist, chair-coolies are the recognised means of passenger transport; it would scarcely be an exaggeration to say that half China spends its time carrying the other half about on its back.

About noon we crossed a nine-thousand-foot range and plunged into a great valley. Its walls, at first steep and rugged, soon took on a gentler aspect. Pretty little villages began to appear, and bean-fields in flower, and clear streams tumbling down in little waterfalls. The landscape was oddly reminiscent of a Pyrenean valley. Towards evening we passed through the formidable-looking gates which guard the small town of Fumin, where there is a curious bridge with a roof over it. The local children turned out in force to escort me noisily through the streets, a sure sign that the place was not often visited by foreigners. I was amused by their gesture of welcome, which consisted of holding up their fist with the thumb uppermost and yelling: *"Ting hao!"* This means "Very good!" and now seems to be the standard formula for greeting foreigners all over China—or at any rate in those parts of it where American troops were stationed during the war; *"ting hao"* was about as near as the average G.I. got to being a sinologue.

The next day was tough. It was terribly hot, and we did a stage of twelve hours without rest (except for a short halt at midday) and without anything to eat or drink. The going got steadily worse, and we climbed eight stiff passes, one after another. I was tired, vaguely depressed and horribly chafed by the pack-saddle; despite the beauty of the scenery, morale was low. On top of all this, I failed to get a bed in the only inn at Wuting, a little village which we reached at the end of the stage. I had to make do with a straw mat, and I had the greatest difficulty in making room for myself among the prostrate bodies which already packed the room that was used as a dormitory. People kept coming and going all night, and at any moment I expected to have my hands, feet or face trodden on. My fellow-guests shouted and chattered without stopping, and amid all this hubbub I had a far from restful night.

We were still two days' march from Yuanmow, but I was beginning to get fit. We were right up in the mountains; the air was cold, but the sky was unbelievably blue. The trail wriggled up and down along the hillside through a forest of giant rhododendrons, now in full bloom; we looked down on a pretty wooded valley. Our small party had been reinforced by four soldiers who were supposed to protect us against bandits, but who did not look particularly apt for this duty. With their straw sandals and straw hats they did not present a very martial appearance; one of them had an umbrella slung across his back. They contemplated the mountains with ill-concealed apprehension, and from time to time discharged their revolvers into the air for morale-building purposes. As a matter of fact, although one occasionally passed a decapitated human head tactfully fastened to a tree-trunk beside the trail, I did not take the alleged bandits very seriously. And in the end, after climbing a high pass and scrambling down an appalling path for about five thousand feet, we found ourselves on the floor of an immense valley, and reached Yuanmow without any untoward incident.

In this place, where we stayed for two days, the caravan split in two. I set off to explore the picturesque old town, protected by great walls of brownish, rather attractive stone, mellowed by the passage of centuries, but my leisurely progress was arrested by a soldier, who took me along to the police station. Dealings with officialdom monopolised the rest of my stay in Yuanmow. I trudged endlessly to and fro between the police station, military headquarters and my lodging, at each of which lengthy conversations took place and innumerable cups of tea were drunk. I was fed up to the teeth with answering the same questions over and over again, but it all taught me a lesson in patience which was often to prove of the greatest value later on. After two solid days of argument, they stamped a new set of hieroglyphics on my passport and authorised me to carry on with my journey; but I had to accept their offer of two soldiers who were detailed to act as my bodyguard.

At dawn on December 24th I left Yuanmow with my insignificant caravan. We began by crossing a sort of plain, oddly scarred and eroded by ravines between which jutted

up great bastions of ochre-coloured earth which reminded
me of the Dolomites.   Then we entered the broad valley of
the Yangtse, known, at this early stage of its career, as the
Kincha Kiang.   I was thrilled by the sight of this mighty
river, which for years had been so often in my thoughts; its
waters ran swift and clear and pleasant to behold—very
different from the turbid flood which I was to meet again
later at Nanking and Chungking.

The valley, getting steadily more inhospitable, narrowed
into a passage between towering cliffs; we advanced along a
track which zigzagged capriciously over patches of sand,
round rocks or through little scraggy woods; sometimes it
dropped steeply down to cross a ravine.   We halted for the
night in a tiny village, where there was an outcrop of little
adobe houses on a broad ledge between the river and the
cliff overlooking it.   There was no inn, but I managed to
install myself in a wretched building; it consisted of a small
stable and a large, dirty, smoke-filled living-room.   The
place was cluttered up with human beings, animals, piles of
firewood and primitive farm implements, all barely dis-
tinguishable from each other in the dim light of oil lamps.
The noise and the smoke were too much for me; my two
bodyguards—nice men who took my personal welfare
seriously—helped me to settle down on a pile of hay outside.
Night fell, and after it, less precipitately, silence; I lay there,
curled up in my warm sleeping-bag, savouring the cold, still
darkness, enjoying a tranquillity which sounds from the
stable—the stamp of a hoof, the tinkle of a bell on a headstall
—were powerless to disturb.

It was Christmas Eve.   That I should be spending it in
so poor and so remote a place was (I reflected) the sort of
thing that often happens to travellers.   You could not have
asked for a lovelier night, a clearer sky.   I lay there, embedded in hay, on a bare shelf of rock suspended in nothingness; my eyes looked beyond the stars towards infinity.   I
found myself thinking about that night in Bethlehem.

Christ's parents, too, must have done a long stage and found at the end of it a miserable quarter. The stable in which Jesus was born cannot have been very different from the one in which, just beside me, much the same animals were making much the same noises as they had made two thousand years ago. I was probably the only person awake in this wretched hamlet, tucked away in a cranny of the mountain wall which bounds the limitless land-mass of China. I was certainly the only person who knew that it was Christmas Eve, the anniversary of an event which was to shake—though not, alas, decisively to change—the world. The great festival, from the depths of my sleeping-bag, seemed to have no connection with the life I was leading; but I found myself recalling past Christmasses—some sad, some happy—spent among human beings whom I loved. Memory conjured up a remote world—a world, almost, of dreams. It was not without emotion that I sought asylum in it.

I slept badly. At first light I woke shivering; I wanted to start quickly, so as to get warm. Soon after we did start we branched off from the river and struck up the course of a tributary. Before long we lost touch with this stream in an endless valley: an arid, rocky, desolate place, laced with a series of ravines. Every time we climbed out of a ravine I though we were out of the valley, but there was always another ridge ahead. We finally emerged on to the plateau at six o'clock in the evening. By then it was dark. For another hour, hunched against an icy wind, we pressed on past woods and lakes, half-seen and wholly mysterious. At last, through the darkness, I made out the walls of a little town; and a few minutes later the men were knocking vigorously on its enormous but prudently bolted gates. Knock, knock, knock: a good deal of shouting: a long discussion: an endless wait. At last the gates were opened, and we stormed into the little town of Kiangyi, desperate for the warmth of an inn.

We had a comparatively dull journey from Kiangyi to

Hweili, though the scenery—pretty little fir-clad hills with high peaks in the distance beyond them—was pleasant enough. We were passing through a more prosperous region, with plenty of cultivation and frequent villages. On December 27th we debouched once more into the main valley, and shortly afterwards reached Hweili; this town marked the end of the first phase of a long journey.

I went round to the Catholic Mission, where I found Father Flahutez, of the Missions Etrangères de Paris, and Father Miguelez, a Spanish Redemptionist; after my long, lonely trek I was greatly touched by the warmth and friendliness of their welcome. It was the first time I had stayed with missionaries in China. I was often to do so again, not always as the guest of my compatriots; everywhere I found the same wonderful hospitality. In remote places missionaries are real fairy godmothers to the traveller, who would be —figuratively speaking, anyhow—lost without them. With them he is among simple, kindly people, who know the country and the people backwards, who can tell him what to do and what not to do, who go out of their way to help him in all his tiresome dealings with officials and police and in the endless bargaining involved in buying stores and arranging transport for the next stage—with all the things, in fact, which make life in China so complicated for a foreigner.

3. A CHINESE FUNERAL

1946 was ending; I saw the new year in at Hweili. It did not take me long to see the sights, such as they were, of the town; and I soon found that whenever I appeared in its streets all the local children formed up behind me in a solid and well-disciplined phalanx which, if I stopped to look at anything, stopped to look at me. So I gave up sight-seeing, and spent most of my time in the Mission, reading the books they had there or talking to the Reverend Fathers. They can hardly have been more delighted than I was by the chance of gossiping with somebody from one's own country; but they had been in this outlandish part of China for a very long time, cut off from all contact with Europeans, and they had forgotten quite a lot of French words. For these they substituted pidgin-*chinoiseries*, full of local colour, but seldom comprehensible to me.

At Hweili I was invited to a funeral. I had never attended one of these functions in China and was keen to do so. The setting was a biggish house in the country; its four wings, all of one storey and supported by stout lacquered beams, surrounded the inner courtyard. The place was crammed with relatives, friends of the family and neighbours who had come from gastronomic motives; we had some difficulty in getting in at all. The next-of-kin were clustered round the coffin; they had all put on, over their best clothes, the loose smock of coarse white cloth which is the standard garb of mourning in China. The women wore a sort of white turban, the men a much odder-looking head-dress, like a *tricorne* with complications, but also white. They took charge, as they wept and keened, of the mourners' tokens of esteem: banners, pennons and samplers of silk embroidered with estimates of the deceased's character in which understatement played no part. There were other offerings, too; all were received with sobs. When we appeared, however, those who knew Father Flahutez beamed at us with every appearance of delight; this was, no doubt, in accordance with the time-honoured Chinese social axiom that "my insignificant grief does not merit the sympathy of exalted persons."

We had hardly arrived when dinner was announced. Everyone instantly stopped crying and bustled off to establish a bridgehead at the groaning board, which in practice comprised a lot of little tables dotted about all over the place.

From then on the funeral rites merged into the uproar of a Chinese banquet, uninhibited, deafening and gay. Everybody feasted until night fell, and the flow of talk was punctuated only—but not infrequently—by alcoholic toasts.

The actual interment took place next day, and an endless procession wound its way through the streets of Hweili. In China it is always desirable to make a certain impression; in terms of "face," the ostentation of this morning's *cortège* was as important as the succulence and profusion of last night's banquet. At the head of the procession paced a long file of men and boys. They carried funerary inscriptions: life-size portraits of the deceased, framed and borne upon trestles; grotesque or comical dummies, gilded litters made of cardboard. All these stage-properties were to be burnt as part of the burial rites. Behind them came a dozen stout fellows making an absolutely deafening noise—blowing brass trumpets with all the strength of their powerful lungs, thumping drums and gongs and cymbals for all they were worth. Next came the dead man's family, all in white, with the eldest son in his funny-looking white hat at their head; he sobbed, wailed, wept and screamed, and so great was the burden of his grief that he had to have two other members of the family to support him. It was a beautifully acted charade. The other relatives trailed behind him, bearing banners and long linen streamers which writhed in the air like huge white snakes. Finally there was the coffin, an enormous affair: solid, ponderous, a real monument in polished black wood embellished with gilt. It was slung from a great beam carried on the shoulders of twelve sturdy men who laughed, sang and cracked jokes to keep their courage up. On the beam perched a cock, very conscious of the important part he played in the proceedings; at a later stage of them he would be sacrificed. Bringing up the rear came a rabble of friends and acquaintances, chattering and gossiping. The spectacle—so curiously compounded of real grief borne with unobtrusive dignity, and loud, ostentatious, theatrical lamentations, the whole set against a background of junketing—was the sort of thing which Westerners find it almost impossible to understand.

Flahutez and I moved off with the procession, then took a short cut to the North Gate, near which the corpse was to be buried. It was some time before the *cortège* reappeared. It continued its stately progress until, all of a sudden, everybody stopped dead. The coffin was dumped unceremoniously by the roadside, surrounded by its ghostly escort of paper effigies, while the family and their guests disappeared into a nearby house for another enormous meal. We would have liked to wait and see the climax of the ceremonies—the great *auto-da-fé* of the dummies and the other paper gadgets—imitation bank-notes, and bars of silver made of cardboard, and all the rest of the bogus offerings which the credulous and deluded gods were, somewhat cynically, expected to put up with; but we lacked the stamina and in due course made for home.

4. LORRIES AND LOLOS

AT nine o'clock on the morning of New Year's Day I heard that a lorry was about to leave for Sichang; it was a chance not to be missed. I rushed up to my room with the two missionaries, we packed up my things at top speed and, accompanied by a train of young converts carrying suitcases and kitbags, galloped off to the lorry, which, needless to say, was right at the other end of the town.

It was the first time I had travelled on a Chinese lorry; I was soon well acquainted with the peculiar delights of this form of transportation. The reader must disabuse himself of the idea that in China they have lorries, on the one hand, for freight, and buses, on the other, for passengers; unoriginal arrangements of this kind are met with only on

routes—generally between one large town and another—
where there is heavy and regular traffic. In the interior the
normal system is for passengers and freight to travel
together, crammed on top of the same vehicle. The lorry is
first loaded up with merchandise, though "loaded up" is an
inadequate way of describing this phase of the operation.
What actually happens is that the lorry is stuffed to bursting-
point with a cargo twice as heavy as that which its manu-
facturers intended it to carry; it is usual to continue loading
until the lorry's springs are observed to be concave where
they ought to be convex. After this, the passengers launch
a determined assault on the mountain of freight and with
any luck establish some kind of foothold upon its towering
summit; here, jostling each other, scrambling over each
other, squashing each other and testing to the utmost the
remarkable adaptability of the human frame (especially the
Chinese frame), they eventually settle down. Everyone
clings for dear life to something—to the man next to him,
to the bale underneath him or to one of the cords with which
the cargo is lashed in place; once under way, the swarm of
human beings sways from side to side in open defiance of
the laws of equilibrium. One is apt to suppose, at the
moment of departure, that the maximum degree of over-
crowding has been attained; but just outside the town the
lorry stops to pick up a few additional passengers. These
furtive and equivocal individuals, known by the rather
charming sobriquet of "yellow fish," contrive to infiltrate
into the solid mass of humanity.

I was fortunate enough to secure a place on the corner of a
packing-case, flanked by a huge bundle of scarlet pimentos
on which three of my fellow-passengers were already sitting;
the pimentos struck a gay note against the uniform dark
blue of everybody's clothes. Gradually the swarm got itself
organised, and we found ourselves clamped like limpets to
whatever claim we had managed to stake, totally incapable of
altering our position. On the numerous occasions when the

telephone line, sagging slightly, crossed from one side of the
road to the other, everyone had to lie down flat; feats which
would have earned the respect of a contortionist were performed in an effort to avoid being dislodged or decapitated
by the wire.

We left Hweili at two o'clock. Our first breakdown
happened a quarter of an hour later, and soon after that we
had a puncture; so by the evening we had covered hardly
any distance at all. We stopped at Yimen, where I was
invited to spend the night in some quarters where the
engineers from a porcelain factory were lodged. For two
more days we continued this leisurely progress, regularly
interrupted by breakdowns and punctures. The tyres were
in such a deplorable state that in the end we were repairing
them with the soles of old gym-shoes, held in position by a
leather thong and a chain.

This was not, however, our only form of amusement.
The road crossed a large number of bridges, of which in
most cases only the rudiments remained. After they had
been built, several years ago, the authorities felt that they
could rest on their laurels, and nobody since then had done
anything about maintaining them. The aprons had rotted,
the beams and cross-pieces had done likewise, and generally
it was only the stone piles which were still sound. So the
lorry had to cross the river on a ferry—whenever it was
possible to do so—and, since the banks were soggy, it was
extremely difficult to drive up the one on the far side. The
tyres would not grip, the wheels ate their way into the soft
ground and the lorry stuck fast. All the passengers
clambered down from their perches, and everyone started
pushing, pulling, arguing and issuing directives. Stones and
branches were collected and wedged under the wheels, and
in the end the lorry got back on to the road somehow.

Even when the bridge was still standing, we prudently
stopped. The driver got out and reconnoitred the bridge,
examining it minutely. If his verdict was favourable, the

lorry went at it full tilt; the passengers alighted first, for there was no sure means of knowing how the bridge would react. The great thing in favour of these manœuvres was that they gave the passengers a chance of restoring the circulation in their legs, numbed by long periods of immobility in postures for which nature had not designed them; the drawback to them was the savage struggle for *Lebensraum* which took place when we had to get back on the lorry again.

At first, in the valley of the Anning Ho, the country was lovely; but as we approached Sichang it grew dull and featureless. Ten kilometres from the town yet another breakdown brought us to a halt. I had more or less given up hoping of arriving that day when, by a great stroke of luck, a jeep appeared. It was driven by an American officer, whose passenger was none other than Father Catel, with whom I had travelled from Marseilles to Saigon in 1945. I transferred my luggage to the jeep and we drove off, abandoning without regret the lorry, now clearly on its last legs. At the Mission the Bishop, Monsignor Baudry, welcomed me with great affability. There is nothing very striking about Sichang, though the country round it is attractive. Father Catel took me to see the large Buddhist shrine at Lushan, about ten kilometres outside the town. There are some interesting old pagodas there, romantically situated above the clear waters of a lake.

At the Bishop's residence I had a long talk with Father Arnaud. He has spent more than thirty years in those parts and is the greatest living authority on the Lolos, of whom large numbers live in Kienchang, between Sichang, Fulin and the marches of Kangting, to the north. He told me a lot about these people; he is extremely fond of them and speaks their language.

The Lolos are entirely different from the Chinese, with whom, although they live at such close quarters, they have practically no intercourse. They are the descendants of one of the many aboriginal tribes which used to inhabit Yunnan, Sikang, Burma, Laos and Tonking before the spread of Chinese colonisation. When, in comparatively recent times, the Chinese came down from the north-east and took effective control of a vast region which up till then had only been a sphere of colonial influence, the indigenous tribes—Lolos, Lissus, Miaos and others—abandoned the fertile plains and valleys to the invader and fled to the mountains. There were thus brought into being, in the most westerly parts of China, sizeable enclaves where the aboriginals—savagely resisting attempts to penetrate their territory and refusing to submit to foreign domination—have kept their civilisations alive. Some of them have been gradually subdued, and finally tamed; but there are still plenty of Lolos who lead a completely independent life behind the protection of great mountain-barriers. Driven back by the invading Chinese into wild, infertile tracts of country, they grow opium poppies, breed a few cattle and hunt; but their real *métier* is banditry. I imagine that this is an occupation which not only provides them with a livelihood but at the same time satisfies their deep, primordial thirst for adventure and freedom. It is certainly a fact that their own economy, their dependence on poor lands which are surrounded by prosperous Chinese settlements, fosters, if it did not actually create, their lawless tendencies. These are now so integral to their way of life that no young Lolo can take a bride until he has been out on a foray; a similar convention is observed in some parts of Tibet.

Physically the Lolos are quite different from the Chinese. They are tall, strongly built, well-knit people, with dark skins; their eyes are not noticeably slanted, and their noses—instead of being small and snub, like Chinese noses—are often hooked, in the Red Indian style. They have several characteristics in common with the aboriginal population on the mountainous frontiers of Annam and Cambodia and, like them, are believed to have been originally of

Indonesian stock. They make good fighters, brave and well armed—generally with rifles captured (or purchased) from the Chinese regular forces. They frequently raid the neighbouring valleys, burning the peasants' houses and looting their belongings, their grain and their cattle; sometimes they take the owners away with them as slaves.

The Lolos represent not only a continual threat to law and order but a serious loss of face for the Chinese authorities, who are completely incapable of controlling them. While I was in Sichang, fighting broke out in the north of the province between the Lolos and the Chinese, but the former, as usual, proved much braver and better soldiers than the Nationalist troops. From their mountain strongholds, inaccessible to the faint-hearted Chinese, they launched murderous attacks on the Government forces. These were in any case of poor quality, consisting of wretched youths—some of them no more than children—who had been forcibly impressed during recruiting drives through the villages. Badly fed and rarely paid, these miserable conscripts lived off the country and thought only of deserting. They were armed with almost every known type of rifle, but had only the vaguest idea how to use them; for, in order to husband their scanty stocks of ammunition, they had never been given any firing practice.

There was an American colonel at Sichang. He was looking for men of the United States Air Force who had been lost during the war in that part of the world—sometimes, perhaps, because their maps of it were inadequate—while keeping open the dangerous supply route from India to China over the Hump. Most of these men had been killed, and the Colonel's main concern was to recover their bodies; but he hoped also to find any survivors who might have been taken prisoner by the Lolos. So far, although he had taken endless trouble, the unfortunate man had found nothing at all, and he was bitterly disillusioned by the attitude of the Chinese officers who, after officially pledging

A Chinese funeral

themselves to further his efforts, did nothing but obstruct him. Whenever he did receive news of the whereabouts of a corpse, every kind of complication arose, and the authorities would do nothing to help him until they had been bribed.

5. THE OPIUM RACKET

On January 5th I started off again on another lorry; it was pretty obvious, from the condition of its tyres, that our progress was going to be erratic. The valley of the Tatung River, which we followed after leaving Sichang, was spectacular; the road, boldly engineered, clung to its rocky face and sometimes projected from it. It was built during the war and several thousand of the coolies who worked on it lost their lives; but nobody maintains it now, and it will soon be out of commission. The scenery, with its lovely jagged ridges soaring up above huge forests of pine and larch, reminded me of the uplands of Vercors. We met a lot of "civilised" Lolos—inoffensive people, who come down from their homes in the hills to shop in the villages; they have kept their own customs and their own style of dress. At one of our halts I found myself in the centre of a group of Lolo women, looking very pretty in their brightly coloured finery, quite different from anything worn by the Chinese; but when I tried to photograph them they covered up their faces and giggled like schoolgirls. A moment later, however, their lord and master appeared. He was a fine-looking fellow in his long, fringed cloak; he had an arrogant face, overhung by a great coif of hair which among the Lolos is a kind of talisman, not to be touched by anyone else under pain of death. He was in the best of tempers and ordered his womenfolk to pose for me—a duty which they performed with obvious gratification, for they were all coquettes, well aware of their own youth and good looks. Finally the man

Chinese village on the upper reaches of the Yangtse

himself posed, and was so tickled by the whole business that he did his best to make me go back with him to his far-away village. I would have been delighted to do so, but my destinies were, alas, inextricably linked to the lorry—and, of course, to my luggage.

On the morning of the 7th we crossed the Tatung by a big suspension bridge. The Chinese did not seem to be over-confident of its stability; before the lorry ventured on to it, the passengers were all debussed and an army of coolies carried the freight across—a process which took several hours to complete. After that we climbed a high pass under exceptionally disagreeable conditions; the clouds were low, the hills were covered with snow and on the lorry, with nothing to protect us against the icy wind, it was bitterly cold. It was eleven o'clock at night before we reached Fulin, where I was welcomed at the Catholic Mission by Father Le Roux, a very likeable man whose brother I was to meet later on in Sikang.

I would have liked, at this point, to have left the main road, hired coolies and struck up north toward Kangting; but at the time this route was closed by bandits. Many of these are, of course, only peasants who have been ruined in the opium racket. Fulin is a big opium centre; the cultivation of poppies and traffic in the drug which they produce are all too often the basic reasons for the troubles which intermittently break out in Sikang and for the banditry which is endemic there. Most of the local Chinese officials actively encourage the peasants to give up growing food-crops by dazzling them with visions of the untold wealth which will be theirs if they grow poppies instead. Then, when the poppies are in bloom, the peasants are visited by a magistrate or a police-officer who reminds them that both the cultivation and the manufacture of opium are strictly illegal in China (which is perfectly true on paper). This starts a long argument which always ends in the same way: in return for official connivance at their misdemeanour the peasants hand over a considerable sum of money and agree to forfeit part of their crop. This process is repeated, by a different set of officials, when the juice is being extracted from the poppies; and the net result is that the peasants' profits are completely swallowed up by this double-barrelled form of blackmail. Very often the poor wretches, punch-drunk by centuries of extortion and misrule, bow with a reasonably good grace to the inevitable; but sometimes they rebel and murder the official in cold blood. If the latter gets warning that this is liable to happen, he quickly makes a large *ex gratia* payment to his victim in order to avoid any unpleasantness; for he knows that he himself is hopelessly compromised and has not got a leg to stand on. After all these vicissitudes it generally pays the peasant to leave his village, and, having grown no crops except the opium, he has no resources of any kind; so, rather than starve to death, he turns bandit, loots caravans for a few years, and generally finishes up as a soldier in the Chinese Army.

That is the background to the chronic lawlessness which ravages Sikang; and the fighting which, while I was there, was going on between Government troops and the Lolos also had some of its origins in the opium racket.

The livelihood of almost everyone in Fulin depends on this racket or on the gun-running which is linked up with it. The small dealers, having bought the drug from the men who produce it, go off with it to Chengtu, where they sell it to the big dealers; these transactions are carried out under the protective auspices of army officers, the value of whose patronage and the scale of whose rake-off are in direct proportion to the eminence of their rank. This traffic is also carried on along the road from Kangting to Chengtu via Ya-an, where once, some time later, I met a long military convoy under the command of a well-known general. The convoy consisted of some twenty litters, each loaded with rectangular packets, neatly packed and sealed, and each closely escorted by soldiers carrying their rifles and sub-machine-guns at the ready; the head and the tail of the column were protected by men armed with American carbines, while several officers brought up the rear. I learnt afterwards that the convoy was transporting a large consignment of opium belonging to the fabulously wealthy General W——. There was nothing very unusual about this. In those days almost all Chinese armies more or less belonged to their generals, who employed them as far as possible on duties of a useful and constructive kind. Times, after all, were hard; to neglect one's own or one's dependants' interests is not a mark of discernment.

My lorry started off again on January 9th for Kiating. The weather was lovely, and we began a long climb up a steep road covered with frozen snow. The view from the top was dramatic. Through a great gap in the hills we could see, far away in the distance, a tremendous snow-covered peak, radiant and glistening in the bright winter sunlight. This was Minyakonka, twenty-three thousand feet high; behind it the Tibetan mountains stretched to the horizon like an angry sea.

We halted for the night at Wangmuchang, a little village pleasantly situated on a sunny plateau. It was a very cold night. Our driver, somehow managing to overlook this fact, omitted to let the water out of the radiator before going to bed, and next morning, after a quarter of an hour's run, he noticed that the water, not unnaturally, had frozen. Quite unperturbed, he pulled into the side of the road and methodically proceeded, in the gelid air of dawn, to dismantle the bonnet, the water-pump, the fan and various other bits and pieces, with a view to removing the entire radiator. Somebody went and fetched a bucket of water from a stream which ran, invisible to us, at the bottom of a deep ravine, while others collected dry sticks; a large bonfire was made, and while the passengers huddled round it, chattering and warming their hands, the driver and his mate hung the radiator over the fire until it had thawed out. They then put the whole bag of tricks together again with the same unruffled air of routine, warmed up some more water with chunks of ice in it, poured it into the radiator and off we went again, delighted with the auspicious outcome of this *contretemps*. The whole operation was completed in very little more than two and a half hours; it would have taken five minutes, last night, to empty the radiator. But what does time matter, anyway?

The journey to Kiating was an impressive experience; it must be one of the most remarkable stretches of road in China. Its construction was a *tour de force*, for it is cut out of the cliff-side into which it even, from time to time, burrows in a tunnel; in some sectors the workmen had to be let down on ropes to put the blasting charges in position. To the traveller it offers an endless series of ups and downs and hair-pin bends. Far below us, at the foot of an almost sheer precipice, we could see the thin silver ribbon of the Tatung Ho; at times we were close on three thousand feet above it. Above us loomed the great bulk of Omeishan, whose peak has for centuries beckoned devout pilgrims of the Buddhist faith.

Eventually we dropped down—it was a long, tortuous and hair-raising descent—to the floor of the valley, and soon afterwards passed through the village of Omei, from which the pilgrims set out for the mountain. It was full of little Buddhist shrines; pious expeditions told their beads as they moved off to begin the long climb.

Beyond Omei the stage became less interesting; at the end of it we forded the Ming Ho and reached Kiating. Here I found myself committed to a brisk but aimless tour of the municipality in a rickshaw. The man between the shafts, though he failed entirely to understand the directions I gave him, went off like a stag, and it must have been more by good luck than good management that we finished up outside a paper factory where I had been told they might be able to put me up. Here I found the friendliest of hosts in the person of a Chinese engineer who had spent ten years

studying the craft of paper-making in Paris and Grenoble.
He gave me a good room to sleep in, and next day took me
round his very up-to-date factory: after which we spent a
pleasant evening exchanging reminiscences of the Quartier
Latin.

Kiating, situated at the confluence of the Ming Ho and
the Tatung Ho, is an attractive little town. The water-
front swarms with life. If you go on down the Ming Ho,
which flows southwards from Kiating, you come to a gorge.
The cliffs of sheer rock which flank it are about three
hundred feet high, and each is crowned with a dense crest of
evergreen trees; it is as if twin silvicultural follies had been
established on either side of the gorge. Its towering walls
are honeycombed with Buddhist shrines, the oldest of them
dating from the T'ang dynasty and monopolising a big area
of the cliff-face overlooking the river. Out of this was carved,
centuries ago, a gigantic effigy of the seated Buddha. It
still looks fairly imposing at long range, but the workmanship must have been unusually crude. Time has blurred its
outlines, and erosion of the rock-face has reduced the great
image to a shadowy pastiche. Though its dimensions are
more impressive, this Buddha, one hundred and twenty
feet in height, is far less striking than the two comparable
but smaller images carved out of the cliffs at Bamyan in
Afghanistan. There are other examples of rock-sculpture
round Kiating; they were first described by Ollone in 1911
but they, too, are not particularly good.

6. THE HOLY MOUNTAIN

On January 12th I went back on my tracks to Omei. The
chief of police there, to whom my friend in the paper-mill
had given me a letter of introduction, placed at my disposal
a soldier who was to act in the dual capacity of guide and

bodyguard. This warrior, without even giving me time to have something to eat, shouldered my bedding-roll and whisked me away into the mountains; before I knew where I was I had done an hour's forced march and stood before the great gates of the temple of Paokuossu. This is the starting-point of the path used by pilgrims who climb Omeishan. We entered, passing a gatehouse on whose walls Tibetan texts were painted and beyond which a pleasant avenue of trees led to the main buildings. Here we spent the night.

Omeishan is one of the seven holy mountains of China and as a centre of pilgrimage is held in as much veneration by the inhabitants of that country as by the Tibetans. It is not difficult to understand why this peak should have captured the imagination of those peoples and assumed, for them, a religious significance. Although to the westward it links up with the sprawling mountain ranges of Yunnan and Tibet, to the eastward it juts up sharply between two great river valleys; from this quarter no foothills mask it. Out of the fertile plain of Kiating the great mountain soars upwards almost perpendicularly for some nine thousand feet, an awe-inspiring bastion towering towards the sky. With its fantasticated outline and its curious flat summit, it might have been specially designed to capture the fancies of the Chinese, whose love of nature, though deeply felt, tends to centre on its freakish aspects; they have a passion for wild, unusual scenery in which their lively imaginations can identify the shapes of beasts and dragons and characters out of their folklore.

Omeishan ranks third in the hierarchy of China's great holy places, each of which is sacred to a particular divinity in the Buddhist pantheon. The most celebrated is Wutai-shan, in the north of Shensi Province, which is dedicated to Manjusri, the God of Metaphysical Wisdom; next comes Putoshan, situated on a little island in Hangchow Bay, not far from Shanghai, and sacred to Kwangyin, the Goddess of

Mercy. Omeishan, the third most important in the whole country but much the most notable in the west, is presided over by Puhsien; this is the name given by the Chinese to the Indian Samantabhadra, one of the five great contemplative Buddhas in the pantheon. In Tibet (where they call him Kuntuzombo) this deity is accorded a special reverence by several of the unreformed sects, which is doubtless why so many Tibetan pilgrims find their way to Omeishan.

The great, lovely mountain is dotted with pagodas, strung out along the path by which pilgrims make the ascent. Built in the conventional style, they are singular in that a figure of Puhsien always occupies the central position of honour. Among his other distinctions is that of having founded the Mitsong sect—the so-called "College of Mystery" to which all the priests on Mount Omei belong; it corresponds to the esoteric sect known in Japan as Shingon.

The temple of Paokuossu is one of the most important pagodas and is typical of all those on Omeishan. You enter it through a gatehouse in which, back to back, stand statues of Wei-to and Mi Li-fu. The latter, a popular figure of the Chinese Buddhist hierarchy, is familiar to many Europeans, who often mistake him for the Buddha; he is in fact the amiable Pu-sa. Beaming, obese, seated at his ease and surrounded by plump, jolly babies, you meet him all over China; but he is only a representation of Maitreya, the Buddha-to-be.

The gatehouse opens into a spacious courtyard, flanked on two sides by living-quarters and leading to the main temple, a fine large rectangular building, its roof supported by huge red-lacquered timber beams, almost on the scale of the pillars in a cathedral. In the centre of this edifice stands the ancient throne of Buddha, called Sakyamuni, and, standing with his back to the throne, a colossal figure of Omitofu. He is the God of light, who came originally from Persia and is especially venerated by the "Pure Earth" sect.

To him are addressed countless invocations of *Namo-Omitofu*, chanted daily by the devout as the eight hundred beads on their rosaries trickle through their fingers; for he graciously promised that anyone who thus addressed him at least once before they died would be received into his Western Paradise. These forms of worship, perfunctory and rather cosy, suit the materially-minded Chinese, who are superstitious without being metaphysical, to perfection; also they offer to a people, the majority of whom are poor and needy, some consolation for the hardness of their lives. There would seem to be little danger of the cult dying out.

Beyond and behind the temple there are two more imposing buildings, standing in a noble garden shaded by tall trees. The first houses statues of the seven great Buddhas, six belonging to the past and one—the jovial Maitreya—to the future; in the second Puhsien sits in state among his entourage of the eminent sages who were Buddha's companions.

Nearby is the enchanting old temple of Fufussu, tucked away in a grove of trees above a mountain stream; a flight of mossy stone steps leads up to it. Besides the normal complement of images, one of its great chambers contains no fewer than five hundred of Buddha's associates; this great concourse of statues—some with merry, some with scowling faces, but all full of animation—produces an astonishingly lifelike effect.

When I got back to my lodging that night, a drum started beating somewhere, and I went in quest of it; it signalised the evening rites, and the sound, coming out of the darkness, had an eerie potency. The monk who made it was alone in a temple, its ambient gloom enhanced rather than dispelled by a few primitive oil lamps. First he beat a gong with a long series of slow, deliberate strokes; then he began a precise, rhythmical tattoo on a huge drum, accompanying it with an endless dirge, monotonous but infinitely sad; a big brass bell tolled at the end of each verse. Other monks answered his lonely summons. Silent as shadows, they glided into the temple and took their places in two ranks beside the altar. For a few moments there was complete silence; then they began to intone the rites to a sad, slow refrain, which gradually became faster and faster and was punctuated by the ringing of large wooden hand-bells. The scene had a quality of mystery to which I found myself yielding; and later I was scarcely aware that the ceremony had ended, and the monks, departing as noiselessly as they had come, had melted away into the darkness outside.

7. "BUDDHA'S GLORY"

ON January 13th we set off, at an early hour, through the fertile and well-populated countryside, in which at that season fields of flowering beans make pleasant patches of colour. Before long, however, the valley narrowed abruptly and the flagged path, worn smooth by the feet of generations of pilgrims, plunged into the Dragon's Gate, a narrow gorge through which a clear stream ran swiftly. We crossed a wooden bridge and began to climb a series of very steep flights of steps which zigzagged upwards through the fir trees. A remarkable thing about this pilgrims' way is that practically the whole way up the mountain it consists of these staircases; their little stone steps are beautifully made, and a prodigious amount of work must have gone into their construction at that great altitude. Every now and then we passed a temple, half hidden among the trees, with a red-and-gold ceremonial arch standing in front of it; and in all of them we were given a courteous welcome by the priests, with their shaven pates and grey robes. They really seemed to enjoy showing one round their temple, especially when they discovered that one did not regard them as curious sort of animals, but was interested in their religion and actually knew the names of their gods.

At the top of a particularly long and gruelling flight of steps we came to Wannienssu, the Temple of Ten Thousand Years; it had been recently burnt to the ground and was being rebuilt. On the great ledge of rock where the central shrine had stood nothing was left but rubble, over which brooded the incombustible iron skeletons of eighteen large images. A brand-new throne, which had been dumped down in the middle of this group, looked singularly out of place.

A thatched shelter temporarily housed some of the gods who had been rescued, but a little way off I saw a great iron Buddha, badly damaged by the fire and written off as a total loss. A funny-looking brick building in the background had been given a new roof; this consisted of a cement dome and was crowned by four plaster gazelles, a traditional Buddhist symbol. These improvements were revoltingly ugly, but they at least provided shelter for a huge Puhsien, seated in the lotus position on an elephant with six tusks, a form of transportation much favoured by the gods.

From here to the summit was a ten-hour climb up dizzy flights of steps flanked by some forty temples, built like eagles' nests on ledges in the cliff. We had a meal, and set off on an exacting stage which brought us to a terrace on which there was a shrine to Kwangyin. In front of it stood a very fine, very antique wooden statue, but except for a dog and a small child the shrine itself seemed to be deserted. We climbed on and stopped to rest at a little temple called, not inappropriately, Inner Tranquillity. Shortly after this it began to snow, and we completed the ascent of Omeishan through a layer of icy snow which made for tricky going on those steep flights of steps.

Passing various sizeable pagodas, we came to the great temple of Huanientin, where we were to spend the night. It has a magnificent situation, clinging to the cliff-face on a ledge so narrow that its balconies jut out over nothingness.

The weather had turned nasty and the clouds were down to the tree-tops; we got only occasional glimpses of the abyss below us when the wind tore aside for a moment the mist that veiled it, but this did not make it look any less fantastic. The whole mountain, with its precipitous gorges, its pine forests and its twisted rocks, has—especially when the mist is down—an irresistibly romantic aspect.

Our temple was the customary place for travellers to put up. They gave me a good meal and a clean room with sheets as well as blankets, an unheard-of luxury in China. I was moreover almost the only person there and could wander as I pleased round the temples and the large colony of images which they housed. One shrine near the main entrance was dedicated to the King of the Mountain, who turned out to be a panther, enclosed in a little sanctuary fashioned like a cage where pilgrims came to do him homage. As a matter of fact there are quite a lot of real panthers on Omeishan, and to burn a few sticks of incense in honour of this one is regarded by the Chinese as a sensible form of insurance.

Before we moved off next morning I took the precaution of substituting a good, solid pair of shoes for my flimsy sandals. The snow, as things turned out, got steadily deeper; one could not see where the steps were, and the only thing to do was follow the tracks of one's fellow-pilgrims. There were a good many of these. They seldom travelled singly, but preferred to keep together in parties from the same village. I was greatly struck by the seriousness with which they took the whole business. Nothing gives the Chinese greater pleasure than conversation or, failing that, meditation; but these pilgrims hardly ever halted, never dawdled and scarcely exchanged a word. They pressed on steadily in single file, wasting no time. The skirts of their robes were girt up above their knees, their backs were bowed under the weight of their belongings, they wore straw sandals on their feet and many carried, slung across their backs, an umbrella and the inevitable thermos, from which the Chinese traveller seldom allows himself to become separated. They did not miss out a single shrine or a single temple, and they paid their respects to every image with the same dutiful formula, lighting one stick of incense and prostrating themselves once.

I saw, too, a good deal of the coolies who bring supplies up to the temples, and I much admired the way in which they dealt with the prevailing conditions. They were heavily loaded, and in order to avoid slipping on the icy steps they fastened climbing-irons underneath their sandals with string.

Passing the Temple of the Stone Lotus, we came to the Temple of the Elephant's Bath, where—according to legend —Puhsien's pachyderm performed its ablutions. The worst part of the climb was over, and henceforth the path led up a comparatively gentle slope, zigzagging off through the trees in order to bypass huge outcrops of rock. The sun, a stranger for the past two days, gradually got the better of the mist, disclosing a prospect of startling beauty. The tree-tops everywhere were blanketed with snow, but at the slightest puff of wind the white sheath in which the branches were encased disintegrated in a glittering cloud of particles.

We looked in on several more temples and then embarked on the last lap of the climb. Here we overtook a number of pilgrims who had given way to exhaustion and were travelling in a style that was new to me. On these steep flights of steps it is out of the question to use an ordinary litter, so the coolies have devised a wooden frame, consisting of a seat flanked by two arm-rests. This they carry on their backs like a rucksack, and in it sits the unfortunate victim of fatigue. It would take a lot to make me use one.

Shortly afterwards we reached the wide plateau which forms the summit of Omeishan and on which stands the famous Golden Pagoda. This, I fear, has come down in the world and now comprises only a desolate barrack in which languish Puhsien and a handful of lesser personages, all in

an advanced state of dilapidation. The main chamber, however, opens on to a remarkable little balcony carved out of
the rock. It juts out into space; the sheer precipice below
falls uninterruptedly for several thousand feet, its base
vanishing into the treetops which clothe the foothills. This
balcony has no parapet: only an old rusty chain, hung with
Tibetan prayer-flags.

The Golden Temple was uninhabitable, but I found
quarters in another shrine quite near it. My room opened on
to a tiny terrace, with nothing between it and the precipice
but a wooden balustrade. I spent a long time there, half-
hypnotised by the void below me and vaguely hoping to see
the phenomena known as "the tongues of flame," a spectacle
which everyone hopes will reward his pilgrimage to Omeishan. Fireflies abound all along the sheer rock-face below
the summit and—very occasionally—you see a great swarm
of these little creatures streaming upwards in formation.
The pilgrims, much impressed by this mass-flight through
the darkness, long ago decided that it must be a form of
homage paid to Buddha by the insect world. The phenomenon is most frequent during the warm summer nights.
When I was there it was bitterly cold, a circumstance which
may have discouraged the fireflies and which certainly drove
me back to the warmth of my room without having seen
anything resembling a tongue of flame.

I had no better luck, next day, with "Buddha's Glory."
Soon after sunrise the shadow of the peak is—again very
occasionally—projected on to the sea of mist in the valley
below. This shadow gradually grows larger till it seems to
reach up to the sky, and a sort of luminous rainbow forms
round its edges. This is what they call Buddha's Glory; it
sounded to me much the same sort of thing as the famous
Spectre of Brocken in the Hartz Mountains. The phenomenon, although a purely natural one, has a certain majesty
which is enhanced by the solitude of the place, its religious
atmosphere and the vastness of the abyss below it; a curious

thing about it is that no two people describe what they have seen in the same way. The pilgrims, athirst for marvels, look forward eagerly to this vision which may provide a grand finale to their pious journey; if they do see it they are beside themselves with excitement. It has even happened that men, completely carried away by their emotions, have cast themselves over the cliff, their arms outstretched towards the celestial emanation; the spell it casts on them is strengthened by their belief that those who answer its summons will be granted admission to the paradise of Amithaba. I was obviously unworthy of this distinction, for my pilgrimage was not rewarded with this auspicious vision, and I was even denied the more sublunary satisfaction of looking down on the incomparable view which, in clear weather, you get from the top of Omeishan. Mist shut us in on all sides, and the great white mass of Minyakonka remained obstinately immured in clouds.

I went diligently round all the temples strung out along the topmost ridge of the mountain; at its western extremity this ridge ends in a projecting crag, on which, like an outpost in eternity, stands a curious little hexagonal temple. We started down from the summit on the following day and, after two hours' march, came to a place where the path forked. Instead of branching left along the route I already knew, I took the right fork, which promised a fresh lot of temples and unfamiliar aspects of the mountain. The snow, which had been a major obstacle on the way up, was rather a help on the way down.

We soon reached Lijessu, an extraordinary little miniature temple cocked up on top of a bluff with a gorge on either side. The whole thing is on such a small scale that there is no room for a path, and travellers walk through the middle of the temple. Apart from a cell where the priest lives, there is only one room with an altar at the end of it. Being a highway as well as a place of worship, this temple has a rather countrified and informal atmosphere; grass grows all over the place, and chickens forage equably without taking any notice of the pilgrims.

From this place a steep flight of steps took us down to the beginning of a long uphill stretch through forest. The landscape had a nightmare quality. The mist, swirling out of tremendous gorges, allowed one glimpses of the depths below, looking sinister in that uncertain light; snow lay everywhere, and there was a continual sound of dripping water. The silence was oppressive. There was no one about —not a coolie, not a pilgrim, not an animal: only a large black bird which hopped along the path in front of us. After a while the trail passed between two huge rocks, at whose base a few sticks of incense smouldered; they were the only sign of life up here.

Soon we were below the snow-line. The endless flights of thousands of little steps finished up by having a hypnotic effect on me as I tripped interminably down them. But at last we found ourselves in a pretty wooded valley, where we spent the night in a temple overlooking a mountain stream. A fire was burning a little way off, where some Tibetans were encamped. A huge kettle of tea was boiling over it, and it was surrounded by packs and pilgrims' staves; an enormous dog growled throatily at me, and his master had to hold him in.

It was my first contact with a race in whose favour I was predisposed in advance. There were about a dozen of them, great strapping fellows, wrapped in sheep-skin *shubas* which left their chests exposed to the cold. Two of them were lamas, easily identifiable by their red robes and shaven heads; the others were herdsmen who had travelled here on foot from the interior of Sikang. We exchanged a few words, and afterwards my mind was filled with thoughts, conjured up with great vividness by the mere sight of them, of the vast and empty land from which they came.

We were back at Paokuossu quite early the next day, and a little further on, in the village of Omei, a young Chinese

ABOVE: *Lolo women* and *A Lolo warrior*. BELOW: *A Tibetan nomad and her children* and *A Tibetan caravan-boy wearing a shuba.*

ABOVE: *Dressing hair in 108 plaits (Note the typical Tibetan boots)*
BELOW: *An old Tibetan and his daughter with a prayer-wheel and a rosary*

tudent took charge of me, arranged for us to be photo-
graphed together, reserved me a seat on a bus and bought
my ticket for me. A few hours later I reached Kiating,
where I looked up the charming engineer from the paper-
mill. On January 18th I left for Chengtu in a reasonably
comfortable bus. The country looked prosperous and fertile.
Everywhere you saw fields of beans, corn, radishes and rape,
little market-gardens, green paddy-fields, and long, narrow
plots of sugar-cane. The road ran through several small but
thriving towns; one of them, Pengshan, looked particularly
attractive behind its great wall of pinkish stone. Children
were paddling happily about in the rice-fields, fishing with a
sort of bottomless basket which they suddenly thrust down
into the shallow water; it was very much the same technique
that I had often watched in Cambodia. The fields are irri-
gated by a complicated system of water-wheels which raise
the water from one level to the next in little bamboo cups;
the wheels are worked with their feet by two boys, each
sitting on a saddle and looking for all the world as though he
were bicycling.

We crossed the great ferry at Sinching. We were getting
near Chengtu, and the road became more and more con-
gested. It was thronged with pedestrians, cyclists and people
using more exotic means of transport—huge carts drawn by
eight monotonously chanting men, jolting rickshaws, funny-
looking wheelbarrows whose axles emitted deafening
squeaks; these carried either an old Chinese lady demurely
perched on the narrow cross-piece, or a gigantic pig, lashed
to the barrow on his back, beating the air with his trotters
and uttering heart-rending squeals. Overburdened coolies,
sometimes carrying an entire suite of furniture on their
backs, jostled each other in the gutter.

We reached Chengtu at three o'clock. I got a rickshaw,
but the coolie's navigation was faulty and I had been bump-
ing through the crowded streets for a long time before he
found the French Consulate. I had just decided that we

D

were completely lost in an obscure quarter of the town when, on the corner of a mean alley, I happened to notice a street-sign which had a little tricolor painted underneath it. I was simply delighted by the sight of my national emblem, even though it was so apologetically displayed; and, after picking my way with some difficulty through the wheelbarrows which cluttered up the lane, I at last reached, and was admitted to, the Consulate. I was welcomed with great kindness by our consul, M. Auvynet, a retired naval officer, and spent a delightful evening with him and a friend of mine, M. Cazanave, the commercial councillor from our Embassy, who by an astonishing fluke happened to be there too. Like me, Cazanave is a keen mountaineer, and we proceeded to swap reminiscences, including one of the time, years ago, when we had both stayed in the hut at Midi-d'Ossau in the Pyrenees. After so many days spent entirely on my own in the back-blocks of China, it was a wonderful experience to be suddenly able to conjure up memories of mountain-tops that meant so much to both of us.

PART TWO

A Slight Case of Banditry

8. LIFE IN CHENGTU

It appeared that idiotic formalities connected with visas and currency regulations would keep me much longer in Chengtu than I wanted to stay there, so I decided to cope with this long delay as best I could. Next day the consul took me round to call on Monsignor Rouchouse, the Bishop of Chengtu, and the Franciscan Sisters who run the hospital there. One of the doctors was on leave in France, and I agreed to deputise for him until he got back. I moved over to the hospital the same day and was installed in a small, quiet room, where one could work in peace; although I was busy with patients in the mornings, I had plenty of time left to read, explore the town, visit Buddhist centres, pick up a smattering of the Tibetan dialect which they speak in Sikang, work in the library and generally prepare for the next stage of my journey.

I did not care for Chengtu. My memories of the works of Legendre and Gervais led me to expect a romantic old town, with machicolated walls enclosing a Tartar city as well as a Chinese one; but all the really attractive features of this lay-out have disappeared. Of the Tartar city, which has been demolished, nothing remains but a nondescript expanse covered with a warren of huts made of planks and old petrol-tins and surrounded by fœtid piles of garbage. The battlements of the Chinese city have also vanished, leaving behind them nothing but ugly outcrops of masonry surrounded by an untidy no-man's-land of mud. Although it is a big place with an enormous population, Chengtu struck me as an overgrown village rather than a proper city. I always think of cities as living entities which have developed characters of their own. The centuries have stamped marks on them that still survive—a temple or a

53

palace, a tower or an old gate; on top of that the inhabitants
have added, in some feature which has been influenced by
their tastes or their occupations, their own contribution to
the city's character. In China the results of this process
have too often been lost. The boundless, pullulating energy
of the people tends to obliterate everything; historic monuments and ancient ruins have a shorter life than they have
elsewhere. Except, perhaps, for Peking (whose most notable
beauties are, as a matter of fact, not particularly old), the
cities of China are all rather the same: all have this air of big
villages swollen to many times their natural size. The
Chinese have a gift for reducing things to their lowest
common denominator.

Some of the streets in the centre of Chengtu have been
at pains to assimilate the more regrettable characteristics
of up-to-date European municipal architecture. The results
are unfortunate and bear much the same relation to the
original article as the olde-worlde stucco on a trade-stand in
an exhibition does to the well-tailored exterior of an old
country house. In the main shopping street the finest
buildings are terrifyingly ugly—ghastly erections which
derive their inspiration from pre-war German architecture
at its worst, built of inferior concrete which crumbles
readily, undermined by that stealthy pox which soon infects
so many modern buildings in China. Practically all the
other streets consist of row upon row of little shops, exactly
like what passes for the business centre of any other Chinese
town.

The unpaved streets are reasonably clean when the
weather is dry, but a shower of rain transforms them into
treacherous quagmires, through which you slither precariously or wade in mud up to your ankles. Since either
drizzle or a damp mist envelops Chengtu for at least half the
year, the pleasures of a stroll round the city, through a
seething mass of rickshaws, coolies, hawkers and pedestrians, may be readily imagined.

One cannot, all the same, pretend that the place is wholly lacking in the picturesque. Half a million people live in Chengtu, but they have no form of organised water-supply, piped or otherwise; there is plenty of water in the subsoil, but nothing has ever been done to ensure its efficient distribution, although it is encouraged to accumulate in shallow wells. These sumps are all over the place. You are equally likely to find them in a muddy lane somewhere, or in the middle of a pretentious boulevard, and they consist merely of a hole in the ground about three feet wide surrounded by the most perfunctory of stone parapets, into which the citizens in need of water dip the long bamboo containers with which each well is provided. These containers are removed at night, but the wells, of course, are not; in the dark streets, lit only by a feeble form of street-lighting in which the current is continually failing, they represent dangerous mantraps.

Then there is the problem of sanitation. The total volume of human excrement produced every day by half a million people—even if they do live mainly on rice—is bound to be formidable. No drainage of any kind exists; its place is taken by an old-established guild of public servants, who can be seen every morning in large numbers making their way through the streets. The casks or buckets which dangle from the bamboo poles across their shoulders smell no better than you would expect them to; they are always full to the brim, and their contents, which are eventually sold to smallholders on the outskirts of the city, are a constant threat to the legs of passers-by. In Chungking the inhabitants draw their water from the Yangtse, which runs past the base of the steep bluffs on which the city stands; the buckets in which they carry their night-soil down the hill are used, after being briskly rinsed, to carry their water up it.

I was slowly acquiring an understanding of the Chinese character. Basically, the people are easy-going, innocent of malice and likeable; their cheerful outlook, their even temper and their inexhaustible patience provide a sound foundation for their relationships with their fellow-men. They are merry, gregarious and quick to make friends; and they are much addicted to talking and making jokes. The parties which they give are always distinguished—even if the hosts are persons of consequence—by this quality of almost child-like simplicity; there is never a trace of conceit or affectation. Their proverbial courtesy is an integral part of their make-up; it is seen to best advantage among Chinese of a certain age, who have been moulded in the ancient casts of tradition; in young people it is often only a façade behind which it is easy to discern a callous egotism. (No one can doubt this who has done a certain amount of travelling by lorry in China.) The peasant, the coolie, the man who pulls your rickshaw, the itinerant pedlar—all those millions of under-privileged but invincibly optimistic people who make up the great mass of the population are lovable, natural, generous and staunch. All this is equally true of most of the intellectual classes—the artists, the writers, the professors— from whose society the foreigner in China can derive such a tremendous amount of pleasure. But in the younger genera-tion, among the half-baked intellectuals and the minor bureaucrats of the Kuomintang, that childlike simplicity is apt to degenerate into a casual, "couldn't-care-less" attitude; of their capacity for unbounded self-esteem, for sly malice and for bullying someone who is completely at their mercy merely in order to show how important they are, I was to acquire later some first-hand experience. These young people have rejected the old traditions which gave their race its strength, substituting for them a façade of Western culture, whose ill-digested essentials too often include the less admirable features of American civilisation, which exerts upon many rootless Asiatics so irresistible a spell.

At this stage of my journey my plans were to get, first of all, to Kangting, and thence to push on across Eastern Tibet to Kantze, Derge and Jyekundo; what I hoped to find was some sort of jumping-off point for an attempt on Lhasa. If I got there, I would make for India. If I failed, I would strike up to the northward, hoping to get on to the route through Sinkiang to Kashmir which was pioneered, some years ago, by Ella Maillart and Peter Fleming. These plans called for a lot of complicated preparations.

As regards passport formalities, the situation as far as Tibet proper was concerned was not in the least complicated; an application for a visa through official channels was certain to be refused, and would have the additional disadvantage of arousing curiosity about me. My only chance of success was to get through without being spotted. I would, on the other hand, have to have visas for each of the Tibetan provinces under Chinese control. In order to obtain them I had sent my passport off to the Ministry of Foreign Affairs at Nanking as soon as I got to Chengtu; but weeks passed and nothing happened.

Things were not very much more promising on the financial side. The Exchange Control in Indo-China had given me credit facilities in United States dollars, which have a high value in China, but, although cheques in dollars can be cashed readily in big centres like Shanghai or Hong Kong, the form was different in Chengtu, where nobody would touch them. The banks would, of course, have taken them like a shot, but only in exchange for Chinese paper currency and at the official rate of three thousand Chinese to one U.S. dollar, which was between four and five times less than the black-market rate. The last thing I wanted to do was to acquire vast sums of this unstable currency which was daily depreciating in value and which would be useless to me once I was past Kangting, since the only forms of currency which the Tibetans regard as legal tender are either silver dollars or bricks of tea, neither of which (needless to say) were available in Chengtu. If I got as far as Sinkiang, even silver dollars would be useless; I should need gold, which is the accepted form of currency all over that province. On top of all this, the last stage—India—would require either U.S. dollars or sterling.

All these ghastly complications made things particularly difficult for a person (like me) lacking even the most precarious grasp of finance, economics or commerce. After endless negotiations, throughout which exasperation alternated with despair, I managed—by accepting a crushing loss on the transaction—to convert some of my traveller's cheques into gold. The remainder, transferred to Shanghai, assured me a reserve of American dollars. This left me with a few pounds and some Chinese dollars which, I reckoned, I should be able to convert in Kangting into the tea and silver which would pay my way across Tibet. I was, in short, equipped for every contingency—except, as luck would have it, the one in which I was shortly to be involved. If I had foreseen its nature I would not have bothered so much about these tiresome matters.

9. BUDDHISM AND VISITING-CARDS

I USED often to go and watch the Buddhist ceremonies at the temple of Wenchuyuen, near the North Gate. They were an impressive sight. Some of the monks who took part in them were young novices, their shaven heads marked with fresh scars by the nine ritual brandings which are part of the ordination service. The ordination of Chinese Buddhist priests has a curious climax. The young novices kneel before the oldest monk, who places on their cropped skulls nine little charcoal cones fixed in position with wax. The cones are then lighted and proceed to smoulder, finally making deep burns, which leave lifelong scars, on the scalp of the novice. This rite is part of the Buddhist Vow which binds the man to take upon himself the sufferings of all living creatures. All the celebrants wore, over their ordinary

grey robes, splendid cloaks of dark red cloth whose folds
were gathered at the shoulder by a large silver clasp of
exquisite workmanship; on their heads they wore curious-
looking mitres, wider at the top than at the bottom. They
entered the great lofty chamber in procession and took their
places round the high altar on which an image of Buddha
sat enthroned; before it stood tables laden with offerings
of flowers and fruit. After all had prostrated themselves,
the rites began with the chanting of an invocation. Though
this went on for a long time, the sound was not at all monotonous; the monks' voices rose and fell in rich, majestic
harmony, punctuated by the pealing of great bells and the
thunder of immense bronze drums. Every now and then the
tempo quickened; then, against a background of utter
silence, the slow, solemn voice of a single chorister would
ring out through the stillness of the holy place, which was
hung with long curtains of purple silk.

The noonday rites often included a sacrificial ceremony
which I found very striking. The service would suddenly
stop, and an old monk, after prostrating himself before the
altar, lit in the flame of a candle a long stick of incense,
which he held with his hands clasped in the manner prescribed by ritual. Flanked by two novices carrying a long
stole of yellow silk, he advanced towards the huge censer
which stood in the courtyard and reverently placed in it the
incense thus consecrated. Then another monk brought a
bowl of rice; with slim, expressive hands he traced in the
air symbols which would ensure that his offering was
acceptable, then he dropped the rice, a grain at a time, into a
vessel placed in front of the censer. This gift is for the
preta, spirits of the nether world whose throats are too
narrow for them ever to be able to swallow enough food to
satisfy their hunger (this form of torture, a variant of that
to which Tantalus was subjected, is a punishment for greed
and gluttony during one's earthly existence). The ceremony
was brought to an end by a monk who made an offering of

fire by lighting a large paper torch at the altar-candles and then thrusting it into the incense-burner in the court-yard.

After this all the monks rose and set off in a long pro-cession whose files wove in and out of each other as it moved slowly forward to the sound of chanting and the tolling of bells. Their rate of progress steadily increased until every-one was out of breath and quivering with exertion; then suddenly the whole thing stopped. The monks went back to their stations round the altar, prostrated themselves and then withdrew in silence, their mien serious and abstracted, while, as the curtains were drawn and the shutters closed, darkness welled up again inside the temple where only the small, bright flames of the candles kept vigil on the altar of Buddha.

On March 19th my passport came back from Nanking. Unfortunately, in spite of the telegrams with which I had bombarded the Ministry of Foreign Affairs, it was in exactly the same condition as when I had sent it off; they had given me none of the visas I required. I had been kept hanging about for two months and had achieved nothing. The official excuse was that Nanking had been unable to get any reply from the governments of the provinces I wanted to visit—Sikang, Chinghai and Sinkiang. This may well have been true of the last two, but was almost certainly untrue of Sikang; the whole thing was a typically Chinese method of passing the buck. On the consul's advice I decided to ask the Chengtu police for a local visa to go to Kangting, and this they granted me without demur.

When I reached this town, which is the capital of Sikang, I asked for a similar visa to go to Chinghai, the province beyond, and got it without difficulty. I learnt in time that this is far the best way of doing things. The control authorities, who are chronically suspicious, hate the idea of issuing visas for provinces in the interior, especially for very remote ones; but if one merely applies, in the capital of one province, for a visa which permits one to go on to the one next door, nobody thinks anything of it, and one can travel the whole length of China by sticking to this formula. Another useful tip is never to put forward, as the purpose of your journey, a scientific—and above all an archæological—objective. The authorities have a deep and perhaps not altogether unjustified distrust of foreign technicians, whom they suspect of having come to prospect their country with ulterior motives, and this distrust extends to archæologists; they have not forgotten the thousands of manuscripts and paintings which Aurel Stein and Pelliot "collected" in the Tunhuang caves. "Business" is, and always has been, far and away the best reason to advance for making a journey, for it makes sense to the Chinese.

The consul also made me out a *laissez-passer* for the various places I was heading for, including Tibet and Sinkiang. It had no official validity, but it was translated into three languages—Chinese, Tibetan and Mongol—and it was plastered with those imposing seals which have such a salutary influence on ignorant policemen. And anyhow China is an odd sort of country, where it is perfectly possible to be arrested even though your passport is in order, whereas visiting-cards bearing your name in Chinese, followed by a high-sounding description of your appointments or professional qualifications, often work like a charm. I quickly got a large supply of visiting-cards printed and distributed bushels of them as I went along.

10. MY AMATEUR COOLIES

IT took me two days to wangle a seat on a lorry, but at long last I left Chengtu for Ya-an, the terminus of the motor-road; from there I hoped to make my way, on foot, to Kangting and the marches of Tibet. I was so delighted to

be on the move again after two months of immobility that I
found myself actually enjoying being bumped along in the
lorry, perched dizzily on top of a pile of luggage and wedged
tightly between my equally uncomfortable fellow-passengers,
of whose national characteristics I had by now a good working knowledge. On the outskirts of the town we picked up
the inevitable contingent of "yellow fish," those semi-
clandestine travellers who get themselves taken on as super-
cargo by bribing the driver.

The landscape, judging from the glimpses I had of it
between the heads of my neighbours, was as opulent as all
landscapes seem to be in Szechwan: graceful hills, their
crests picked out by widely-spaced lines of trees, golden
fields of rape, pale green fields of rice. We slept that night
in the little village of Kinglai. With great difficulty I got a
tiny room to myself, and was fast asleep when another guest
arrived to share it. Without worrying in the slightest about
disturbing my rest, he immediately began to bellow for the
boy; then he started his toilet. He washed, cleared his throat
and spat promiscuously, after which, feeling better, he burst
into song at the top of his voice with a lack of self-conscious-
ness and self-restraint to which I was now pretty well
accustomed. In China, and for that matter all over the Far
East, privacy, so indispensable to the individualistic
Westerner, simply does not exist. You are never alone;
people burst into your room in the middle of the night and
start shouting, yelling and arguing as though you were not
there at all. They themselves are totally unaware of the
row they are making and would be quite capable of sleeping
soundly through a much louder uproar.

As we got nearer to Ya-an the country began to change.
The well-tilled fields were replaced by a harsher terrain, and
yesterday's gentle hills by mountains, high, naked and inhospitable; I even thought I could see, far away in the
distance, peaks with snow on them. The pastures were
dotted with spring flowers, and the great valley of the

Chingkiang reminded me of the valley of the Arve, near Sallanches.

Before long we reached Ya-an, and I clambered down off the lorry with feelings of unqualified relief and legs that were swollen from hours of cramped immobility. From now on, and for months to come, I would be free to travel through the wilds on foot or on horseback, far from the main roads and the unspeakable vehicles that use them.

The busy little town was full of life, for its market is the only trading-centre for the Chinese and Tibetans from Kangting. Accompanied by two coolies, I crossed the long suspension bridge which oscillates alarmingly over the Ya Ho. I got separated from my coolies in the dense crowd which swarmed along the main street, but in the end found them, and my luggage, at the Catholic Mission, where two venerable Fathers welcomed me with the flowery courtesy of mandarins.

I had now to organise my journey to Kangting. Most people who go there travel in *hua kans*, those carrying-chairs of which I have already given some account; but I was so badly in need of exercise, and so intensely disliked being carried on the backs of my fellow-men, that I decided to set out on foot, with two coolies to carry my things. I spent two days at Ya-an, buying various stores that I needed, while the Chinese Fathers scoured the place for coolies. In the end they produced two of their converts, one of whom was getting on in life. They looked pious enough, but had not the build of professional coolies. The loads they were prepared to carry were much smaller, and the wages they demanded much bigger, than those recognised by custom; but they were all I could get, and I preferred to give way on both points rather than prolong the usual sordid and tiresome arguments.

Ya-an is the main market for a special kind of tea which is grown in this part of the country and exported in very large quantities to Tibet via Kangting and over the caravan routes through Batang and Derge. Although the Chinese regard it as an inferior product, it is greatly esteemed by the Tibetans for its powerful flavour, which harmonises particularly well with that of the rancid yak's butter which they mix with their tea. Brick-tea comprises not only what we call tea-leaves, but also the coarser leaves and some of the twigs of the shrub, as well as the leaves and fruit of other plants and trees (the alder, for instance). This amalgam is steamed, weighed and compressed into hard bricks, which are packed up in coarse matting in sub-units of four. These rectangular parcels weigh between twenty-two and twenty-six pounds—the quality of the tea makes a slight difference to the weight—and are carried to Kangting by coolies; a long string of them, moving slowly under their monstrous burdens of tea, was a familiar sight along the road I followed.

I set off from Ya-an on March 24th. After passing through the usual sewage-disposal area on the outskirts of the town, my two coolies and I followed for a time a track hewn out of the bluffs which dominate the right bank of the Ya Ho. After a while a primitive sort of ferry took us over to the left bank, where we rejoined the main route. It ran through a lovely valley, flanked by high, wooded mountains to whose slopes clung a number of peasants' huts looking remarkably like Alpine châlets. Light though their loads were, my coolies were making very heavy weather of the march, and my misgivings about their physique increased steadily. There was, on the other hand, something to be said for the slow rate of progress which they imposed on me; I could meander along, sit down when I felt like it, enjoy the scenery, take photographs, pick flowers; after those fearful ordeals by lorry I felt like a schoolboy on the first day of his holidays.

There was a lot going on, too, along this track: long convoys of coolies, peasants going home from market, caravans of pack-ponies, army officers or minor bureaucrats travelling in litters, wrapped up to the eyes in blankets and urs. We stopped for luncheon at Feichenkuan, a pretty little hamlet over which, and over the valley below it, towers a huge crag with a little fort perched on top of it.

When we started off again after luncheon, I noticed that my coolies had recruited an assistant; he was a miserable specimen, lame already and so near starvation that he could hardly stand upright. On his back they had piled the greater part of both their loads, reserving for themselves only one light suitcase which—whistling cheerfully, and with their hands in their pockets—they took it in turns to carry. I was frightfully upset by what they had done; but I was unable to express, in terms intelligible to them, my disgust at their behaviour, so there was nothing for it but to resume the march without comment. It was only then that I understood why the Chinese Fathers had foisted off these two bogus coolies on me at an exorbitant price. Taking advantage of the freemasonry which is one of the foundations of their Church, they had hired me a nondescript brace of converts, who—thanks to the high rate at which they were being paid —could now hire somebody else to do their work for them. They had almost certainly extorted a premium from the lame coolie; and they almost certainly hoped for a tip from me. This neat little transaction was shortly to involve me in something like disaster.

We trailed on for several hours down a wide valley where the land was cultivated. There was no shade, and the coolies showed signs of distress as they plodded on through the oppressive heat; but at last we began to climb a twisting path up a thickly wooded hillside. Reaching the top, we plunged steeply down into another valley. Night was falling when we came to Tienshuan, a sizeable town where we slept in a reasonably comfortable inn.

We left it at seven o'clock the next morning. The road passed through a series of villages, in some of which I stopped for a cup of tea while waiting for the coolies to catch me up. The peasants were extraordinarily friendly, and

E

I deeply regretted my inadequate command of their
language; I would have given much to be able to talk freely
to them, but as it was we could do little more than beam
amicably at each other. The men all wore either a jacket or
a gown of blue cloth; the latter had to be hoisted up for
walking or for working in the fields. The women dress quite
differently from the way they do in the towns. Their jet
black hair is gathered into a flat bun at the nape of the neck
and this is transfixed by a huge pin—either of iron or of
imitation jade—which is their only form of personal adorn
ment; on their heads they wear a rather becoming sort of
turban, made of white cloth and having the shape of a
crown. Their costume consists of a jacket of coarse, dark
blue cloth, buttoned down the side, which reaches almost
to their knees and is caught at the waist by a cord or girdle
of yellow wool. Short, wide trousers of the same dark
blue cloth come down to a little below their knees. When—
much later—I saw for the first time fashionable European
ladies wearing slacks tailored in what I believe is known as
the "pirate" style, it was amusing to recall these Chinese
women who for centuries have worn trousers cut in this way
without giving a thought to their potentialities as a means of
attracting the opposite sex. On their feet both sexes in this
part of the world wear the traditional sandals of plaited
straw, which are both comfortable and inexpensive. They
are highly expendable, so the coolies always carry two or
three spare pairs; you can buy them in all the little country
shops, and their frayed skeletons litter every roadside in
China.

Round about noon the whole appearance of the valley
altered as sharply as though we had stepped across the
frontier between two different worlds. It was good-bye to
the big arable fields, the pastures, the rich and fecund villages.
Landslides or, in the winter, avalanches had mauled the
road; it was seldom more than a mule-track cut out of the
wall of the river-gorge whose course it followed, and along

t one found only squalid hamlets, comprising three or four deserted and ruinous hovels. Round these there were poor fields of rape or buckwheat and odd plots of cultivation, reluctantly yielded up to human endeavour by the inhospitable hillside. The population of this disenchanted valley was sparse; its members were as forlorn and desolate as their dwellings and the wild country in which their dwellings stood.

11. ROBBERY UNDER ARMS

THERE came a time when I was a long way ahead of my coolies. I had eaten nothing since we started, and my empty stomach made the great valley seem still more forbidding. At last—it was about four o'clock—I sighted a little village, and eventually found that it possessed an inn. An old woman and a sad little boy gaped at me for a long time before I could make them understand that I wanted something to eat; then they went away and came back with a bowl of cold rice and a cup of tea. While I was doing justice to this miserable snack, the coolies turned up; they were so exhausted that they refused categorically to go any further.

The place inspired no confidence, the people less. After the coolies had rested and eaten some rice, I had another shot at persuading them to finish the normal stage, and thus reach a place where we could enjoy a proper meal and reasonable security, but they were determined to stay where they were, and insisted that the next village was three hours' march further on and that it was even now too late to reach it before nightfall. (They were, as I found out later, lying; we could have got there in less than an hour.) Not for the first time, I cursed those amateur coolies; but what could one do about them? There was no point in going on alone and leaving all my kit behind; so there was nothing for it but to spend the night in this dreary inn, situated in the middle of the loneliest and most desolate stretch of this lonely, desolate valley. I had another bowl of rice with a bit of fat pork in it, and then retired for the night to a remarkably squalid little room. The next one was full of coolies; some were smoking opium while the others jabbered incessantly, but I was tired, and after a while fell asleep in these nightmare surroundings.

I was up at six, longing to get clear of this village into sunlight and clean air. I was rolling up my sleeping-bag in my room when one of my coolies came rushing in; pale and shaking, he poured into my ears a recital of which I could not understand a word, but which obviously meant a great deal to him. I went out, and found that the main room of the inn was occupied by a gang of swashbucklers of an unmistakably criminal appearance; they were armed to the teeth and were busily engaged in ransacking my luggage. As soon as they saw me they asked for the key of my suitcase.

At first I took them for soldiers engaged in the prevention of opium-smuggling, of which a great deal is done in these parts; however, before I could find my key, one of them swung my suitcase on to his shoulder and disappeared into the street. I dashed after him, leaving the coolies huddled in a corner and shaking with terror, caught up with him and somehow managed, by making signs, to induce him to return to the inn. As I crossed its threshold two of the bandits (by this time I had no doubt about the nature of their vocation) grabbed hold of me and emptied my pockets, a third tore off my jacket, which had my Leica in it, and a fourth removed my shoes; I was, in a word, systematically fleeced. At the back of the room the rest of the gang were busily engaged in dividing up the contents of my luggage; I had to help them sort out three pairs of shoes and show them the difference between the right foot and the left. I made an effort to salvage my Leica and my reserve stock of fifty films, but they suspected that the little boxes were some

sort of magic and probably contained treasure; in spite of
my protests they opened every single one and commandeered
the camera as well. The one who had taken my suitcase,
and who appeared to be the leader, hung on to his booty;
I failed to recover anything at all.

Meanwhile the main body of the detachment had not
been idle. The bandits turned the whole place inside out—
not merely the inn but every house in the village—and
appropriated everything that could be carried away: rice,
clothes, blankets, cooking-pots, even some panic-stricken
chickens and two pigs which screamed like lost souls. As I
watched them bustling about, I reckoned that there must be
something like fifty of them, all heavily armed with daggers,
Mausers or Chinese rifles; one of them had an American
automatic carbine. I spotted my Leica, my hat, my spectacles
and my leather wallet as their new owners bore them past
me; one man was using my tent-pole as a swagger-stick.
From time to time some of the bandits would come back
and run their hands over me, to make quite sure that nothing
had been overlooked; one of them gazed long and wistfully
at my trousers, almost made up his mind to take them, but
finally decided (they were in a very dilapidated state) that I
might as well be allowed to keep them. One party came back
to the inn and cooked some of the eggs they had stolen; I
watched them enviously, for in spite of all I had been
through I was ravenously hungry. They must have read my
mind, for they promptly invited me to share their meal;
their hospitality cost them little enough, but I appreciated it
greatly.

Shortly afterwards they gave the whole tragi-comedy a
suitably ironic climax by requisitioning my two coolies to
transport to their remote mountain fastness the things they
had stolen from me. The two rascals, bone-idle as ever, pre-
tended not to understand what was required of them, but
the blade of a knife, pressed gently against their ribs,
brought a sudden flash of comprehension, and they

shouldered their loads with the utmost docility; no suggestion was made, this time, that the loads were too heavy or that they were being inadequately rewarded for carrying them. The poor supernumerary coolie was, I imagine, considered too miserable a specimen to be worth kidnapping and was left in peace; he must have been the only person in the village who lost nothing in that foray, which shows that there is some justice in the world.

At last a whistle sounded and the whole gang disappeared down the path, covering their retreat with a *feu de joie.* The inn-keeper and I, left to our own devices, took one look at each other and roared with laughter. The bandits had taken his gown and left him with nothing but his underclothes, which were not in the best of repair. My costume consisted of an ancient pair of trousers, a very thin shirt and a pair of socks; as the excitement ebbed away, I began to shiver, for it was still only March, and up in the mountains the early mornings were bitterly cold.

12. A GRUELLING MARCH

WELL, that was that. There I was, alone in this god-forsaken village, without shoes, clothes, luggage, food or money; and I could not speak the language. I had been completely cleaned out. Everything had gone—all the money for my journey, the gold bars, the U.S. dollars, the Chinese dollars, the pounds sterling: my clothes, underclothes, sweaters, shoes, raincoat, camping kit, blankets, sleeping bag, Leica, films, medicine-chest, books, revolver, carbine, ammunition. Every single thing I possessed. The bandits had done remarkably well for themselves.

In the end I did recover some books which they had thrown away, a certain amount of salt, some tins of jam and —most valuable of all—my tent; presumably they had not been able to make out what it was. For months afterwards, when I crawled into it at night, I felt grateful to the bandits for leaving it behind. I also realised with a shock of surprise that the bandits had somehow overlooked my wrist-watch, which was covered by the sleeve of my shirt; and later I found, scattered along the track, my visiting cards and my passport, from which somebody—possibly wanting a souvenir of a happy occasion—had torn out the photograph.

I was in a curious mood. I felt indifferent to my plight, almost as though it was somebody else's; physically and emotionally I seemed to be drugged; I had, nevertheless, to make up my mind what to do, and, since it was obviously out of the question to continue my advance over the mountains in a state of destitution, I turned back towards Ya-an, accompanied by the coolie, shivering with cold and fright and carrying in an old sack the pitiful remainder of my possessions. As we started out I discovered a coin in my pocket; worth (in Indo-China) twenty-five centimes, it represented for the time being my entire capital.

Not being used to walking on a stony path in nothing but my socks, I had a pretty gruelling time of it. Still, I minced along, picking the best places to step on, and finally reached a hamlet where some soldiers—reacting without undue precipitation to the sound of firing—had also just arrived. They gave me a good hot bowl of rice and a pair of straw sandals in which I could make less agonising progress as far as Chussekuan, where their headquarters were. When I got there, the lieutenant in command was extraordinarily nice to me; he produced an admirable meal, fitted me out with an old army greatcoat, wired to the French Consul in Chengtu to say what had happened and gave me a room to rest in until the next day. I could not in any case leave until I had collected the two missing coolies. I was, as a matter of fact, pretty worried about them, and I knew that the last thing the soldiers wanted to do was to go chasing all over the mountains and braving the fire of bandits for the sake of two wretched coolies. So I had a breathing-space in which to take stock of the situation and decide what to do next.

That morning the shock of losing everything I possessed had brought on—understandably, perhaps—a mood of despair. I felt that my journey had ended in disaster, that there was nothing for it but to limp back to Ya-an, scrounging food like a beggar as I went. But by now I had pulled myself together; it seemed idiotic, after all the effort I had put into getting this far, to call everything off when one was within a few stages of Kangting. I might as well go on at least as far as Kangting. It is, after all, the gateway to Tibet; if I got there, the journey would not have been a complete waste of time. The bandits had failed to make much impression on the spirit of adventure, which is a tough sort of imp and was stirring again inside me.

I realised that I should have to scrap all my ideas of getting through to Sinkiang, and thence on to India; I no longer had the resources for such a journey. But there was one alternative to this ambitious programme which might prove feasible. I had, as luck would have it, arranged for a considerable sum in Chinese currency to be forwarded to Kangting; it would be waiting for me when I got there, and it might be enough to see me through to Jyekundo and the Kokonor. Meanwhile, I could cable to Indo-China for more money and have it sent to Sining; with it I could meet the expenses of the last lap to Peking. And what, in any case, was the point of worrying? If my recent experiences had taught me anything, it was that you cannot provide for every contingency.

Nevertheless, I slept badly that night, and the next day seemed as if it would never end. But at last, as it was getting on for dusk, my two coolies suddenly turned up, dirty, ragged and exhausted, but alive. They had been forced to carry their loads over steep mountain trails to the bandits' village, which was about five hours' hard going from the place

where we had been robbed. They had been beaten at intervals to keep them up to the mark and had had (they said)
nothing to eat for two days; they were lucky to have escaped
with their lives. But their afflictions loomed less large after
they had eaten—at the Chinese Army's expense—a heavy
meal. I had nothing left for them to carry, and the more
elderly of the two was in any case in no condition to go on;
I sent him back to Ya-an and kept the younger coolie as a
guide.

It so happened that a party of senior Chinese officials,
travelling to Kangting in litters, arrived at this place next
day. My adventures, which provided the sole topic of local
conversation, scared them out of their wits; they were determined that nothing of the kind should happen to them, and
our joint departure assumed the outward appearance of a
full-scale military expedition. The column comprised eight
litters with bureaucrats in them, twenty more laden with
their personal effects, one hundred soldiers with their gallant
centurion, and a wide variety of firearms. This formidable
mass of manœuvre made, for me, a slightly ridiculous contrast with the shoe-string style in which I had set forth, a
day or two earlier; but I realised, of course, that VIPs have
got to be looked after.

The VIPs themselves were, alas, caricatures; their pom-
posity and their conceit affronted the stark poverty of the
valley through which we travelled. One of them, a wealthy
magistrate, epitomised, in a slightly exaggerated way, com-
placency and ostentation. He travelled in tremendous style.
A magnificent tasselled silk skull-cap was clamped to his
head, and he wore a splendid silk gown lined with fur; on
top of all this he swathed himself in a capacious cloak—also
of silk, and as richly embroidered as a bishop's vestments—
which was lined throughout with the pelts of otters. This
garment was set off by a wide collar of ermine; and his boots
were lined with fur as well. This sort of get-up is not, as a
matter of fact, uncommon among rich Chinese *en route* for

Kangting, though the standard of magnificence rarely
reaches these dizzy heights; they are so genuinely frightened
of the cold and the other rigours they expect to face that they
feel obliged to dress as though for the Antarctic.

As a mere pedestrian, my status in this caravan was somewhat invidious. I had a hard time keeping up with the
chair-coolies, who moved at a brisk, rhythmical trot; they
monopolised the good going in the centre of the track, so
that I often had to trudge through the bad going on either
side. All the haughty officials in the litters knew about my
misfortunes, but their blank, unsympathetic faces never
relaxed into a smile of understanding; for them, I was just a
penniless down-and-out on foot, and as such I came in for
my share of the contempt with which they regarded the
coolies who carried them distressfully on their backs. I
never saw one get out of his litter, even on the stiffest climb,
to relieve the bursting lungs and straining muscles of the
coolies; they had hired the men, and they were going to get
full value out of them, even though it might cost one or two
poor brutes their lives. Their attitude was typical of the
Kuomintang bureaucracy at its worst.

I was, of course, retracing the route which I had followed,
so blithely and hopefully, three days ago. We made a longish halt in the village where I had been robbed and I
realised, seeing it for the second time, that the bandits'
attack could hardly have been a bow at venture; they must
have found out that an unescorted foreigner was coming
that way, otherwise they would never have made a considerable expedition—to a village which was not a recognised staging-place—on the very night when I happened to
be there. It also dawned on me that if the Fathers had found
me two professional coolies (of whom there were plenty at
Ya-an) we should have completed the full day's march to an
adequately guarded village and nothing would have happened. Professional coolies might have been unregenerate
heathens, and opium-addicts into the bargain; but what I

wanted was two strong men, not a couple of choirboys. However, the whole business was over now; it was no good crying over spilt milk.

After a time, since nobody seemed to be making a move, I went on ahead, only too pleased to be away from my uncongenial companions. It was a lovely day, and the air was full of the scent of violets. I was alone for once, and I found myself toying with the idea of a world where there would be sunlight, mountains, streams, flowers, birds and beasts, but no men—none of those mischievous and destructive creatures whose capacity for evil perverts all that is good and gentle on our planet. But soon the convoy of litters caught up with me again, its strength considerably reduced by the loss of its heroic escort, who had prudently decided to return to base. I let the long file of straining coolies trot by, then, when silence returned to the mountainside, followed them at a comfortable pace. That evening I reached Lianluku, a big hamlet at the foot of the pass, where my army greatcoat created a mild sensation. A nice little Chinese merchant, bound for Kangting, lent me a small sum of money, so I was able to pay for my board and lodging.

The next day was tough, for we had to cross the great pass of Feiyuling, nearly nine thousand feet above sea-level. The route was uninteresting to begin with, but soon led us into a wild, deep, cañon-like valley. Here snow was still lying and waterfalls were fantastic stalactites of ice, but sunny corners where the snow had thawed were dotted with early primroses, a lovely and a touching sight. Unfortunately their charm was slightly lost on me as I floundered miserably through the mixture of mud and snow on the trail. We soon turned sharply off this to climb up an exceptionally steep path. The coolies' tracks had made a sort of staircase in the deep, hard snow which covered it. My straw sandals, sodden and disintegrating, gave me no grip and were always slipping; my feet, bleeding where the skin had been rubbed

off them, were half-frozen; the climb was torture for me
However, my lot struck me as less hard than that of the
coolies laden with brick-tea. They had to dump half their
burden and make two journeys of it; even so, each half-load
weighed nearly a hundredweight, and they had to fix iron
crampons to their sandals to avoid slipping on the frozen
surface.

Presently we reached a shoulder where the path joined up
again with the main trail. The coolies wolfed down a flat
cake made of maize, then shouldered their loads again
Most of them were carrying thirteen or fourteen packets of
brick-tea—in other words, something like two hundredweight; one was actually carrying eighteen, or over two-and-
a-half hundredweight. These poor wretches move forward
with tiny little steps, their heads lowered; every thirty yards
or so they stop, propping their load on a staff shod with a flat
iron head which they rest on the ground behind them
They only pause for a moment, then a whistle starts them
off again and they crawl on to the next halt. In this way
they cover the hundred and fifty miles between Ya-an and
Kangting. They eat nothing except maize cakes, but at
the end of every stage they smoke a pipe of opium, which
seems to strengthen their powers of endurance as well as
bringing solace to their minds. The drug is a passport to
oblivion; they are to be pitied for needing such a passport
but they can hardly be blamed for using it. They live
like beasts of burden; opium is the only happiness they
know.

The trail wound on in long zigzags until another precipitous short-cut brought us up on to the wide, flat col. I
had a splendid view from here, although the high mountain
ranges towards Tibet were largely hidden by cloud.

Nothing seems to have altered since Huc and Gabet
travelled through these regions more than a hundred years
ago. The fashion in those days was for high-flown descrip-
tive writing; but after making allowance for the "fearful

chasms from which the most intrepid traveller needs must recoil in horror," on whose brink "a single false step spelt annihilation on the jagged rocks below," I found any number of things which were exactly as Huc and Gabet described them: the way the chair-coolies lived, the maize cakes, the unchanging landscape, the views from the peaks, and especially their account of the tea-coolies roused to renewed efforts by "a long whistle which sounds like a mournful sigh." That was precisely the impression the noise made upon me.

After a short rest on the pass, we began the descent. My coolie set off down a steep path leading towards a valley, some way off, which stretched as far as the eye could see. I had a vague idea that we were not going in quite the right direction, and it seemed odd that there were no other coolies about. Presently we met two young herdsmen who told us that, sure enough, our path did not go to Luting but joined the valley much lower down. So we had to climb back again for about three hundred yards, and once more I cursed my wretched coolie who was not only incapable of carrying a load but did not even know the way, for it was the first time he had been there.

However, we finally got back on the right path. Night was falling and the lights in the valley were still a terribly long way away. We had to slacken our pace, for fear of losing the path again. My straw sandals were only a shadow of their former selves and my feet were giving me hell. The coolie was in even worse case; it was the first time in his life that he had done a stage like this through the mountains. Presently he lost his bearings, had no idea whether to go back or go on, and burst into tears; I had to go and rescue him.

Finally, about eight o'clock, we stumbled on a hovel made of planks into which a large Chinese family had squeezed themselves; by squeezing themselves a bit tighter they made room for us to lie down on the mud floor and we both fell

asleep like animals. Next day a few hours' march brought us
to Luting and the plateau of Chapa; here there was a Catholic
Mission, where a young Chinese Father gave me a hospitable
welcome.

13. PRESSING ON REGARDLESS

I HAD a day's badly needed rest on a sunny terrace which
overlooked the valley of the Tatung Ho. Above me soared
the great range which we had crossed the day before; it
divides Szechwan from Sikang, of which Kangting is the
capital. Next day we set off at an early hour along the right
bank of the Tatung Ho, below a towering cliff-face. Stunted
palms jutted from the skyline above us; there were banana-
palms, too, struggling against heavy odds to bear fruit.
There was a lot of traffic on the road: Tibetans on horseback
going to Ya-an to buy tea, coolies jogging slowly in long files
following one behind the other like a procession of caterpillars, other coolies resting by the side of the road.
Occasionally we passed through a little village; in front of
every inn there was a tall bench, made of clay and about the
height of a man, on which the tea-coolies could dump their
loads without having to stoop. I was walking along, thinking
of nothing in particular, when suddenly, as I rounded a
corner, I stopped dead with an exclamation of wonder; to
the south, through a gap in the mountains, a huge snow
mountain reared up, resplendent against the deep blue sky.
It was not Minyakonka herself, but one of her secondary
spurs. I could distinguish three separate peaks and the
highest of them, a noble pyramid rather like the Dent
Blanche, wore an elegant sheath of ice which plunged down
into an enormous glacier. Even at that distance—and I was
a very long way off—I could pick out quite clearly the scars
of the seracs. This dramatic spectacle banished all my

worries, but it was, alas, only a transitory glimpse; round the next corner the heat, the dust and my sore feet returned to plague me.

Just beyond the village of Penpa, about fifteen miles from Luting, I saw on the other side of the river a great white *chörten*, completely Tibetan in appearance.* It was the first I had seen, and it came as a reminder that Tibet was not so very far away. Immediately afterwards the road, across which lay deep drifts of sand, branched off from the main river and struck up a narrow valley down which a tributary, the Kangting Ho, flowed swiftly.

That night, in a little inn, I was woken up by insects crawling about on my face. The coolie, who had been suffering from them himself, got up and lit a candle to see what we were up against. A dense swarm of bed-bugs, in various stages of maturity, teemed in the cracks between the planks which formed a partition along one side of our room. The coolie beat a retreat, but I merely shifted my position and lay with my head towards the outside wall, which was less thickly infested.

During my stay in China I had acquired a good working knowledge of the various types of parasite and had made some instructive comparisons. Fleas are easily the most irritating bedfellows, for they insist on carrying out exhaustive reconnaissances which make you itch unendurably everywhere. Bed-bugs, on the other hand, do not worry me much, though they are temperamental creatures and quick to take offence. If, when they start strolling about on your face, you brush them off in a rough, boorish way, they leave a most revolting smell on your fingers. The least uncongenial guests are, in my view, lice; they are placid, well-behaved little fellows, who only give trouble when you have

---

* *Chörten*—from the Sanskrit *Chaitya*. A shrine or monument, normally of stone or brick, having a formal and traditional design. Generally erected on a spot of especial holiness or to mark the grave of a saint. The author gives a detailed description of two *chörtens*, one old and one comparatively modern, on p. 231. P. F.

too many of them at a time. One quickly gets used to them
which is just as well, for in China—and even more in Tibet—
it is virtually impossible to avoid their society; everybody ha
lice, and whenever you see a caravan at rest, a good many o
the people in it are sure to be engaged on a louse-hunt—the
only form of blood sport, as an Englishman once said, ii
which you provide the blood.

Before starting next day I tried to doctor my feet, which
were by now a mass of bleeding sores. When I saw how bac
they were, I told the coolie to go on to Kangting and send
back a *hua kan* for me as soon as he got there; in the mean
time I hobbled on, treading delicately. The valley, strait
laced by its towering walls, was extraordinarily beautiful
It was shut in by parallel ranges of hills, but on the left
hand side you got, if you looked up a corrie at the righ
moment, glimpses of a glacier poised in eternity, or of a
great snow-covered mountain with its peak buried in the
belly of the clouds. If you looked below, there was the
Kangting Ho: a mighty torrent, swollen by the melted
snows, plunging down the valley with a deadly purpose and
a deafening noise, exploding, as it surged over the huge
boulders in its course, into far-flung panoplies of spray in
which the sunlight picked out delicate rainbows.

At Hokiu I stopped to rest and stayed there long enough
to study in some detail one of the Tibetan bridges which I
had so often read about. Its basis was an enormously thick
cable made of bamboo fibre; this was slung across the river
and fixed to a huge rock on either side. On the cable rode
what sailors would call a block—a big bamboo ring fitted
with a pulley—beneath which dangled the seat on which the
traveller sat. A cord, running through the pulley, was
connected to a small platform at either end of the bridge. As
I watched, a little girl was using this primitive contraption,
and she did it with the disarmingly matter-of-fact air of one
who is used to doing a difficult and slightly dangerous thing
for fun. She sat herself down on the seat, hooked it on to

ut; he immediately set off to try to recover Liotard's body,
nd did in fact manage to bring back some of their kit.

I soon realised that the Chinese authorities were genuinely
vorried about what had happened to me; the light which my
xperiences threw on the state of law and order in a province
or which Nanking was responsible threatened them with a
rave loss of face. Acting on the advice of Father Yan (who
vell understood his compatriots' dilemma) I told the
Governor, in mild but rather wistful terms, that I should now
be obliged, for lack of funds, to abandon the task with which
ny Government had entrusted me; it would, of course, be
ecessary to include in my official report my reasons for
oing so.

All this—and especially the first part—was no more and
o less than the truth; but I did not care for this indirect
orm of blackmail, however closely it might conform to the
ustom of the country. It did, in fact, conform so closely
hat, a few days later, the Governor asked to be informed
ow much, in terms of money, I had lost as a result of my
egrettable encounter with the bandits. The next time we
net, at a banquet, he insisted most courteously that I should
  he put it) be so gracious as to do him the honour of
cepting a trivial measure of compensation, offered in the
ope that I should be able, with its help, to continue my
urney.

His trivial measure of compensation represented, in
hinese currency, quite a lot of money. It would not enable
ne to replace everything I had lost—the gold, for instance,
nd the photographic equipment, and the other things you
ould not buy in China—and its value would, of course,
epreciate almost hourly. It would, nevertheless, adequately
nance my attempt to traverse the Eastern Marches of
Tibet. I felt rather pleased with myself for having "pressed
n regardless," instead of giving up when I had all too many
good reasons for doing so.

What I completely failed to find in Kangting was either

camp equipment or European clothes; so I fitted out m
expedition on Tibetan lines. The Sisters at the Catholi
hospital knitted me some sweaters and the local Chines
doctor lent me an American raincoat; with these, and wit
my little tent which the bandits had left behind, I was no
going to be too badly off. The loss of my camera, on th
other hand, was a major disaster; but Father Richard ler
me his Kodak-Retina for the journey, and the last of m
administrative troubles was over. Now all I had to do was t
complete my preparations and find a caravan bound for th
right destination. This last item on the agenda proved to b
a matter of some difficulty.

PART THREE

The Gateway to Tibet

14. TIBETANS IN KANGTING

KANGTING is the capital of the Chinese province of Sikang. It is a market town, situated nearly eight thousand feet above sea-level, on the floor of a narrow valley. Chinese governments have always had a mania for altering place-names, and until a short time ago Kangting was called Tatsienlu; it still is on most maps. The old name is a corruption of the Tibetan Dar-Tsen-Do; the syllable *do*, which you often find in Tibetan place-names (Jyekundo, Chamdo), indicating the confluence of two rivers—in this case the Dar and the Tse. The little town is closely shut in on all sides by high mountain ranges which during much of the day— and in winter very inconveniently—shut out the sunlight. Kangting lies so low in relation to the surrounding hills that when you are in it you cannot see the peaks beyond them and you do not feel as if you were high up on the surface of our planet; but you have only to climb the grassy slopes to the northward to see Minyakonka proudly asserting herself against the sky. The highest point on this splendid, ice-sheathed mountain attains (according to her first conquerors) a height of 24,900 feet above sea-level.

Kangting was only recently promoted to the dignity of a provincial capital and still has a slightly *parvenu* air. The new cinema and the hideous municipal buildings have only incompletely imposed a veneer of modernisation on the ancient city of the Chala kings; its atmosphere lingers on in the narrow alley-ways of the Tibetan quarter. Coming from Ya-an, you enter the town by a long, characterless street, flanked by tea warehouses, customs sheds and police stations; the amenities of this thoroughfare are not improved by a concrete pillbox, heavily loopholed, which will theoretically deny access to potential invaders. This is the New City, built on the right bank of the river and downstream from the point of confluence; it suffers regularly from flooding during the spates of spring. The business centre of the town differs little from its counterparts elsewhere in the interior, and consists of a long, straight street lined by hundreds of small shops. They are all in the hands of the Chinese, who can be relied on to crop up wherever there is money to be made.

Eventually you reach a little square; this is the heart of Kangting, and on it practically everyone converges— Tibetans, pedlars, men hawking firewood or charcoal and many others. Beyond it lies the Tibetan quarter, less animated but more interesting. Here you find the crafts- men who build those noble boots, black and red in colour with the toes turned up like the prow of an old ship, and the travelling-chests bound in fine rawhide like morocco, and all the other things that they make out of leather—belts bandoliers, tobacco-pouches, saddles and bridles studded with silver. Here, too, are the Tibetan pawnbrokers, with their diverse and exotic stock-in-trade: images of Buddha, bells and ritual sceptres, beautifully worked silver talismans, wooden eating-bowls, saddle-cloths, sacred pictures and enormous Tibetan daggers, which are really more like broad swords and whose hilts are bedizened with silver-work. These great swords are—like his amulet, his tinder-box and the big wallet dangling from his belt—among the very few items of personal equipment which the Tibetan regards as indispensable; he would feel incomplete and unhappy with- out any one of them.

Every narrow street in this part of Kangting has several inns in it; and these, whenever a caravan arrives, are loud with the objurgations of muleteers, the grunting of yaks and the clamour of overburdened tea-coolies who have reached their destination at last. On the opposite bank, on the tongue of land formed by the confluence of the two big rivers, stands the administrative centre of the city—the offices of the provincial government, the cathedral, the schools and a good many of the big business houses.

Kangting is essentially a clearing-house for brick-tea. It comes in from Ya-an and goes out on caravan routes which serve the whole of Tibet as far as Lhasa. The town (which otherwise would be a place of no importance) depends for its prosperity entirely on tea; the yaks and mules which in one year set out from it laden with this commodity are numbered in tens of thousands. And yet, if you walk about the town, you are barely conscious of the part which tea plays in its life. The stocks are held in warehouses, or else in the court-yards of the inns frequented by the caravans of the big Chinese and Tibetan merchants. These spacious buildings are built round an ample courtyard with stores and stalls open-ing off it; the living-rooms, which give on to a wide gallery, are on the first floor. The brick-tea is packaged either in the courtyard or in the street outside; it is quite a complicated process. When the coolies bring it in from Ya-an, the tea has to be repacked before being consigned up-country; in a coolie's load the standard sub-unit is four bricks lashed to-gether, but these would be the wrong shape for animal transport. So they are first cut in two, then put together in lots of three; this leaves you with what they call a *gam*, which is half a yak's load. Tea which is going to be con-sumed reasonably soon is done up in a loose cover of matting, but the *gams*, which are bound for remote destinations, perhaps even for Lhasa, are sewn up in yak-hides. These hides are not tanned, but merely dried in the sun; when used for packing they are soaked in water to make them pliable and then sewn very tightly round the load; when they dry out again, the tea is enclosed in a container which is as hard as wood and is completely unaffected by rain, hard knocks or immersion in streams. The Tibetan packers are a special guild of craftsmen, readily identifiable by the powerful aroma of untanned leather which they exude. Another prominent guild in Kangting is that of the women tea coolies who shift the stuff from the warehouses to the inns where the caravans start. They have a monopoly of this work, and the cheerful gangs of girls are a picturesque element in the city's life. They need to be immensely strong to do a job which consists of carrying anything up to an entire yak's load, several times a day, over a short distance. Many of them are quite pretty (and well aware of the fact); they look very gay and rather brazen as, giggling and chattering among themselves, they carry their heavy burdens, which are held in place by a woollen girdle round their chest.

I liked the Tibetans enormously. They are quite different from the Chinese, with whom, despite the close quarters in which they live, they have hardly anything in common. Against the background of a bustling throng of small Chinese traders, all uniformly clad in dark blue so that no individual stands out, your eye cannot help being caught by these handsome, gentle giants, caravan-men or nomads who have come in from the interior to sell their wool and buy tea with the proceeds. They move slowly through the crowd, dwarfing it, their massive, muscular frames lounging along with an easy, athletic gait. In appearance they are not in the least like the Chinese. With their deeply tanned complexions, almond eyes, salient cheek-bones and noses which are prominent and often aquiline, they might almost be Red Indians. Except for the lamas and certain laymen who shave their heads, the Tibetans generally wear their hair either long, or else in a plait wound round their skulls and embellished with a complicated pattern of lesser plaits which make the whole thing look like some sort of crown. They very often wear a huge conical felt hat, whose shape varies according to the district they come from; sometimes its peak supports a kind of mortarboard from which dangles a thick woollen fringe. In order to prevent their hats being blown away, they attach them to their heads with the long plait which I have just described, and which has to be unwound for the purpose. In their left ear they wear a heavy silver ring decorated with a huge gaud of either coral or turquoise.

Their costume is not elaborate; it normally consists only of a *shuba*, a long, capacious robe with wide, elongated sleeves which hang almost to the ground. This is caught up at the waist by a woollen girdle, so that its skirts reach only down to the knees and its upper folds form an enormous circular pocket round its wearer's chest; this is called the *ampa*, and in it are stowed a wide range of impedimenta—an eating-bowl, a bag of *tsampa* and many other small necessities. Many *shubas* are made of wool—either the plain grey wool that they spin in Sikang or the splendid, warm, soft stuff from Lhasa, dyed a rich dark red. The nomads, on the other hand, generally wear a sheepskin *shuba*, hand-sewn and crudely tanned in butter, with the fleece on the inside. The town-dwelling Tibetans—prosperous merchants for the most part—supplement this garment with cotton or woollen drawers and a cotton or silk under-shirt with long sleeves; but the nomads normally wear nothing at all under-neath it, though in winter they sometimes put on sheepskin drawers. The Tibetans hardly ever do their *shubas* up over their chests; the right shoulder and arm are almost always left free; and when they are on the march or at work the whole top part of the robe is allowed to slip down so that it is supported only by their belts; this leaves them naked above the waist and clad in a very odd-looking sort of skirt below it. They hardly feel the cold at all, and in the depth of winter, heedless of frost or snow or wind, they trudge imperturbably along with their bosoms bared to the icy blast. Their feet, too, are bare inside their great top-boots. These have soft soles of raw, untanned leather; the loose-fitting leg of the boot, which may be red or black or green in colour, has a sort of woollen garter round the top of it which is fastened to the leg above the knee with another, very brightly coloured, strip of woollen material.

The Tibetan women—tall, well-proportioned and graceful

—are in general not less impressive than the men. They hav
the same prominent cheek-bones, the same almond eyes
They look nice, and they also sound nice; their deep, sultr
voices could hardly be more different from the shrill
strident fluting of the sing-song Chinese girls, which seldon
falls very beguilingly on European ears. At Kangting mos
of the Tibetan women wore their long, jet-black hair in
plait twisted round and round until it made a sort of turban
being women, they had broken up this sombre, formal mas
by interlacing it with strands of red and green wool, thu
making a striped and garish halo which set off their dark
burnt faces very well indeed. Further north, up in th
Derge territory, they twist their hair into a fringe of ver
long, very narrow plaits which make them look as if the
were wearing a veil over their heads; these plaits ar
gathered behind their backs and end in a long horse-tail o
black hairs and strands of black wool. Standing on th
terrace outside her house, her slender figure closely en
veloped in her *shuba*, a Tibetan woman looks like a mediæva
princess.

Outwardly and inwardly, she and her sisters differ i
every way from the small, willowy, unforthcoming Chines
women in their characterless, ill-cut uniforms of blue, th
graceless fatigue-dress of modern China. (It will be clea
to the reader that I am describing the female population o
the interior, not the elegant expatriates of Hong Kong an
Shanghai.) But of course in China a woman inherits a
immemorial tradition of domestic serfdom, of automati
subjection to her lord and master: whereas in Tibet she is
free agent, who does indeed work very hard but who i
allowed—and does not hesitate to take—plenty of initiativ
in running her house (or her tent) and is never afraid o
speaking her own mind. She wears much the same clothe
as the men. Her *shuba*—as long, anyhow, as she is leading
sedentary life—is not kilted up; it is, moreover, fastened a
the throat and shows off her figure. The dangling sleeve

are rolled up to her wrists, so that their blue silk lining stands out brightly, like an exaggerated cuff, against the drabber background of the robe itself.

The nomad women, on the other hand, wear, like their menfolk, coarse sheepskin *shubas*. When they go to work on the land they, too, let the top part of the garment fall round their waists, baring in all innocence their strong shoulders and their proud breasts to the gaze of the passer-by. Fashionable Tibetan ladies, on the other hand, wear underneath their *shubas* a voluminous shift of red or green silk with long sleeves which show at their wrists. As for Tibetan children, they can only be described as adorable, especially when they are very small; they wear—even in the coldest weather—either nothing at all or alternatively a miniature sheepskin *shuba* which, bulging unnaturally round the tiny bipeds, makes them look like overgrown little chickens.

The men and the women are equally keen on jewellery, by which I mean heavy—but often very finely worked—silver gew-gaws: enormous earrings, necklaces, rings, and amulets, embossed with complicated pictorial designs which, like so much Central Asian art, are often inspired by animals. The women's best necklaces offer a good guide to the Tibetan taste in jewellery: enormous lumps of blood-red coral: lovely blue turquoises: huge beads of amber: "Tibetan pearls," locally known as *zi*, which are a kind of oblong-shaped agate, olive-grey or *café au lait* in colour but laced with black or chocolate-coloured veins which generally have a white border and are always roughly circular, so that the stone has something of the same aspect as a human eye. The value of these so-called pearls is determined by their conformation and by the pattern of the veins. The commonest type are oblong, comprising (as it were) two eyes with one ring round each eye-ball; if there are two rings, and especially if one of them is slightly scalloped, the stone's value is greatly increased.

These stones are very hard; a knife makes no impression

on them. The best are worth a great deal of money. Unfortunately there are a lot of fakes about. A German
traveller took home some genuine specimens and had them
copied and manufactured in bulk; so that today Tibet is
flooded with imitation "pearls," all made (in Germany) of
plastic. On the coral market, once dominated by the pink
coral from Formosa, the most popular shade is now the
blood-red, which comes from Italy.

You notice the natural good taste of the Tibetans in even
their most ordinary belongings: their big, odd-looking
boots, in which leather of several different colours is used
with the happiest effect; their belts and garters, whose design
is always original and never ugly; their purses and tinder-
boxes, overlaid with finely worked silver. It is the same with
their weapons: the long knife which they use for practically
everything, the great broadsword thrust diagonally through
their belt, the musket with a long forked rest attached to its
barrel—everything in this primitive armoury is treated as an
objet d'art and embellished with silver-work and with uncut
coral or turquoise. Even their humblest household utensils
—the nomad's wooden bowl, beautifully shaped and often
lined with silver; the charming tea-cups, with lids shaped
like little pagodas and decorated with coral and silver; the
teapots and beer-flagons, the big copper braziers on which
the tea is kept hot, the richly coloured carpets, the simple
furniture—the Tibetans allow nothing to look dull, let alone
ugly. I often used to see, in the kitchen of an ordinary
lamasery, huge, fantastic saucepans and kettles which, by
the perfection of their design and the grace of their symbolic
decorations, could fairly claim to rank as works of art.

And of course one should not forget the real, the deliberate
works of art: the life-size images, the statuettes of gilded
copper, the splendid paintings on silk—all those inspired
manifestations of religious art of which the West is beginning
to know something and which play so dominant a part in
Far Eastern æsthetics. Tibetan art may have its roots in

he cultures of China and India, but it has developed a dis-
inctive and easily recognisable character of its own. There
an, I think, be very few races in whom the artistic sense—
eriving almost wholly from religious inspiration—is so
cute and, far from being the prerogative of one small class,
s a common heritage of the whole community.

15. FRONTIER TROUBLES

T would not be possible to tell my story, such as it is, with-
ut some reference to the political relations between Chinese
nd Tibetans in the little buffer-state of Sikang, to the lack of
ffection (to put it mildly) of the latter for the former, and to
he inability of the Chinese Government to maintain any
orm of effective control over the province. A brief survey of
he history of this region may prove helpful to the reader.

Frontier troubles are a chronic form of political malady
ll over the world, and the Sino-Tibetan frontier provides no
xception to this rule. We have it on the authority of
Chinese historians that, a hundred years before the Christian
ra began, the Tibetans had established themselves in the
erritories which today form the provinces of Sikang and
Chinghai. At that time Chinese suzerainty was asserted
nly by the bestowal of Chinese titles on the Tibetan chief-
ains, whose executive powers were not interfered with; this
delicate form of vassalage provided a formula which was
qually satisfactory from the point of view of Imperial
prestige and Tibetan independence. It was not until very
much later—the end of the seventeenth century—that the
territories were annexed by the early Manchu emperors in
accordance with their policy of unifying the whole of China;
and even then annexation, though a fact on paper, was
largely a fiction in practice. In those days Buddhism, which
had gained a strong hold over most of Central Asia, had been

adopted by the Manchu dynasty as their official religion
and the emperors even posed as protectors of the Tibetan
Church.

Although there was a short military campaign, as a result
of which Chinese garrisons were established at Tatsienlu, at
Batang and at key points along the road to Lhasa, Peking
formally recognised and even proclaimed the Dalai Lama as
the sole temporal sovereign authority in Tibet; the Manchus
contented themselves with appointing to Lhasa two special
commissioners, called *ambans*, in whom were vested power
to influence decisively the selection of all future reincarna-
tions of the Dalai Lama. By way of reparation, the Emperor
regularly distributed handsome grants of money to the
lamaseries and the local chieftains. These comparatively
urbane relations between the two countries, which had unobtrusively given the Tibetan priesthood a vested interest
in the Chinese administration, lasted until the Manchu
dynasty fell; and, while they lasted, Chinese armies from
time to time entered Tibet on the pretext of protecting the
country against Mongol invasions from Dzungaria. The
Sino-Tibetan frontier was marked by the erection of a
pillar on the Bum-La, a pass which lies two and a half days'
march to the southwest of Batang; thence the frontier ran
north along a line parallel to, and slightly west of, the
Yangtse. All the territory to the west of this line was under
the direct authority of the Dalai Lama, but to the east of it
the petty chieftains of the local tribes retained—although
they paid tribute to Peking—a considerable measure of
independence.

These arrangements failed to survive the blow dealt, in-
directly, to China's position in that part of the world by the
British expedition to Lhasa in 1904. In order to offset the
damage done to their interests by the treaty between England
and Tibet, the Chinese set about extending westwards the
sphere of their direct control and began to colonise the
country round Batang. The Tibetans reacted vigorously.

The Chinese governor was killed on his way to Chamdo and his army put to flight after an action near Batang; several missionaries were also murdered, and Chinese fortunes were at a low ebb when a special commissioner called Chao Yu-ong appeared on the scene.

Acting with a savagery which earned him the sobriquet of "The Butcher of Monks," he swept down on Batang, sacked the lamasery, pushed on to Chamdo and, in a series of victorious campaigns which brought his army to the gates of Lhasa, re-established order and reasserted Chinese domination over Tibet. In 1909 he recommended that Sikang should be constituted a separate province comprising thirty-six sub-prefectures, with Batang as the capital. This project was not given effect until later, and then in a modified form; for the Chinese Revolution of 1911 brought Chao's career to an end, and he was shortly afterwards assassinated by his compatriots.

The troublous early years of the Chinese Republic saw the rebellion of most of the tributary chieftains, a number of pitched battles between Chinese and Tibetans and many strange happenings in which tragedy, comedy and (of course) religion all had a part to play. In 1914 Great Britain, China and Tibet met at the conference table to try to restore peace, but this conclave broke up after failing to reach agreement on the fundamental question of the Sino-Tibetan frontier; this, since about 1918, has been recognised for practical purposes as following the course of the Upper Yangtse. In these years the Chinese had too many other preoccupations to bother about reconquering Tibet, things gradually quietened down, and in 1927 the province of Sikang was brought into being; but it consisted of only twenty-seven sub-prefectures instead of the thirty-six visualised by the man who conceived the idea. China had lost, in the course of a decade, all the territory which the Butcher had overrun.

Since then Sikang has been relatively peaceful, but this short synopsis of the province's history makes it easy to

G

understand how precarious this state of affairs is bound to be
Chinese control is little more than nominal; I was often to
have first-hand experience of its ineffectiveness. In order to
govern a territory of this kind it is not enough to station, in
isolated villages separated from each other by many days'
journey, a few unimpressive officials and a handful of ragged
soldiers. The Tibetans completely disregard the Chinese
administration and obey only their own chiefs. One very
simple fact illustrates the true status of Sikang's Chinese
rulers: nobody in the province will accept Chinese currency
and the officials, unable to buy anything with their money,
are forced to subsist by a process of barter.*

16. ELEMENTS OF BUDDHISM

KANGTING is rightly called The Gateway to Tibet. There
can be very few other places in the world where the transi-
tion between two races, two cultures and two religions is
made so brusquely.

On the way from Ya-an to Kangting one passes nothing
but Chinese villages, hears nothing but Chinese spoken, sees
only Chinese temples; the few Tibetans that one meets are
transients, who have made the journey to Ya-an to buy tea
but are eager to get back to the mountains and the valleys of
their homeland. But once one is west of Kangting, one has
done with China. Henceforth only Tibetan is spoken, only
Tibetans are to be seen, even the landscape alters; the
religious monuments are all Buddhist, the temples are all
lamaseries. Chinese money ceases to circulate, and the only
Chinese one meets are officials or soldiers or little merchants,
all seemingly lost in a land which they do not understand

* I am writing about the Chinese Nationalist régime between the years
1947 and 1949. I believe that the Communists have made an effort to base
their administration on social and democratic reforms. A. M.

nd in which they keep themselves to themselves, living in the Chinese fashion, having as little as possible to do with the weird and (to them) barbarous world around them, beings isolated and benighted in the empty immensity of the high plateaux.

Kangting is the point at which two worlds touch. It is a good place to make one's first direct contact with the religion which has left so deep a mark upon the life of Tibet. Its streets are full of red-robed lamas; in and around the town are dozens of lamaseries, with their white *chörtens* and their prayer-flags, and often, in the silent hours of darkness, you hear the long, low blasts of the great ceremonial trumpets and the melancholy notes of the hautboys. This music, so sad and yet so simple, seems to express the very soul of Tibet.

It is a country where religion rules men's minds, pervades and shapes their lives; it is no exaggeration to say that Tibet is—except perhaps for India—the most religious country in the world. One cannot attempt to describe it without describing the main essentials of its faith.

Lamaism, which exists only in Tibet and Mongolia, is a specialised form of religion, an offshoot of the main corpus of the Buddhist faith. Although it differs greatly, especially in externals, from Buddhism as practised in Ceylon, Cambodia and elsewhere, it derives its virtue—however dissimilar its rites and even its beliefs may be—from the same source: from the doctrines of Buddha and from the fundamental principles which he himself laid down.

Buddha (who was, it is perhaps hardly necessary to point out, a real person) lived in India in the seventh century B.C. Unlike most men who have founded a religion, he never claimed to be either an emissary or a son of the Deity, but only a human being who—having, unaided, solved the problems of sorrow and deliverance—dedicated his life to sharing this secret with his fellow-men; it was only later that his disciples deified him. This problem of deliverance, which obsesses the Hindu mind, is linked with the equally fundamental idea of transmigration. The life we live is not the gift of a god, but merely an episode in a sequence of different lives, an instalment in an endless serial. We have lived before, we shall live again; from birth to the death which follows it, from death to another birth, the thread of our personal existence runs on, linking each life to the next.

The sequence of these lives is not fortuitous. It is controlled by the law of *karman*, which is merely an extension to the immaterial world of the law of causality, which has long been recognised in the material one. In each life a man's share of grief and joy is determined by the amount of good or evil that he did in the life before it; and his conduct in his current life will decide the kind of existence which will follow it. In this way happiness, or the failure to achieve it, are due, not to the arbitrary decrees of a God, but to a man's own actions. This is a rational and a consoling creed, wholly free—since it makes us directly responsible for our own destinies—from the apathy and fatalism which are often charged against it. A third conception, characteristic of and integral to Buddhism, is merely the rationalisation of something which everyone can see for himself—to wit, that suffering is inherent in life, is indeed one of life's chief characteristics, dogs life's footsteps from the moment of birth to the moment of death, despite fleeting and illusory moments of happiness. If a man believes that suffering is a part of life and that for him—since he is always going to be reincarnated after death—suffering will never cease, he has the strongest of motives to escape from this terrible treadmill, to achieve salvation by meritorious conduct which will progressively lessen his burdens in the future.

Buddha was able to bring to the problem of man's unending dilemma a lucid and precise solution, because he discerned the starting-point of the chain of cause and effect which leads from one life of suffering to the next. This starting-point is desire. Every desire inspires action to satisfy it; every action involves a man in fresh contacts with the world, and these awake new desires. At death it is desire—the desire for more life—which launches the vital spark into another existence and keeps the treadmill turning. To achieve deliverance a man must suppress his desires; with them will go the desire for more life. When he is completely detached from the world, he will stop living, as a lamp which has run out of oil stops burning. He will have attained the supreme tranquillity of *Nirvana*, free from desire and free, equally, from the penalties attendant on rebirth.

This doctrine, the core of Buddhist teaching, was bound to leave the great mass of believers unsatisfied; for only a select few of them could attain salvation, and its rather arid asceticism repressed the human heart's instinctive longing for mysteries and marvels. So, about the beginning of the Christian era, a new form of Buddhism emerged; it was known as "The Great Vehicle." The former conception of the wise man striving to attain *Nirvana* was replaced by that of the Bodhisattva, a being who renounces the peace of *Nirvana* to devote himself to the salvation of mankind by taking on himself the burden of their sufferings. This goal could be reached by all, whether they were monks or mere laymen.

Buddhism continued to evolve and develop until, in about the fifth or sixth century A.D., a new Vehicle was recognised —the Tantric Vehicle or the Vehicle of the Diamond. Although Western minds find its conception disconcerting, it was in fact the logical outcome of centuries of religious speculation. When one has grasped that the world is a void, that nothing exists except thought, and that thought is the Absolute and the world only its reflection, one is drawn to the conclusion that all the phenomena of the cosmos are closely inter-related. Prayers are no longer offered to a divinity who is distinct from mankind, for mankind is part of the Absolute; hence the practice, during meditation, of *visualising* a divinity in order to identify oneself with it. This accounts for the multiplicity of the Tibetan gods;

ignorant people believe in their reality and credit them with powers for good or evil, but enlightened people (and there are many in Tibet) know that they are only an illusion, and thus in accordance with traditional Buddhist doctrine.

From this conception derive various rites which often seem ridiculous to Westerners. Tantrism, like Brahmanism, has always attributed a magical significance to certain mystical patterns and formulas. These are reproduced in speech or in writing all over Tibet. Since all the phenomena of the cosmos are comprehended in the Absolute, every gesture and every word makes an impact on its totality. Words have the power of influencing the world; and, if the formulas are repeated with the mind fixed on their true meaning, they act as agents of the creative imagination.

It is not even necessary to speak the formulas, for the written word is no less powerful than the spoken, and this is the justification for what Westerners call "prayer-wheels." The lama who turns his prayer-wheel is not praying *himself*, he is releasing the power contained in the formulas printed on the wheel. This power can be released even if the lama is thinking about nothing at all, even indeed if the wheel is turned by the wind or by running water.

The doctrines of the Tantric Vehicle dominated the form of Buddhism which was introduced into Tibet in the seventh century. What sort of conditions did it find there? It is obvious that a people's mentality and its religious beliefs are influenced by the sort of country it lives in and the sort of life it leads there; Buddhism could never develop in Tibet along the same lines as in the warm, benign climate of Ceylon. Tibet is like no other country in the world; for those who do not know it, it is impossible to form a just conception of its grandeur, of the wild immensity of its desolate uplands, its mountain peaks, its tremendous gorges. Apart from a few populated valleys, it is a vacuum, a bare boss on the earth's crust where man, encompassed by the hostile forces of nature, is a cipher.

The country had, before the seventh century, developed a form of religion well suited to the needs of its scattered population of mountaineers and herdsmen. This was Shamanism, the worship of good and bad spirits, who had to be honoured or propitiated with sacrifices. So Buddhism, when it came to Tibet, met with strong opposition; the demons of Shamanism were strong enough to prevent the new cult from spreading. Buddhism might, indeed, have disappeared altogether had not King Thri-srong-det-san, in A.D. 747, summoned from India the famous teacher Padma Sambhava, a leading exponent of the Tantric doctrines. This sage was a potent magician. Armed with his ritual sceptre, he embarked on an all-out campaign against the evil spirits and in the end got the better of them; but he realised that it was hopeless to try and cure the Tibetans of their taste for the supernatural, and thus Lamaism came into being as a result of the fusion of Tantric Buddhism with Shamanism, Padma Sambhava being to this day regarded as its founder.

One of the institutions of Lamaism which is imperfectly understood in the West is what we generally, but misleadingly, call the Living Buddhas. This is a meaningless appellation. These beings are Trju-kus, or manifestations in human guise of personages—men or gods—who have left the world. Although this conception is an ancient one in Buddhist lore, Living Buddhas were not officially recognised until the seventeenth century, when the fifth Dalai Lama discovered, under divine guidance, that he was the re-incarnation of Chenrezi, long venerated as the saviour of Tibet. The Panchen Lama, head of the great monastery of Trashi Lumpo, was identified as the emanation of another famous Bodhisattva called Eupamé, and before long every lamasery was presided over by a Tjru-ku, who was either the reincarnation of a well-known historical figure or, more modestly, of the last abbot of the place. The Living Buddhas are almost always men of great benignity, deeply versed in

Buddhist lore; I formed a warm friendship with several of them.

There is no rivalry between the various sects of lamas. They are generally differentiated only by the identity of their founders, by their choice of a protective divinity or by some nicety in their interpretation of doctrine. They do not compete with each other, and Lamaism has never been rent by the disputes—let alone by the sanguinary wars—which have sullied the history of the Christian Churches.

The last peculiarity of Lamaism is the politico-social nature which it confers on religion and for which no analogy can be found elsewhere in the world. The life of every Tibetan is dominated by religious preoccupations. He is conscious of being surrounded by demons who can be appeased by certain rites and ceremonies. Only the lamas have the knowledge and the authority to perform these, and this gives them a status of supremacy. Moreover, in a country so sparsely populated, the lamaseries are far the most important communal centres, often housing several thousand monks; the average Tibetan town consists of a large monastery with a few peasants' houses and a market clustering round it. The lamaseries are rich, and when a peasant needs butter or *tsampa* or silver, the lamas are always ready to help him. It was therefore inevitable that, in a country organised on feudal lines, power should have been concentrated in the hands of the leaders of these great religious communities. They have used their power wisely and humanely; Tibet, where social harmony prevails and wars have been rare, deserves to rank as one of the best-governed countries in the world.

PART FOUR

Caravans and Lamas

17. BRICK-TEA AND *TSAMPA*

HAD been three weeks in Kangting and had still, in spite of strenuous efforts, failed to get into touch with a caravan bound for Kantze, the next destination of importance on my route. The spring is the worst possible season for travelling in Tibet. It had been raining and snowing solidly for a fortnight, and the mountains were once more covered with a thick white mantle; all caravans were held up at the foot of the Haitsushan, a pass which lies a few stages north of Kangting. The weather was not particularly cold—the temperature was only a degree or two below zero—but it was chilly and damp and thoroughly disagreeable.

I made the most of the delay by paying long visits to the lamaseries in the town; they were the first I had seen, and everything about them was fraught with interest. In all there are seven at Kangting, but none of them is particularly important; the largest of them only houses sixty monks, a trivial total by Tibetan standards. Two of the lamaseries belong to the Gelupa sect, two to the Sakyapa and three to the Gnimapa. This last sect—"the Sect of the Old Ones"— goes back to Padma Sambhava, the founder of Lamaism, and has never been reformed. The Sakyapas, who date from the eleventh century, enjoyed at one time a period of great prosperity, when their chief lama was the temporal ruler of Tibet. The Gelupa, or "Virtuous," sect was reformed in the fifteenth century by Tsongkhapa and is today the most powerful in Tibet, for both the Dalai Lama and the Panchen Lama belong to it.

It is a fallacy to suppose that Tsongkhapa wanted to convert Lamaism back to orthodox Buddhism; he merely tried to carry out the disciplinary reforms which were necessary at that period. He made celibacy compulsory for the whole

priesthood; up till then, in the unreformed sects, only thos
who had been ordained were sworn to chastity, the lesse
clergy being allowed to marry. Otherwise the doctrinal and
ritual differences between the reformed and the unreformed
sects are insignificant. People sometimes refer to th
Gelupas as "Yellow Lamas" and to the rest as "Red Lamas;"
this, too, is misleading. All priests, whatever sect they belong
to, wear the same garment of coarse material, brick-red o:
garnet-red in colour; this consists of a voluminous robe tied
round the waist with a woollen girdle, a sleeveless jacke
which leaves the arms bare, a toga-like vestment called th
zen, and the usual heavy Tibetan boots. The head is closely
shaved and is generally bare, though during ritual observ
ances a hat is worn; it is only by the colour of this hat tha
the reformed sects, who wear a yellow one, can be dis
tinguished from the unreformed, who wear a red one.

On March 21st Father Yan appeared at the Mission with
two Tibetans who were starting out with a caravan to
Kantze next day. After the usual bargaining I arranged to
travel with them, and early next morning, after saying good-
bye to the kindly missionaries at the North Gate, I climbed
on to my overloaded pony and rode off at the far-from-
spanking pace which yaks impose on those who travel with
them.

A fair number of European travellers have come up to
Kangting from Szechwan or Yunnan to sniff the air of Tibet;
but for them Kangting was a goal, a terminus, and few have
ventured beyond it along the lonely trails that lead to the
Tibetan uplands. For even fewer has Kangting represented,
not the end, but the beginning of an adventure. Once you
are outside the North Gate, you say good-bye to Chinese
civilisation and its amenities and you begin to lead a different
kind of life altogether. Although on paper the wide territories to the north of the city form part of the Chinese
provinces of Sikang and Chinghai, the real frontier between
China and Tibet runs through Kangting, or perhaps just

outside it; the empirical line which Chinese cartographers, more concerned with prestige than with accuracy, draw on their maps bears no relation to reality.

It is perfectly obvious that, in an ethnological, a religious and a linguistic sense, these two provinces form part of Tibet; and their geographical affinity to that country is not less apparent. The great mountain-ranges and the high plateaux which form the watersheds of the Yalung, the Yangtse, the Salween and the Mekong extend without any major variations, and at roughly the same altitude as the massif of central Tibet, until at last they meet the formidable barrier of the Himalayas. In the same way the deserts of Chinghai foreshadow the empty, snow-covered uplands of Western Tibet. You have only to look at the map of Central Asia to recognise the essential geographical unity of the whole land-mass of Tibet, and to see how artificial are the political boundaries which man has sought to impose on it. No frontier has been more often drawn and redrawn than that between Tibet proper and those parts of it annexed by China, for the simple reason that this frontier corresponds to nothing at all, its only purpose being to separate, in the light of arbitrary and ephemeral political considerations, a population of which all other considerations emphasise the fundamental unity.

I was thinking of all this as I set out along the road which follows the bank of the Tse Chu. The road is reasonably well maintained, for it leads to some hot springs, about five miles from Kangting, which are a favourite resort of the Chinese. Here a few dilapidated pavilions house baths full of extremely hot and sulphurous water; the concrete walls of a deserted road-house were beginning to crumble, afflicted by that mysterious rot which seems to attack all modern buildings in China. I crossed the river by a wooden bridge and found that the road came to an end on the further bank— or dwindled, rather, to a mule-track, very picturesque and very rough. The first corner hid the road-house from view;

with it, unregretted by me, disappeared all trace of th
civilisation of which it was the unattractive symbol.

I caught up with the caravan just as it was halting for th
night. This was my first camp with Tibetans; I thoroughl
enjoyed it, and was initiated into the age-old routine whic
thenceforth was so largely to dominate my life.

They had stopped on a stretch of greensward beside th
river-bank, and the animals were quickly relieved of thei
loads and their pack-saddles. The yaks, mules and ponies
who had been looking forward to this moment, wandered of
in search of grazing. The men stacked the loads so that the
formed a wall round three sides of a square; since they wer
all composed of bales of brick-tea, very compact and sym
metrical, this wall gave excellent shelter from the wind
Meanwhile one of the Tibetans had drawn water from th
river, another had collected firewood and dried yak's-dung
and a third was making a fireplace with three big stones; i
no time at all, a great cauldron of tea was brewing.

I was constantly amazed by the skill with which th
caravan-men got a fire going whatever the conditions were—
even if it was pouring with rain and the wood was damp
With their tinder-box—an indispensable item of equipmen
in Tibet—they lit a bundle of moss which they had carefull
kept dry, then they brought a huge pair of leather bellows int
action and very soon the flames were crackling away
Yak-dung, which they used whenever there was no wood t
be had, is a splendid form of fuel, burning with a clear an
steady flame. Brick-tea is made by methods only distantl
related to those employed in China or Ceylon. When th
water boils, a great handful of the stuff is crumbled into i
and allowed to stew for between five and ten minutes, unti
the whole infusion is so opaque that it looks almost black
At this stage a pinch of salt is added; the Tibetans alway
put salt, never sugar, in their tea. I have been told that the
sometimes add a little soda, in order to give the beverage
pinkish tinge, but I never saw this done in Sikang. The

ery seldom, on the other hand, drink tea without butter in
t. If you are at home, you empty the saucepan into a big
wooden churn, straining the tea through a colander made of
osiers or horse-hair, then you drop a large lump of butter
nto it; after being vigorously stirred, this brew is trans-
erred to a huge copper teapot and put on a brazier to keep
t hot. When you are travelling, you do not normally take a
churn with you; so everyone fills his wooden bowl with tea,
scoops a piece of butter out of a basket, puts it in the bowl,
tirs the mixture gently with his finger and, finally, drinks
he tea.

Apart from tea, *tsampa* is the staple, indeed often the only
diet of the Tibetans; it is a kind of flour made from roasted
barley. This is how you eat it. You leave a little buttered
ea in the bottom of your bowl and put a big dollop of
sampa on top of it. You stir gently with the forefinger,
hen knead with the hand, meanwhile twisting your bowl
round and round until you finish up with a large, dumpling-
ike object which you proceed to ingest, washing it down
vith more tea. The whole operation demands a high degree
of manual dexterity, and you need a certain amount of
practical experience before you can judge correctly how
much *tsampa* goes with how much tea; until you get these
proportions right the end-product is apt to turn into either
a lump of desiccated dough or else a semi-liquid paste which
sticks to your fingers. Sometimes you lace this preparation
with a form of powdered milk, made from curds which have
been dried in the sun.

The whole process, in a country where nobody bothers
much about washing, has the incidental advantage that,
however dirty your hands may be when you embark on it,
they are generally quite clean by the time you have done.
In the early stages my *tsampa* was mixed for me by Elie, the
Chinese-Tibetan-aboriginal half-caste who combined the
duties of cook, servant and groom, and I used to be slightly
distressed when I saw the splendid fellow kneading my staple

diet with the same pair of hands (never in any circumstance
washed) which he used for blowing his nose, collecting yak
dung, scratching his head, squashing lice and many other
functional purposes; but after a bit, when I had come to
terms with my new way of life, it seemed the most natural
thing in the world. And anyhow, it was not long before I
was mixing my own *tsampa*.

18. THE SPELL OF JARA

ELIE, an agreeable rascal, had been engaged for me by
Father Yan. He spoke no European language and thus
left me with no excuse for not learning the dialect of Sikang.
I had studied classical Tibetan in France, and it was of
course invaluable for reading Buddhist texts or conversing
with learned lamas. But the *patois* of the caravan-men bore
little resemblance to pure Tibetan, and now I had to set
about mastering it.

Darkness had fallen when we finished our meal, but we
stayed on for a little while round the fire, talking and
smoking our pipes. The caravan was made up of lamas
belonging to one of the lower orders of the priesthood, who
were taking a consignment of tea to the monastery of
Kantze, some of it for the use of the monks and some for
their own commercial purposes; in Tibet this sort of active
interest in trade is perfectly compatible with a life dedicated
to religion, although it is true that you will never find a high-
ranking lama engaged in such enterprises. They are left to
junior priests who in this respect fulfil much the same purposes as the lay brothers in European monasteries. Throughout the journey, as a matter of fact, my companions were
dressed as laymen; it was only when we got to Kantze that
they put on their robes and I realised their true status.

I had, however, already been impressed by their piety;

ur leading mule bore the religious emblem which is associ-
ted with caravans and which consists of a big ball of multi-
oloured bits of cloth with sacred texts printed on them and a
taff with a trident on the end of it, its three prongs repre-
enting the Buddhist trinity of Buddha, Dharma (the Law)
nd Sangha (the Community). In camp this tutelary emblem
vas placed on top of the loads. The lamas never drank tea
vithout taking a ladle and scattering a few drops towards
ach of the five quarters of the Universe (the fifth is its
entre). Every morning they made a burnt offering of
trongly scented herbs to the gods; every evening the sing-
ong chanting of their prayers lulled me to sleep as I lay
eside them round the camp-fire.

The process of retiring for the night is not, in Tibet, a
complex one. You spread out on the ground some coarse
elt rugs which by day serve as padding under the pack-
saddles of the yaks; then you undo the woollen belt with
which your *shuba* is buckled at the waist and lie down, using
he *shuba* as bedclothes. When it rains, you merely pull a
saddle-cloth or a sheepskin over your head. I was not, at
hat stage, sufficiently hardened to sleep out of doors in wet
clothes, and I was glad to take refuge every evening in my
ittle tent, which was pitched on the outskirts of our camp.
Everyone was soon fast asleep, leaving only the mastiffs to
keep guard; these were chained up near the loads.

I found the next two days a bit of an ordeal. A fine rain,
which soon changed to snow, fell relentlessly, and my
Chinese raincoat did not protect me from being soaked and
rozen as I rode slowly along. One of my Tibetan boots had
ubbed my heel, so it was out of the question to keep warm
by walking. The going got very difficult. The track consisted of a sort of stairway cut out of the rock which zigzagged up and down the mountainside, and the animals
could make only very slow progress. My pack-horse lost his
balance and finished up at the bottom of a ravine, and we
had to take his load off to get him up to the track again.

H

The whole caravan moved at a snail's pace, for the animal
were always bunching and stopping altogether on par
ticularly difficult sections of the track, and everyone had to
wait until the muleteers sorted things out and got them
moving again. Our caravan consisted of only twenty-two
mules and ponies, but we travelled for several hours in
company with another caravan of some forty yaks. It is
quite a common thing for two smallish parties, such as our
were, to join forces so as to be better able to look after them
selves if anything untoward occurs.

We passed a little village, after which the track became
even harder to negotiate. Two of our mules, completely
exhausted, foundered and could not get up again. They
were unloaded and we tried to get them on their feet; after
a series of attempts had failed it was obvious that they were
done for, and the poor creatures were left by the side of the
path to add their bones to the countless whitening skeleton
with which Tibetan trails are strewn.

Snow now lay everywhere, and we moved forward through
a mist so dense that one could not even see the head of the
caravan; only, every now and then, one got a glimpse of a
towering rock-face plastered with snow or of a tremendou
chasm—a wild, forbidding, awe-inspiring sight. About
noon both the going and the weather improved; the snow fell
less implacably, the sun shone palely through it. We halted
in a wide, grassy glade. I cleared a space in the snow and
pitched my tent. I was frozen and exhausted but soon, to
my great relief, the sun came out properly and I was able to
warm myself and dry my clothes.

The next day we stayed where we were, for the snow lay
deep and barred our way. The weather continued to im
prove, everything dried out, and I spent a pleasant day sun
bathing and improving my command of Tibetan with the
help of Elie. I also managed to establish diplomatic rela
tions with the two enormous black mastiffs attached to the
caravan.

In the end we spent three days in that glade, because the animals had wandered off into the hills in search of grazing and the men had a hard job rounding them up; it was a miracle to me how they managed to collect them all. Ahead of us, in the direction of the Jara pass, we could see a high mountain with a jagged peak. The camp was a delightful place, and the lamas were the gayest and friendliest companions imaginable. Several times a day they collected round the fire, drank buttered tea and then chanted their slow litanies while the men of the other caravan told their beads.

But at last, on the evening before our departure, the animals were rounded up and hobbled to a long yak-hair rope. A Tibetan lit some aromatic herbs, put them in a big copper ladle and went round all the animals as though with a censer. At dawn we set off for the pass. The weather was fine and the track, winding through little woods and stretches of heath, was a great improvement on the previous stage. All of a sudden I saw ahead of us the noble peak which we had first sighted from our camp in the glade; it made me eager to reach the top of the high pass at the end of the valley which we were slowly approaching. We camped at a height of about twelve thousand feet, near a huge mass of rock scarred by crevices and rising to a summit which was hidden by the mist. Ahead of us lay the path leading up to the pass. Another trail forked off right-handed. It led to Tampa, and a small party of Chinese coolies followed it. They were the last men of their race that I was to see for a long time. We had left China far behind, and were in a country where nobody—since there were ponies and yaks to do the job—saw much point in acting as a beast of burden.

We moved off again at six o'clock on April 29th under a cloudless sky. The night had been cold, but soon, by way of indirect compensation, the glaciers of Minyakonka were incandescent against a background of deep blue. I found

good going on the frozen snow and kept ahead of the
caravan; the animals floundered in the trampled slush along
the track. I reached the neck of the pass about half-past
eight and climbed a knoll which overlooked the path.
Behind me, under this amazing sky, the caravan wound in a
dark and tenuous file across a smooth, limitless expanse of
snow; in front of me, the great peak of Jara unveiled the
frozen mask of her north face. I shall never forget that sight.

A little frozen lake glittered in the sunshine. We climbed
a second, higher pass, and found on top of it a *la-tsa*; this is
a religious monument which is a familiar sight on the trails
of Tibet and consists of a huge cairn of stones, most of them
carved with the inevitable *Om ma-ni pad-mé hum*. Multi-
coloured pennons, printed with Buddhist texts, flew from
tall lances projecting from the top of the cairn. Round its
base were strewn the skulls of animals and the horns of
sheep and yaks; one was constantly noticing the important
part played by animals in Lamaism. We conscientiously con-
formed with custom, which demands that everyone as he
crosses the pass must add a stone to the cairn. As they did
this, the Tibetans scattered handfuls of scraps of paper to
the four winds; stamped on each was a representation of
lung-ta, the legendary horse who carries on his back the
Jewel of Jewels and is a charm in whose protective efficacy
everyone believes. At the same time they sent echoing round
the mountains the great cry of joy and gratitude, "*Cha-so-so,
tcha-tchal-lo!*" It means "homage to all the gods;" there was
something very touching about the devotion of these simple
men to deities who symbolised the latent hostility of a harsh,
cruel world.

On the far side of the pass we began to drop down, first
over grassy slopes where snow still masked the path, through
a gorge-like valley. To the left, our view of the great
mountain became steadily clearer and we could see the tremendous ice-walls on its northern face. Geographers know
it as Jara, the highest peak to the north of Minyakonka, but

e Tibetans always call it Sha-dja-ta. Presently the path
nce more became steep and rough, another of those rock
taircases of which the caravan made heavy weather; there
were places where we had to lead the animals one by one
cross particularly slippery stretches. The valley here was
densely wooded, but after several hours of difficult going we
debouched into a much wider one, down which ran the
'an Chu. Crossing this, we halted and made camp on a
grassy terrace shaded by trees.

It was a perfectly lovely place. The peaceful river-valley
was dominated by serried ranks of mountains, which
stretched to the horizon and reminded me of the Pyrenees;
but straight ahead of us everything else was blotted out by
he great north face of Jara. Its beautifully proportioned
peak is formed by a huge, ice-clad pyramid, fringed with
cornices and linked by gigantic buttresses of rock to the
moraines above the pass. To the right, the crest is rockier
and less precipitous; but the north face plunges sheer down
n one awe-inspiring wall of ice, scarred by seracs and fur-
owed by couloirs, to finish up among the sprawling débris in
he bottom of our valley, only a short distance from the camp.

We were lucky in the weather; the towering peak stood
out with exquisite effect against the deep blue sky. I had
pitched my tent under a tree and could have stayed there
for ever, feasting my eyes on a spectacle which evoked so
many mountaineering memories. The air was dry and
stimulating; it was a joy to watch the play of sunlight on the
mountain-tops, the shadow deepening on the great wall of
ice beneath them. I was attacked by the mild dementia to
which mountaineers are so vulnerable, and spent hours
working out possible lines of attack on this unclimbed peak.

felt pretty sure that a well-trained, well-equipped party
could get to the top, and one or two of the approaches looked
as though they ought not to be unduly difficult, though it
would be an exacting climb at that great height. Towards
evening, clouds came down and hid the tantalising summit.

The journey down that valley was a rest-cure. The pat
wound through the woods or dawdled across lowland wher
the spring flowers were beginning to appear. I often stoppe
to look back at Jara, for I was under the mountain's spel
framed between the walls of the valley, it seemed to gain i
majesty as we got further away from it. At last the valle
twisted, we crossed the river by an old mossy wooden bridg
and Jara was seen no more. For a long way the path le
downhill through more woodland, until we came to the ruin
of a big fortified staging-post. Here the path forked, an
we set off up a little side-valley leading to the Ke-ta pass
This was to prove the threshold of a new world.

Beyond it the whole landscape altered completely. W
were now on the Tibetan plateau. Hills, grass-covere
but treeless, rolled away before us in infinite succession
herds of yaks, horses and sheep grazed on their slopes. Her
and there we saw the camps of the herdsmen, their big
black yak-hair tents spreadeagled like spiders. Up her
there was much more traffic on the road; we met caravans
drovers, women on their way home to their huts or thei
tents. We went slowly on across the plateau, climbed a littl
pass and saw houses in front of us. There was a tin
lamasery, too, with a lot of people bustling round it. Thi
was the village of Taining.

19. AN ALIEN WORLD

It was an odd little place. Its walls—three parts demolishec
—formed a square, enclosing a wide, bare, neglected piece
of ground; here, looking completely lost, stood variou
Chinese administrative buildings. The market was in one
corner of this great compound—a picturesque little trading-
place, the terminus of Taining's one and only street, on
either side of which stood the poor houses of the Chinese

and Tibetan merchants. The larger business concerns were established in more impressive flat-roofed houses outside the compound; we were lodged in one of these. While the Tibetans made themselves and their animals comfortable in the courtyard I found in a sheltered corner of the balcony a pile of straw which made a splendid bed. It was a cold night, and next morning even the water inside the house was frozen.

We stayed two days at Taining, which gave me a chance to see something of life in a Tibetan village. The ground floor of our house consisted of a yard for the animals, surrounded by sheds for storing fodder or for housing the animals in bad weather; this was where our caravan was accommodated. A wooden ladder, made of a tree-trunk with slots cut in it, led up to the balcony where I slept and to the proprietors' quarters, which comprised three rooms, built with thick beams of timber and painted ochre-red. It was very dark indoors, the windows—on account of the cold—being tiny; the only form of chimney in the kitchen was a hole in the ceiling, so that the residents lived in a dense and peculiarly evil-smelling cloud of smoke. The big, flat, adobe roof did duty as a rickyard, a threshing-floor and a place to stroll about on; above it, sacred pennons and prayer-flags fluttered from long poles.

The châtelaine of this establishment was a well-developed Tibetan lady with a sociable manner and a strong sense of humour. I helped her roast some barley in the kitchen to make *tsampa* with, thus learning in some detail how this important operation is carried out (her children and I helped ourselves to some of the barley, which is delicious when it has been heated). The process works like this: a big round iron pan is placed on a hot fire, and into this is put a handful of corn which is stirred continuously with a little sort of broom made of twigs. As soon as the neutral-coloured husk of the grain splits and the paler berry inside it can be seen, you stop stirring. Meanwhile your eldest daughter—at least that was what happened here—operates a crude mill made of stone through which the barley is passed after roasting.

After the main meal of the day we—that is to say, our hostess, the two leaders of the caravan, Elie and I—settled down on the balcony for some polite conversation, to which my command of the language did not permit me to make a major contribution. The sun was warm and, as we talked, everyone let down his *shuba* and embarked on a louse-hunt in its well-stocked coverts. It was a very humane form of sport, since Buddhism forbids its adherents to take the life of any living creature, however humble; whenever, there-fore, anyone found a louse he placed it tenderly on the floor beside him. Elie, unfortunately, had been a hanger-on of the Catholic Mission in Kangting for some considerable time, called himself a Christian and thought it would be a good idea to advertise his superior status by squashing his own lice; it was all too clear from the horrified glances of those present that this was not quite the *beau geste* he had meant it to be.

We were closely watched by various honorary and non-human members of the household, among them a pair of choughs, with their red bills and legs; they lived next door to me on the balcony and were half-tame. One of the charms of this strange country is the friendly terms on which the Tibetans live with wild animals, which are of course never hunted in Buddhist countries. Riding along on a pony, one often got quite close to them—hares, marmots, foxes, otters, wild asses and once even a magnificent leopard; *homo sapiens* did not worry them unduly, for they had been taught no reason to fear him.

There is in point of fact only one animal on our planet which deserves the French epithet *sauvage*, and that is *homo sapiens* himself; it is fear of him that has made the other animals wild and sometimes fierce.

I spent the whole of my second day at Taining in the

CENTRE: *My tent at the foot of Jara*

ABOVE: *Haitsushan: Crossing the pass*
BELOW: *Tea-coolies resting their loads on staves*

ABOVE: *Lamas blowing radongs*
BELOW: *A High lama and his retinue*

small but influential lamasery which stood on the other side
of the river behind a screen of trees. But before immersing
myself in spiritual matters I had secular problems to solve;
butter and *tsampa* for the rest of the journey had to be pro-
cured, and in a small place like this the lamasery, with its
far-flung sources of revenue, was the only place where you
could get supplies. I was welcomed most hospitably by the
bursar (as I suppose you might call him), a great strapping
fellow with a handsome—a really handsome—wife. He
received me in a well-appointed room hung with some fine
paintings on silk. After the usual polite catechism over endless cups of tea—the questions can have varied very little
since the Homeric era and must follow much the same
sequence in every country of the world—about my age, my
name, my place of origin and my intended destination—he
took me off to some outbuildings where I got everything that
I wanted without the slightest difficulty.

There we met an old lama. He was so delighted to find a
foreigner taking an interest in his religion from other than
hostile motives that he invited me to his monastery. Its
main temple was a fine rectangular building, rather like a
fortress and—like most sacred edifices in Tibet—coloured
brick-red. On its high gilded roof, designed more in the
Chinese than the Tibetan style, stood the chief emblems of
Buddhism: the big golden cylinders, symbolising Buddha's
kingship, the cone-shaped columns, and the Wheel of the
Law, flanked by two gazelles and representing Buddha's
first sermon, which he preached in the Park of Gazelles at
Sarnath, near Benares.

The interior of the temple was very dark and was decorated with murals and paintings on silk. The coffered ceiling
was supported on wooden pillars, thick enough for a
cathedral and covered with red and gold lacquer. The altar
was laden with images of Buddha and other gods, with bowls
full of thank-offerings, butter-lamps and *tor-mas*; these are
sacrificial cakes shaped like tiny *chörtens* and made of

coloured butter. To the left of the altar stood the abbot's seat. Between the pillars the floor was covered with the carpets and hassocks on which the lamas sat when rites were celebrated.

A smaller temple, not far from the main one, was dedicated to the malevolent gods; you find a place of this kind in most lamaseries. I entered it through a sort of peristyle, from the ceiling of which hung the crudely stuffed hides of a yak and a mule—a common sight in such places, and another reminder of the important part played by animals in Lamaism. Inside the shrine veils hung over most of the images. In the darkest corner a few butter-lamps were burning before a statue of Do-dié-dji-dié, the tutelary demon of the Yellow sect to whom the temple belonged. This personage has nine heads, the principal one being that of a bull, and his thirty-four arms energetically and realistically embrace the female sprite with whom he is copulating; he did not, as he loomed up in the darkness, look particularly endearing. Before him a lama gravely intoned his prayers, accompanying them by a slow, deliberate tattoo on a big drum hanging from a wooden frame. I suddenly felt as if I had been transported to an alien world which had drawn me irresistibly to itself, a world where everything had altered, where things no longer had the same value or words the same meaning, where reality had changed places with illusion. I stayed for a long time, not moving, squatting beside that calm-faced lama who lived on a different plane of existence. The strange, unreal place had me under its spell.

It was beginning to dawn on me that if in Tibet you do not behave like a tourist in a museum, if you make an effort to get *inside* the life of the place instead of being only a spectator, you cannot help undergoing a profound and unforgettable experience.

When I went out into the courtyard the light dazzled me; it seemed incongruous that there should still be a sun, mountains and flowers and trees, animals and even men, all looking perfectly normal. But what, after all, do we mean by normal? Who can demarcate the frontier between illusion and reality?

A roofed balcony ran round the courtyard of the lamasery, and on to it opened the living-quarters of the lamas; when I got deeper into Tibet, where some of the lamaseries are as big and populous as villages, I found that this was the usual arrangement. Everything was silent, every door was closed; it was the hour of contemplation. Except for my guide, none of the monks were to be seen. Only the solemn beat of the drum fell rhythmically upon the hushed, mysterious precincts.

On May 3rd I woke before dawn. We loaded the animals and took the road as the sun was beginning to rise. As we moved away across the plateau the village of Taining faded into the morning mists. The view to the south was unforgettable. Towering above the pass of Che-to, Minyakonka's splendid pyramid of ice gleamed in the first rays of the sun; its spare outline had a striking simplicity; it dwarfed everything else in that wild landscape. To the left of it there was another big mountain with a blunter summit, and in the foreground—still lovely, but insignificant beside Minyakonka—stood my old friend Jara.

The track led us up and down through a wilderness of hills and broken plateaux. Spring had hardly reached these uplands as yet; snowdrifts still clung to slopes which the sun did not touch, but elsewhere the flowers—particularly edelweiss—were beginning to appear. Before long the pastures would be echoing with the sound of bells as the flocks and herds grazed slowly over them. A long downhill stretch brought us to a well-wooded valley where, after crossing the swift stream in the bottom of it, we halted at noon. While we were eating, Elie upset a bowl of scalding tea over my foot, raising blisters which were a nuisance for the next few days. That night—a very cold one—they gave me hell and I got no sleep.

We got up at half-past two and moved off at three. I never really understood the policy on which our caravan was run. Sometimes we started at ten o'clock in the morning, sometimes—for a short, easy stage—at three o'clock.

The landscape, however, was romantic. We rode through undiluted moonlight and five degrees of frost. The streams were all frozen; the canvas of my tent, when I struck it, might have been three-ply wood. I was frozen with cold, too; I tried walking to get warm, but my scalded foot was unbearably painful. Presently the moon went down and left us to grope our way through the dark; but it was easy going here, along a track which wound upwards to a gently undulating plateau. At dawn we crossed—observing the rites which are appropriate and have already been described— the pass of Songlingkiu, some fourteen thousand feet above sea-level.

Beyond this the track plunged into a wide valley, passing through a forest of tall larch; the trees were covered with parasitic growths, but it was the prettiest bit of woodland I had seen. We passed several caravans on their way up to the pass; but we passed them without dallying, for that stretch of the road has a bad reputation and travellers are apt to be robbed in the pretty woodland. We made camp at eight o'clock in the morning on an admirable site where three valleys met; but I could not help wondering why we had stopped so early in the day, for Taofu was quite close and we could have got there before nightfall. The night was very cold. Next day we followed our valley until it debouched into the much bigger valley of Taofu; and here I had my first sight of the celebrated highway about which there had been so much talk at Kangting.

During the Second World War, for strategic reasons, the Chinese built what was meant to be a motor-road between Chengtu and Kangting; thence it was to run on, via Kantze and Jyekundo, as far as Sining. On this project were squandered not only millions of dollars, but the lives of hundreds—perhaps thousands—of Tibetans who were impressed for a task whose completion would bring no benefit to their people. The road was badly built; most of the money raised, by means of crushing local taxes, for its construction finished up in the pockets of contractors and officials. But at last it was formally opened in great style, with speeches, banquets, fireworks and military parades. After this a convoy of three motor-vehicles set off amid the plaudits of the multitude, who were more than ready to salute the achievements of the Kuomintang, or indeed of anybody else. The convoy did not get very far. One of the vehicles struggled on to Taofu, the luckiest of the three got beyond Kantze before it met its Waterloo, but none of them reached Jyekundo; the last part of the highway remains unsullied by wheels.

After this inspiring effort, the highway was left to stew in its own juice. The reader may remember my description of the motor-road from Ya-an to Kangting, which is now little better than a mule-track. This Tibetan *Autobahn* suffered much the same fate. Rains, landslides and the irrepressible vegetation eroded or invaded its surface; it went native again. No cars now attempt to use it, and caravans still follow the tracks which they have followed down the ages. Occasionally, and always coincidentally, these tracks overlap the trace of the motor-road, so that for a time one ambles, feeling slightly bewildered, along a stretch of metalled road neatly subdivided by milestones; but for the rest of its length the project serves no useful purpose except to remind people of the follies of the Kuomintang. The Tibetans, who bore the brunt of the work on this gigantic white elephant, have drawn their own conclusions from it; it has confirmed their previous estimates of the merits of the Chinese administration and of the kind of benefits they can hope to derive from it. They accept Chinese rule because they are peace-loving people, but they will get rid of it with alacrity if they ever get the chance.

The caravan camped near Taofu in a meadow beside th
stream; and I went off, for the night, to the house of Fathe
Leroux, who belongs to the Mission at Kangting and occupie
one of Christianity's most advanced outposts in Tibet.

The faith which enables men to live under the sort o
conditions which Father Leroux had to put up with alway
fills me with admiration. He had been buried for severa
years in this village, which is eight days' journey from th
main mission station; he made this journey once a year, fo
Retreat, if nothing happened to prevent his going. For th
whole of the rest of the year he was completely alone, neve
speaking his native language and seeing nobody except a few
ignorant Chinese—apart from European travellers. The las
one before me was Guibaud, just before his tragic adventure
and that was three years ago.

Father Leroux can have found few compensations in the
work he was there to do. His "flock" consisted only of :
handful of Chinese traders and a small gang of impoverishec
hangers-on who more or less lived on his charity. The
faithful—who were all Chinese—numbered about fifty, a
total which, thanks to their reproductive powers, remained
fairly constant; but there were never any new converts,
except when yet another little trader came and set up shop in
Taofu.

Every morning Father Leroux held mass in the presence
of a few squawling children; for the rest of the day he worked
in his garden, went fishing, read old magazines, ran the tiny
little Mission school or gave religious instruction to some
aged Chinese. Except for a few officials and business-men,
the whole population of this large village is Tibetan; there
is a lamasery with a thousand monks in it, some of whom are
very learned men. Yet the poor Father lives in complete
seclusion and has no contact with anyone but the Chinese;
he does not speak Tibetan, knows virtually nothing about
Buddhism and, not very surprisingly, has never had a
Tibetan in his flock. We had a long talk, and I could not

elp being sadly aware of the deep melancholy which his air
f dauntless optimism strove in vain to conceal.

The reader will have realised that I hold unorthodox
iews about missionary work, but it really does seem to me
ppalling—even if one only looks at it from the missionaries'
oint of view—that a man of character and intelligence, who
ould be so useful in some other sphere, should be allowed to
vaste his whole life in a place like Taofu. Our Missions in
Tibet, like our Missions in Cambodia, have been a failure;
heir original object—the preaching of Christianity to the
natives—has been for practical purposes abandoned, the
nissionaries having realised that it is a hopeless task to try
nd convert sincere Buddhists in either country. They have
herefore been reduced to proselytising the Chinese, who
re the least religious people in the world but who are often
prepared to go through the motions of being converted.
And, anyway, why should we force an alien doctrine down
he throats of races like the Tibetans, the Cambodians, the
Burmese and the Indians? They are deeply religious, have
a vivid apprehension of the divine and belong to civilisations
steeped in traditions of spirituality; their dogmas rival those
of Christianity in their depth and their piety; their saints and
their philosophers rival ours in stature. There is more
missionary work to be done—and it is better worth doing—
in the West, where religion is only a façade and spirituality
has long disappeared, where civilisation now rests on purely
materialistic foundations, where the pugilist, the film-star
and the millionaire occupy the exalted niches reserved, in the
East, for the hermit, the yogi and the saint. It would really
make more sense if India or Tibet sent missionaries to
Europe, to try and lift her out of the materialistic rut in
which she is bogged down, and to reawaken the capacity for
religious feeling which she lost several centuries ago. But
Buddhists do not go in for missionary work; they are too
tolerant, they have too much respect for other people's con-
victions to want to superimpose their own upon them.

20. FATHER FU

IN the afternoon I visited another lamasery belonging to the Gelupa sect. It was the first completely Tibetan temple that I had seen, for the ones at Kangting and Taining had very noticeably been influenced by Chinese architecture. The lamasery at Taofu, pleasantly situated on the side of a hill, was dominated by a central group of buildings, comprising various lesser shrines, and the living-quarters of the abbots and senior lamas. Round this sprawled the rest of the monastery, like a village with narrow, winding streets, a picturesque warren of a place honeycombed with underground passages, dark corners and mysterious-looking doorways. On either side of its alley-ways stood the lamas' cells with a ground-floor room used as a woodshed, a first-floor living-room with a balcony, one or two tiny little spare rooms and a shrine, full of images, paintings and books, in which the lama prayed or meditated. The monks only assemble in the main temple for certain festivals or for ceremonies at which the presence of the whole community is required. The monastery does not support its inmates with its own funds; the lamas are provided with their cells but have to pay for their own board—unless they are too poor to do so, in which case they act as servants to some more prosperous *confrère*. Some even live outside the lamasery—either with relations or in private houses where they act as chaplains—and only attend there for the more important ceremonies.

My evening with Father Leroux passed all too quickly, and it was very late when we went to bed. The bed he gave me was only a flat slab of wood, but compared with the frozen and sometimes snow-covered ground on which I had been sleeping since Kangting it seemed to me the height of luxury. I had brought Elie and the two ponies with me, so I did not have to make too early a start to catch up with

Cantilever bridge at Yulon

the caravan. Leroux came with me as far as the outskirts of the village.

The trail, which offered good and comparatively level going, followed the wide valley of the Da Chu, a big, swift-flowing river nearly a hundred feet wide. The sun shone strongly and the heat in that windless valley was soon oppressive enough to slow down our rate of advance. We passed a little village under a shoulder of downland and saw peasants working with a primitive wooden plough.

After this the valley got narrower and here the trail ran along the side of the hill over screes which were treacherous going for the animals; below us the Chinese *Autobahn* followed the floor of the valley, as flat as a pancake but never used by the caravans, which clung stubbornly to their traditional routes.

We crossed a little wooden bridge, and on the right bank of the river embarked on a stiff climb which brought us up to a high plateau shaped like an amphitheatre; here we camped, not far from a few isolated peasants' houses. Some women, working on the land close by, had let their sheepskin *shubas* fall to the waist, leaving their breasts bare despite the biting cold.

One of the lamas had realised that I was fed up with our slow progress and the short stages we were doing; he explained to me that the mules were a poor lot and were not getting enough to eat because there was very little grazing so early in the year. On the high ground, where snow still lay in patches, the poor beasts were literally scraping the ground with their teeth in their efforts to get at the young grass which was only just beginning to show. Every day they were issued with iron rations in the shape of dumplings made—with scrupulous care—from a mixture of *tsampa* and tea-leaves; and this was supplemented with a handful of dried peas, which the mules crunched like sweets with obvious relish. I always admired the care with which the Tibetans looked after their animals and the gentle way in

Religious dance at Kantze.   The King of Hell

I

which they handled them; it was in marked contrast with the callous indifference which the Chinese show in these matters.

The next stage, to Charatong, was a dreary one. It rained all night, and when I woke up at two in the morning my tent was soaked through. The rain started again while we were drinking our tea, and we moved off in pitch darkness, further intensified by a thick mist. We squelched through mud on a trail that went up and down like a switchback; I was half asleep in the saddle, and it was a mystery to me why we did not lose any of the animals, which kept on stopping to snatch at the occasional tufts of grass.

Dawn broke dimly behind the mist and, stung by a fine but demoralising rain, we dropped down into the same valley, the valley of the Da Chu, out of which we had climbed the day before. Here it was broad and—by local standards—densely populated, with the river winding along its floor between clumps of stunted willows. We rode, hock-deep in mud, through several villages, and reached Chara-tong at ten o'clock in the morning.

Just as Kangting had advanced an outpost of Christendom at Taofu, so Taofu had advanced a sort of sub-outpost to Charatong. It was in the charge of Father Fu, a gentle, venerable Chinese of the old school, who received me with the utmost deference and amiability. Unfortunately he knew only a few words of French and I knew none of Chinese; we used a kind of kitchen Latin in which to exchange, as best we could, a few rudimentary ideas, but it cannot be said that the art of conversation was displayed to great advantage.

In this rather inadequate *lingua franca* Father Fu gave me to understand that the whole population of Charatong was Chinese, and that every single member of it was a Roman Catholic. This sounded a bit odd to me, since the surrounding countryside was inhabited exclusively by Tibetans; but later I realised that, though odd, it was more or less true.

Charatong was, in actual fact, one of those Chinese
enclaves which the Catholics at one time set out to establish
in the border regions between China and Tibet, and also
between China and Mongolia. The settlers, who were all
Chinese, had to be Christians as well, for this was the object
of the exercise; they were grouped in little agricultural
communities, which did their best to grow crops on land
which had hitherto only provided pasture.

The colony at Charatong had, in its humble way, achieved
a measure of success along these lines; but elsewhere similar
experiments have failed completely, after—in many cases—
producing strained relations between the missionaries and
their Mongol or Tibetan neighbours. The latter believed,
reasonably enough, that the pastures belonged to them; they
felt strongly about their grazing-rights, and were disinclined to subordinate them to experiments, carried out by
aliens, in arable farming, a form of agriculture which, as
nomads, they held in contempt. It was too much to expect
them to take a favourable view of the missionaries' policy of
infiltrating groups of Chinese, generally of rather a low class,
for the sole reason that they were (or anyhow called themselves) Christians.

I had made a small but important improvement in my
personal administrative arrangements by buying from Father
Fu a large square of Tibetan felt, to put over the blankets
with which I padded my saddle whenever I wanted to dismount and walk; this meant that, when I got up on the pony
again, I should be spared the sensations—disagreeable at all
times, and never more so than when the weather is cold—of
sitting down on a large wet sponge.

We crossed the river twice soon after leaving Charatong,
both times by a wooden bridge. Dawn, drab and ominous,
revealed a sky full of large, black clouds; an icy wind was
blowing and during the night snow had once more covered
the peaks of which we occasionally got glimpses. At seven
o'clock we passed below the village of Laho. This looked a

sizeable place, cocked up on a round-topped hill and dominated by a castle, once the home of the Tibetan princeling
who ruled in these parts, now converted into offices for the
Chinese *Gauleiter*. Above and beyond this village there was
a big lamasery belonging to the Gelupa sect.

The pass which we eventually reached was crowned, as
usual, with a big white *chörten*. An extensive valley, which
looked green and seemed to be under cultivation in parts,
opened out beyond the pass. At the far end of it we could see
a snow-covered range of mountains, and I reckoned that
Kantze must lie somewhere at their feet. The second stage
of my long journey was drawing to its close.

21. NIGHT MARCHES

NEXT day, May 11th, we were up at two and off by three.
The night was clear and the moon shone down on us from
a sky full of stars. We rode through a little village perched
on top of a cliff. Everyone in it was asleep, and in the bright
moonlight this poor place became suddenly a romantic
mediæval mountain-fastness. Then the dogs began to
bark, the caravan passed on and the little village was left
behind.

Dawn came and soon after it the kindly sun, to warm
horsemen who were stiff with cold. In the daytime I used
to do as much walking as I could, only getting back into the
saddle when I was tired; this was scarcely possible at night,
when the only sensible thing to do was to go on riding
however cold one got. The night marches seemed as though
they would never end; to pass the time—and to acquire some
badly needed merit—I used to tell the beads on a Tibetan
rosary and chant, over and over again, *Om ma-ni pad-me
hum*. Everybody else in the caravan did much the same thing,
but the Tibetans were naturally much more practised than

was; they could go on reciting, for hours at a time, whole pages from their sacred books. I was amazed by their capacity for memorising words.

The valley was—for Tibet—densely populated, mostly, to judge from the fields of wheat and barley or potatoes, by farmers. At nine o'clock we reached Chuwo, a village clinging to a precipitous spur of rock whose crest overhung (it literally did overhang) the river beneath it. On top of this spur, and seemingly integral to it, crouched a large, squat, square building, simply but forcefully designed and having the air of a keep or citadel; its smooth, sheer façade was broken only by a few windows and a wide balcony which jutted over the void beneath. It was a building which typified the merits of Tibetan architecture—sobriety of line, harmony of proportion and a feeling—despite its massive, rather monolithic design—of lightness and grace. I believe that the secret of this grace (an improbable by-product of a severely geometrical style which ought to be unpleasing) lies in the slight tapering of the elevation. Every perspective is almost imperceptibly distorted, and the final result, though it retains a bleak and solid dominance, achieves at the same time a high degree of elegance; this is a thing which the vast, rectangular products of contemporary European architecture never seem to succeed in doing.

This eyrie is the seat of the former ruler of Hordjriwo, one of the five Hor dukedoms which played a leading part in the history of the province of Khams. Though deprived of his rights by the Chinese invaders, the Duke continues to live in his ancestral residence with the whole of his retinue. He is still, in Tibetan eyes, the fount of authority, and it is interesting to note the contrast between the splendid castle of the deposed Tibetan chieftain and the mean dwelling of the Chinese magistrate, huddled among the poor houses of the village. The magistrate himself lives in a little clique of his compatriots, officials and soldiers who do not take kindly to their exile in a country whose language they speak badly, if at all, and where they cannot even spend the inadequate salaries which their Government pays them.

Djriwo stands on the left bank of the river. We crossed to it by a cantilever bridge, a particularly fine specimen of a form of engineering in which the Tibetans excel. The abutment of the bridge consists merely of a mass of beams—in this case tree-trunks untouched by the saw—which are arranged in layers, one on top of the other, and lashed together by fibre ropes. Each layer juts out by about twenty inches from the layer below it, so that the abutment extends progressively until it meets the other half of the bridge, which has been similarly projected from the opposite bank. If the river is very wide, one or two intermediate sets of piles are driven into its bed, to support a repetition of this formula. The result is a crude sort of arch, over which is laid the apron or surface of the bridge, also composed of tree-trunks; and a bridge thus built is a really solid piece of work, which weathers with no difficulty at all the floods which threaten almost all Tibetan bridges when the snows melt.

It is instructive to compare these cantilever bridges—built entirely by hand, without the help of a machine of any kind—with the modern bridges built in China by trained engineers, with modern machinery and an army of workmen to help them. Whereas the primitive Tibetan bridges stand up to every stress almost indefinitely, the Chinese bridges—as I learnt, all too often, at first hand—quickly collapse or are swept away. In the contrast between their bridges one may, I think, discern the contrast between the characters of these two very different peoples. In Tibet the bridges are built by countrymen, whose object is to produce something which is really well made and will be useful to the community for a long time; the builders are, in short, craftsmen. Chinese bridges are—nowadays—built by unscrupulous officials, wholly indifferent to the interests of the community and intent only on making even more money than they would have made anyhow by using inferior

materials. The Tibetans (you might say) still have a soul;
the Chinese have lost everything except their vices.

Soon after leaving Djriwo we left the valley of the She
Chu; its upper reaches are unexplored. On these high
plateaux live the Ngo-log tribes; Guibaud and Liotard
penetrated their territory in 1946, but after a few days'
march they were attacked by bandits and had to withdraw.
Liotard and two of their men were killed; Guibaud managed
to escape and eventually, after many difficulties, got back to
Charatong, where Father Yan looked after him.

We struck up a steep face on the right bank of the river
and soon emerged on to a plateau surrounded by grassy
hills, where we made camp. The ground up here was marshy,
and while looking for a place to pitch my tent I sank up to
my knees in a bog-hole. A little village was tucked away in a
fold of the ground nearby; at the head of the corrie I could
see the glittering roofs of the great monastery of Joro
Gompa, and after having something to eat I went to inspect
it.

It was nobly situated half-way up a hill with the quarters
of the lamas built all round it. A row of tall white *chörtens*
stood sentinel before its gates, shaded by a belt of trees
planted along the shore of a beautiful lake which filled the
bottom of the valley. The clouds and the hill-tops were
mirrored in the still surface of the water; the reed-beds in
the shallows were full of wildfowl who had nothing to fear
from man in a country where shooting is a form of blas-
phemy. The monastery itself, however, was not particularly
interesting, and its main temple was unimpressive.

Next day, following a trail which led us round the back
of the lamasery, we climbed up to a still higher plateau.
We started soon after midnight, before the moon had risen;
it was a very dark night and men and animals, all half asleep,
blundered forward slowly. We rode for some time through
a maze of hills, bluffs and ravines where it was not easy to
pick out the trail. But at last the moon rose and, no longer

afraid of falling head over heels in the darkness, I got
off my pony and walked, for I was dopy with sleep and
frozen with cold. We crossed a double range of hills by a
pass about thirteen thousand feet above sea-level, and as day
broke reached the heights which look down on the great
valley of Kantze.

A queer sort of track—a sunken road worn deeply into
yellow earth like the loess of North China—zigzagged interminably down to a little village. The valley was in-
tensively cultivated, and this village was the first of many.
To our right, lamaseries clung to spectacular sites on the
cliff-face wherever a narrow gorge debouched into the
main valley. About eight o'clock we stopped for breakfast
at a hamlet from which Kantze was clearly visible. I was
delighted by the prospect of getting there early in the day;
but as soon as we had eaten, the muleteers set about unload-
ing the animals, and I realised that they meant to spend the
night there. This time I really was furious; there was no
reason why, with the whole day to do it in, they should not
have finished the stage. I ordered Elie to put the loads back
on my two ponies; he did so with a very ill grace, but, when
I threatened to dismiss him there and then and send him
back to Kangting, he resigned himself to going on with me.
Shortly afterwards we were at Kantze.

I went straight to the magistrate's office, where I was
received with the usual courtesy. Unfortunately the magistrate spoke neither English nor Tibetan, and for some time
we simply sat there, drinking tea and beaming affably at
each other.

Soon, however, a Tibetan appeared who understood
Chinese, and we got on much better. The magistrate had
had instructions from Kangting to give me any assistance I
might need, and he showed me into a spacious room on the
top floor of the large Tibetan dwelling which housed the
municipal offices. Planks were placed across trestles to
make a bed, two chairs and a little table were produced and

my luggage was brought upstairs—all this in front of a large audience of Chinese and Tibetans who barged in and barged out, sat down and stared at me, jabbered and laughed with that serene disregard of privacy which is so characteristic of the East. An old Tibetan squatted on my bed and told his beads, while a gang of urchins were transported with delight by my tent, which I had spread out to dry, and by the mysterious contents of my luggage.

But daylight began to wane, and with it their curiosity. My room gradually emptied, and at last I was left in peace.

PART FIVE

Yaks and Coracles

NEXT morning I had a welcome surprise. Waiting for me in the magistrate's office was a young Tibetan called Tshering, who greeted me in English. A native of Kalimpong, where he had been educated in a Mission school, he had acted as interpreter for a British official in Tibet. He had travelled widely, and was fluent, not only in English and Tibetan, but in Chinese, Mongol, Urdu and Gurkhali. For some years he had been managing a small business in Kantze, where he had married an extremely pretty Tibetan girl, now the mother of three delightful children. With his help I was able to explain my requirements to the magistrate in detail. I was tremendously pleased at this encounter, for Tshering was a very likeable person and we rapidly became firm friends.

I was kept busy all the time I was in Kantze. I wanted to get to know more about the lamaseries and about Tibetan life in general, for Kantze is one of the most important religious centres in Sikang. At the same time I had more mundane business to transact, for it was once more necessary to find a caravan with which I could continue my journey, and above all I had to get hold of either some Tibetan money or a stock of brick-tea.

Elie and Tshering buckled to and went round interviewing all the people who might have tea to sell. I too did some market research, and during an official luncheon-party given by the local General (he was really only a captain) I met a young Chinese professor who ran a school at Derge. He undertook to find some tea for me through his numerous relatives in Kantze; and at last, by the united efforts of all my friends, I managed to collect about twenty *gams* of tea, which would last me as far as Jyekundo.

Tea is much the most useful form of currency for a traveller in Tibet. Silver coins, though easier to transport, are less convenient, for there are several different kinds, each of which only has its full value in one particular part of the country; moreover, a *gormo* (as the coins are called) is too large a unit with which to make small purchases from nomads who seldom have any change. Tea, on the other hand, is readily accepted everywhere. The only tiresome thing about it is that you need a lot of yaks to carry it about, for a yak can carry only two *gams*, which weigh between sixty and seventy pounds each; but yaks do not cost much to hire, and you can always convert the tea into butter, *tsampa* or even the local currency.

There is, however, one complication about this form of barter, and that is the number of different brands of brick-tea. Each big trading house in Ya-an has its own brand, stamped with its own trademark, and there is a wide variation in local taste, one brand being esteemed above all others in Kangting, another at Batang and yet another at Kantze. On top of all this the Chinese merchants think nothing of forging trademarks or selling *gams* composed of good tea on the outside and bad tea in the middle. Since the outside bricks are the ones you unwrap to check the quality, this swindle is seldom detected until after the tea has been sold and the *gam* opened up. I had personal experience of this sort of thing when I got to Derge.

The Tibetans have a very highly developed palate for tea and distinguish between the various vintages as we distinguish between different kinds of wine, the Indo-Chinese between different kinds of rice and the Greeks between different kinds of water. When they open a *gam*, they scrutinise the dried leaves very closely, chew some of them for a moment or two and immediately know which of the better-known brands they are dealing with. Once they have made up their minds to buy a particular variety, it is practically impossible to sell them any other, except at rock-bottom prices. Needless to say, it is generally the brand which one has not got that they are set on having. For small change it is a good idea to have with you plenty of little things like needles and thread and pocket mirrors, with which you can pay for almost anything and at the same time give pleasure to the Tibetans.

My rather sordid financial worries were more than recompensed by the fascination of life at Kantze. I was delighted with my room, which was quiet and secluded and had a balcony from which I got a wonderful view. Beyond the muddle of roof-tops below me and the wide plain beyond them rose the great mountain range of Kawalori, stretching northward as far as Rongbatsa; at sunset its sparkling glaciers turned a delicate shade of pink.

Behind the house I lived in, the monastery sprawled along the hillside, its temples and living-quarters rising in tiers as far as the ridge. I used to spend the evenings alone on my balcony, in a silence broken only by the distant barking of dogs. Sometimes, out of the dark mass of the lamasery, a strange and beautiful music would steal upon the air as the lamas serenaded their gods. It began with the deep rumble of the ceremonial trumpets, a slow, solemn rhythm throbbing through the night. This ended, there was a moment of silence and then you heard the sweet voices of the acolytes, like dream-music; they begin their hymn on one long-drawn-out note of extraordinary purity, which sometimes seems about to die away, only to well up again with a renewed vigour. Gradually this sound develops into a simple, touching melody, enriched at times with subtle modulations but always reverting to itself—a clear, passionless, gently-flowing volume of sound, expressing simultaneously the essence of human suffering and of the peace that lies beyond it. All the griefs and pains of our existence, with the pity, the tolerance, the love implicit in the Buddhist faith, were here expressed most beautifully, without false emphasis, without repining, without sentimentality. These

harmonies were utterly different from Chinese songs, whic
are fantasticated, staccato and shrill; they might, it is true
be said to have a certain affinity with Indian music, but the
do not have its complex modulations and sudden changes o
register. The religious melodies of Tibet are marked by
simplicity and a freedom from elaboration which are uniqu
in the music of the Far East.

I spent a good deal of time in the monastery, where
was soon on friendly terms with several of the lamas, includ
ing the Living Buddha who had authority over all th
temples in Kantze. The most important of them house
nearly a thousand monks and is one of the largest in Sikang
It is a picturesque place, with its network of alley-ways anc
staircases and quaint little terraces from some of which you
get a splendid view of the mountains. Cells, gardens, bal
conies, and tiny, mysterious shrines from behind whose door
comes the muted, rhythmic thunder of the prayer-drums—
the whole inconsequent miscellany rises in higgledy
piggledy layers. It is crowned, when you get to the top o
the hill, with the houses of the abbots and the senior lamas
in the middle of which rises a jumble of big temples, pilec
one on top of the other rather like a house of cards; from
their balconies you look down into great halls where noble
columns of red-lacquered wood stand out in the half
darkness. To the host of images upon their twilit altars the
flickering light of butter-lamps imparts the illusion of a
secret and mysterious life.

In one of the smaller temples there were four big image
of the Buddha-to-be, the Indian Maitreya; he—and he alone
of all the Buddhist theocracy—is represented, not squatting
but sitting upright in the way that Europeans do, for
legend insists that Buddha's next reincarnation will come
from the West, and not from Asia.

Three lamas were praying before an image hidden by a
veil in a particularly dark temple whose walls were covered
with dust-laden hangings of silk, layers of tapestries.

ABOVE: *Prayer-wheels in the lamasery at Kantze*
BELOW: *The Wheel of the Law at Kantze* and *The master of ceremonies at the dances*

banners and the masks of demons. I entered this holy place
by way of an antechamber unexpectedly cluttered up with old
weapons—blunderbusses and muskets with preternaturally
long barrels, inlaid with gold and silver and studded with
coral and turquoise: broadswords of fantastic design, suits
of armour and coats of chain-mail, helmets which looked
amazingly like those worn by European warriors in the
Middle Ages. I was intrigued to find an armoury in the
heart of a temple dedicated to the Compassionate One, but
the lamas assured me that these weapons had never been
used and had, in their present context, no military significance of any kind.

Kantze is—*mutatis mutandis*—the Mecca of Sikang; the
Tibetans came there in great numbers to perform the ceremonial circuit of the lamasery and to gain thereby much
merit. The pilgrims begin this circuit by prostrating themselves several times in front of the *mendong*, a kind of long
stone wall on which religious texts and invocations are inscribed. At Kantze this wall had one feature which I saw
nowhere else in Tibet—a sort of glacis made of large and
slightly tilted flagstones, on which the pilgrims, supporting
the upper half of their bodies on their hands, prostrated
themselves. Gradually, as the centuries passed, the friction
generated by the hands of the pious had worn in the stone
twin pairs of long, smooth and always rather greasy gutters.

After their prostrations the pilgrims walk round—in a
clockwise direction, as prescribed by ritual—the pretty little
path which encircles the whole of this sacred demesne. The
circuit is punctuated at frequent intervals by simple rites,
most of which involve the turning of a prayer-wheel. Some
of these are enormous machines, twelve or fifteen feet long
and six feet across, installed in little rectangular shrines
whose walls are covered with sacred texts, prayers, banners
and part-worn silk hangings. To get one of these wheels
turning requires a considerable physical effort, so the
pilgrims generally join forces, every member of the party

Tibetan houses at Kantze

K

tugging at one of the handles which project from the cask-like surface. This enables them to give the wheel any number of turns up to the maximum of a hundred and eight, each complete revolution being notified by the ringing of a little bell. Other, smaller prayer-wheels are often disposed in (so to speak) batteries in a long, rectangular gallery, in the centre of which are arranged various symbols or images made of stone or clay. The pilgrim passes through these galleries—never altering his clockwise course—and sets each little wheel spinning with a touch of his hand. The whole of the circuit is dotted with prayer-wheels, *chörtens* and little shrines; and as they go slowly round it the pilgrims unceasingly tell their beads; each bead of the eight hundred on each rosary is equivalent to one repetition of *Om ma-ni pad-mé hum.*

The zeal with which the Tibetans carry out their religious observances is extremely impressive. The pilgrims go through the required ritual in a most conscientious manner, never skipping a prayer-wheel or a sacred monument and telling their beads with devout pertinacity. This circuit is moreover a fairly stiff course—nearly three miles long, with a climb up (and down) of six hundred feet before you get round the whole lamasery. Some of the pilgrims do it several times in the course of a day, often at a spanking pace. Lamaism, though an essentially meditative religion, has its strenuous moments.

I was able, with the help of some lamas who were merchants as well as monks, to buy a number of valuable Buddhist curios (as they would be called in the West). The combination of a commercial career with a religious vocation strikes one at first sight as odd; but the fact remains that the junior lamas—who correspond roughly to our lay brothers—often run little shops where they sell tea or groceries or clothing. It is hardly necessary to observe that it *is* only the lower grades of the priesthood who indulge in commerce; yet I have often heard Christian missionaries criticise this practice in the most scathing terms. But surely Christian Missions own houses which they let, and and—often quite a lot of land—which they farm? And do they or do they not sell the corn, the rice and the other crops that they grow? This surely amounts to much the same thing and often, incidentally, gives rise to law-suits which can rarely, if ever, be said to enhance the spiritual prestige of the missionaries involved in them.

I went to spend a few days in a tiny little lamasery belonging to the Red (or unreformed) sect, perched up on top of a hill not far from Kantze. The head lama was seriously ill and the monks wanted me to stay on there until I had cured him, but the poor old man's condition was beyond hope and all I could do was to keep him alive for a day or two longer.

I have the happiest memories of my stay in this retreat, half-hidden by a grove of trees, in the company of an old lama who was initiating me in the practice of meditation. It was here that I made a discovery which subsequent experience abundantly confirmed; that the unreformed lamaseries are much more interesting from a purely religious point of view than those of the Yellow sect. In the former the actual rites are observed with the same elaborate care as in the latter, but in addition you almost always find, among adherents of the Red sect, certain lamas versed in the mystical doctrines of the "direct way" and in the formulæ prescribed for their celebration.

23. THE ROAD TO THE NORTH

WHEN I got back to Kantze, my friends had not only completed their tea-buying operations but had also found me a caravan; so I could set out once more upon my travels. Henceforth I had no more to do with the big trading caravans to which I had been attached since Kangting; I

rode instead with small private caravans organised on th
system known as *oula*. This system, which is often employe
in Eastern Tibet, is of extremely ancient origin, its inventio
being attributed—rightly or wrongly—to Genghiz Khan.

Based on the requisitioning of transport for each succes
sive stage, its use was once confined to Chinese envoys o
their way to Lhasa; but today it has become more democrati
and is common practice for army officers, officials and—
occasionally—European travellers. A written permit fron
the governor of the province gives you the right to hir
whatever animals you need from the village headman. On
or two men look after them until the end of the stage. Stage
vary a great deal in length; sometimes you keep the sam
caravan for two or three days, sometimes you have to chang
it two or three times in the same day. At the end of eacl
stage your animals are taken back to the place they cam
from, while a fresh caravan is organised for the next lap
The tariff for all this is settled before you start; it is, as
matter of fact, a very low one and travellers are scrupulou
about paying it, often supplementing it with a small tip
Unfortunately the Chinese soldiers—in this respect re
sembling their brothers-in-arms all over the world—ofte
forget to pay, a characteristic which does not endear then
to the Tibetans.

The great advantage of this system is that you can trave
in small, sociable groups; the caravan-men are mostly cheer
ful peasants and are often accompanied by their wives and
children with whom it is easy to get on friendly terms. The
snag about it is that you are liable to get stuck for severa
days in some god-forsaken village where there are no animals
available; but when this happens you can generally find some
lamasery (which you would never have had a chance of
visiting if you had been with a big caravan), and thus gain a
closer contact with the life of the country.

Another, and more serious, snag is that both the animals
and their gear are apt to be very inferior, for the Tibetans

llot the worst of both to work which brings in such a small
return. I did innumerable stages on the backs of lame,
emaciated, listless ponies which were ending long careers in
this semi-public service, while my kit was carried by stunted
and half-starved cows or venerable donkeys to whom,
touched by their sad and disillusioned appearance, I allotted
the smallest possible loads. Their trappings were no better.
Disintegrating wooden saddles held together by string, rope
stirrups, woollen bridles without bits—everything was in a
state of collapse and impossible to fix so that it did not slip
or get twisted or otherwise inconvenience the rider.

I have especially vivid memories of crossing one torrent
in midwinter, when the saddle started turning; I only just
managed to avoid immersion in the icy water and got to the
far bank hanging on to the pony with one leg, clutching the
neck-strap with one hand and holding all my bedding in
place with the other.

We left Kantze on May 20th with three ponies and nine
kéma, a word which Tibetans apply to yaks, oxen, cows and
cross-breds when they are used as pack-animals; these
carried my luggage and my tea. When on the eve of departure I paid for the tea I got a fresh insight into the
standards of probity prevailing among Kuomintang officials.
Before leaving Kangting I had gone to draw some money
from the Provincial Bank of Sikang; they had given it to
me in new, numbered packets, each made up of one hundred
two-thousand-dollar notes. It is not customary to check the
contents of these packets when they are fastened with a
paper band bearing the bank's name by way of guarantee,
but at Kantze the Tibetans, who knew a thing or two about
the Chinese, did not omit this precaution. From the middle
of each packet of one hundred, three or four notes had been
skilfully extracted, without disturbing or tearing the bank's
paper band.

Soon after leaving the little town we rejoined the course
of the Yalung and followed the track along its left bank,

which at first led us steeply uphill by a path cut out of th
mountainside. It was a big, broad valley, with the grea
range of the Kawalori mountains rising unforgettably on th
opposite side of the river.

I overhauled two pilgrims whom I had passed on the roa
several days earlier, on the other side of Kantze. The
were bound for Lhasa and had adopted a mode of progres
designed to acquire additional merit for their journey; the
lay flat on the ground with their arms stretched out in fron
of them and, hoisting their bodies forward with their hand
and elbows, gained about a yard at a time. They then stoo
up with arms outstretched, lay down again and gave anothe
heave towards Lhasa; they still had the best part of fiv
hundred miles to do before they got there. They wor
leather knee-pads and had a sort of wooden runners on thei
hands which made it possible to slide forward, when the
stretched themselves out on the ground, without taking a'
the skin off; but it struck me as a very arduous method o
crossing Tibet, and they were covered with dust and sweat

After a bit we passed the little lamasery of Nyara Gompa
built on a spur overlooking the river. Its ochre walls wer
striped vertically with red, white and black, as are al
lamaseries of the Sakyapa sect, to which this one belonged
It was the first of its kind I had seen since Kangting, but w
were to find a lot of them from now on, for this sect is pre
dominant in Derge. Soon afterwards a village called Ber
came in sight on the left bank; over it towered a great castl
belonging to the princely family of Horberi, one of the fiv
Horpa tribes which I have already mentioned. Here we
had to cross the river, just below an old bridge which hac
been completely destroyed.

Crossing a river in Tibet is an interesting business. Fords
rope bridges and cantilever bridges exist only if the river i
narrow. On wide rivers like the Yalung or the Kinchakiang
you use extraordinary dinghies or coracles made of hid
which are really big round wickerwork baskets covered

with yak-skins deftly sewn together. The middle of the circular "hull" is about six feet across, but the mouth (so to speak) and the bottom of the basket are considerably narrower. Into it you pile men and merchandise, and the vessel, launched upon the flood, is steered by a helmsman with a long wooden paddle.

The voyage is seldom dull, for the coracle spins round and round and rocks violently in rough water or eddies; it has, however, greater stability than its appearance suggests. The current is so strong that you may be carried five hundred yards downstream before you reach the other side, in spite of the efforts of the helmsman. He, when the coracle has been unloaded, picks it up and puts it on his head like an overgrown straw hat and carries it upstream for the best part of a mile, till he reaches a place whence the current will carry him back to his point of embarkation.

On this occasion we found waiting for us, scattered among the boulders on the further bank, a remarkable collection of skinny mules, emaciated horses, cows and even a wretched little she-ass with a foal at foot, a tiny and disarming little beast; this herd of starvelings, which looked like the last assets of a bankrupt circus, were escorted by an uproarious gang of ragged children. They were the next *oula* relay, and were taking over from our first caravan, which had started back to Kantze after leaving us on the river-bank. Fortunately we had only a very short stage ahead of us.

It was uneventful as well as short, and took us to Lintong, where we changed animals for the third time that day. The track ran on through a belt of rich agricultural land, the biggest single area under cultivation in eastern Tibet, with lots of streams and farms, little villages and lamaseries; it is about ten thousand feet above sea-level. At Tadji Gompa I made a brief halt to call on a lama from Lhasa of whom I had heard tell in Kantze; but he was away on a journey. At seven o'clock in the evening we reached the village of Rongbatsa; though small and insanitary, it had a beautiful situation.

It is two days' march from Rongbatsa to Yulong and since there are no other villages on the way, we did both stages with the same caravan. It consisted, luckily, of better animals than we had had the day before. We soon left the cultivated plain for a wild, desolate valley winding between grass-covered hills. There were no houses here, but the landscape was dotted with nomads' tents; their herds of yaks speckled the hillside with black as far as you could see. These steppes were real herdsmen's country.

The nomads were people of striking appearance, whose weather-beaten Aryan features were lacquered with dirt; they wore their hair long save for a fringe cut across their foreheads. They had a big knob of coral stuck in their left ear, two heavy silver amulets hung round their neck, and their only garment was a voluminous sheepskin *shuba*, girt with a belt from which hung a great dagger and a tinder-box. These people are transients rather than nomads in the true sense of the word; they normally move their habitations only three times a year, following the grazing from the valleys up to the mountain pastures and coming down again to the sheltered low ground for their winter quarters.

We met a number of caravans from Chamdo, laden with tobacco and cotton from India. We left the valley of the Yalung and climbed up a rocky gorge which brought us at midday to a fairly high pass. Beyond it a delightful prospect opened up—a huge pine-forest in which we presently found a small house standing in romantic surroundings. Here I renewed my acquaintance with Mr. Chang, the educational-ist from Derge, accompanied by his Tibetan servant-girl and a posse of Chinese officials. I spent a restful night in my tent, free from the usual noise and talk. In this part of the country there is a great deal of gold, and the sandy bed of a little stream nearby glittered with particles of gold-dust, but the dust is so fine that it is almost impossible to extract it by washing. Next day we struck a big tributary of the Yalung and did a dull, rather difficult stage over a track with boggy patches in which men and animals intermittently got stuck in deep mud.

After crossing a wooden bridge we left the valley and reached the small village of Yulong, tucked away in the bottom of a big corrie. It consisted of a large house belonging to the Tibetan headman, an inn where we slept and a few tumbledown shacks.

Big herds of yaks were grazing on the sides of the corrie and I spent the afternoon watching them, for I like yaks. These oddly built, frisky and whimsical animals have very short legs, a very long coat, normally black but sometimes dun in colour, and a huge fluffy tuft on the end of their tails. They have big wooden rings in their noses and a look of mild surprise in their gentle, candid eyes. The calves, which are very endearing little beasts, look like large plush toys as they gambol round their dam or the cow who is suckling them. Near the village I passed a caravan coming down from the high ground with loads of firewood and enormous faggots; the yaks were almost invisible under their burdens and the whole thing looked rather like Birnam Wood advancing on Dunsinane.

Another speciality of Yulong and the surrounding grasslands were some pretty little rodents, very light brown in colour and rather like baby rabbits, except that their ears are shorter, broader, more rounded and set further back on their heads. You see them everywhere, and the cropped turf is honeycombed with their little burrows. They are intensely curious and sit up and watch you as you approach, with their heads slightly cocked to one side, before disappearing into their holes with the rapidity of lightning. One of the odd things about them is that they are always in company with some little brown birds which seem to be inseparable from them. These hardly ever fly, but spend their time running about on the ground at an astonishing speed; when they do fly—as they will if you come too close to them—they keep very low and go only a few yards. The rodents and the birds

are so similar in size, colour and movement that when you
see one of them taking evasive action it is hard to tell which
of the two it is. They live together on the most intimate
terms, the birds nesting close to the mouths of the burrows
and feeding on the seeds and grains that the rodents store
up for the winter.

The direct route to Derge follows the valley which we
had left the day before, afterwards crossing some high
ground and dropping down again to Kolodong; but I
wanted to stop on the way at the big lamasery of Dzogchen
Gompa, whose fame as a religious centre made a powerful
appeal to me. So the next day we sent on to Derge the
luggage, the tea, Mr. Chang's Tibetan girl and the Chinese
bureaucrats and set off for the lamasery in a party of four:
Mr. Chang, his servant, Elie and I. We took with us only
our sleeping-bags and some tea, *tsampa* and butter.

Yulong is the centre of a network of primitive communications, but I never dreamed at the time that in the
following year I should be travelling on one of the tracks
which came down to it from the north. Now we were going
west along a bleak valley which offered us a short cut; it
was full of nomads' tents and herds. We halted for a meal
near the camp of an old Tibetan and his daughter, a bucolic
beauty whose face shone with butter. The old man had a
splendid buccaneering face; he told his beads, turned an
elaborate silver prayer-wheel and seemed to take little
interest in us.[1] We feasted on some delicious sour milk.

Our narrow gorge soon widened out into a deep valley.
High up at the end of it we could see the snows of Nuri La,
the pass for which we were making; to the left rose another
block of high ground, also snow-covered, over which my
caravan of tea would be climbing in a day or two *en route*
for Derge. We clambered strenuously up a steep slope of
screes and huge boulders; an icy wind was blowing and the
ponies, which were feeling the effects of the altitude, kept

[1] See plate facing page 49.

on stopping. I was often surprised to see how much less good animals are than men at adapting themselves to variations in climate and altitude. Although they are bred and brought up on plateaux far above sea-level, Tibetan ponies do not take kindly to the thin air at great heights; their flanks heave like a blacksmith's bellows and they get blown much worse than men on foot.[1]

We found ourselves before long on an extensive, steep slope of frozen snow, and here a savage storm of wind and snow swooped down on us. Riding was out of the question. We plodded slowly forward, bent double, battered by the wind and leading our wretched ponies, which were blinded by the snow clotting over their eyes.

We crossed the pass at three o'clock, after a short halt on the reverse slope to warm ourselves in the sun, which had mercifully reappeared. The pass is nearly fifteen thousand feet above sea-level, or much the same height as Mont Blanc, but it did not give me the thrill that I have so often felt on that noble Alpine peak. On the pass, though we looked down on the valley out of which we had climbed, we were dwarfed by the great mountain ranges towering over us, tumbling away to the horizon in every direction—a lunar landscape of rocks and ice and screes, a treeless, inhuman, mineral world from which all forms of life had withdrawn.

The path scrambled down over loose stones into the valley —an interminable, soggy valley whose peaty floor was dotted with pools of liquid mud and soft patches in which the floundering ponies sank up to their girths; only by combining acrobatics with horsemanship was it possible to remain in the saddle. On our left we had occasional glimpses of a great rocky peak festooned with a glacier. Night fell as we were crossing the stream to climb over a range of hills on its left bank into another valley. We continued this

---

[1] The ponies are, of course, carrying heavy loads; the men, who are better fed and get more sleep than the ponies, carry no extra weight. P. F.

switchback progress over two more watersheds, but it seemed
to get us nowhere and I began to think that we were lost.
At last, late at night, we saw a little cluster of lights ahead of
us; it was the hamlet of Dzogchen, and we were soon installed in the inn where a Chinese official was also lodging.

24. THE HOLY VALLEY

EARLY next morning we were visited by a young Chinese
friend of Chang's. His name was Li Tien-ming, and he had
been living for some years as a lama in the monastery of
Dzogchen Gompa, under a Tibetan name meaning "Chinese
Wisdom." He had studied at the university run by
Canadians in Chengtu and spoke a little English. He took
us round the village, but it is a place completely devoid
of interest, existing as a sort of satellite of the lamasery
which is tucked away out of sight in a cleft in the mountainside. It contains only a few houses, but a large number of
little square pavilions, made of round wooden beams painted
red; they stand in rows along the banks of two streams which
come leaping down the hillside, and each houses a big
prayer-wheel which is worked by the limpid and unsullied
current flowing past it.

We made our way slowly up the narrow defile which
leads to the lamasery. All the way along it stood *chörtens*,
poles bearing sacred garlands, prayer-flags and slabs of
stone on which pictures of the gods had been painted. At
last we emerged into the holy valley. Never have I seen,
anywhere in the world, a place apter for the life of contemplation. Once we had entered it, we lost sight of the gorge
which brought us there, and we found ourselves standing in
a green oasis, which felt as if it was suspended in the sky
and around which was deployed a vast amphitheatre of
forests and mountains. On our right the buildings of the
lamasery rose in tiers with their backs to a gentle slope;

acing them, on our left, lay a lovely wooded corrie, domi-
ated by the tremendous snow-covered peak which towered
n unchallenged mastery over the whole valley.

It is not a particularly big lamasery, for many of the monks
ive in little cells scattered through the surrounding wood-
and. We started to go over it, and on the wide terrace in
ront of the main temple found ourselves unexpectedly wit-
nessing a ritual dance; it might have been specially organised
or our benefit. The musicians were grouped in front of the
entrance to the temple; with their instruments—huge
rumpets, prayer-drums and cymbals—they accompanied the
sweet singing of the acolytes with a muted melody. The
amas were treading a slow, solemn, convoluted measure.
They were not wearing masks nor were they dressed as gods
or demons, as they often are for ritual dances; they wore
heir ordinary robes. Holding aloft the sacred emblems—
the sceptre and the bell—they mimed a scene from the annals
of Buddhism with reverent gestures; then, with a poised and
graceful movement, they spun slowly round on tiptoe with
their robes billowing out around them.

When the dance was over, a lama took charge of us and
led us to the biggest building in the lamasery, where its
chief dignitaries live. We were ushered into a long, light
room, a kind of veranda whence one looked out over a sea
of mountain-peaks stretching away to the horizon. It contained an altar covered with very fine bronze images and its
walls were hidden by shelves of books and silken hangings.
We were received by four lamas seated on cushions, who,
with much decorum, invited me to take my place beside them.

One of them, a lad of fifteen with an alert, intelligent
face, was the Living Buddha of that place and had authority
over two hundred other lamaseries belonging to the Gnimapa sect. The lamasery at Dzogchen belongs to a special
sub-division of the sect, and its monks are considered pre-
eminent for their knowledge of philosophy and for their
practice of contemplation. There are three other lamas of

the first rank at Dzogchen: the young man whom I have just
mentioned and who was the most important of the three;
his brother, who at that time was completing his studies in
Lhasa; and a third, an older man, who was with us in the
room. The two other lamas present were their teachers.
They all looked extraordinarily kind and serene. One had
the noble head of an ascetic; I felt instinctively that he would
be the ideal person to initiate me into the inner mysteries of
Lamaism, but it was not yet time for me to settle down to
intensive study; I had first to learn the preliminary lessons
which I hoped my visits to many different monasteries would
instil in me.

Conversation, thanks to Mr. Chang and his young friend,
was for once an easy matter, and I managed to elucidate
many religious problems which had been puzzling me. We
talked much of meditation, but these wise lamas would pro-
pound no hard-and-fast formulæ to be used; every disciple
develops a relationship with his master so intimate that the
latter can guide him, step by step, in the way best suited to
his character and personality; all instruction takes place in
complete privacy. The monks rise at five o'clock and
during the course of the day devote four periods of an hour
each to meditation; these are preceded by readings from the
Buddhist scriptures. Many do much more than the prescribed curriculum and live in a state of almost continual
meditation in hermits' cells deep in the forest. The Living
Buddha had a gravity of demeanour remarkable in one so
young, but from time to time one glimpsed the charming,
unaffected boy behind the staid mask of dedication. He was
greatly interested in my camera and my Tibetan notebooks;
he could hardly get over the idea of a foreigner reading and
writing the Tibetan script.

His teacher gave me some valuable guidance in matters
of the spirit and was kind enough to invite me to return and
study under him for an indefinite period. One day, I
promised myself, I would take him at his word, for what he

ad to offer me was, ultimately, what I had come to Tibet to
eek. I took some photographs of my hosts and left them
with a keen sense of regret, for deep within me I felt that,
n the short time we had spent together, a strong bond had
been established between us. In the main temple, lit by
nnumerable butter-lamps, I was once more filled, as the
monks performed their evening rites, with the serenity that
comes from two hundred deep, reverent voices intoning
their slow, harmonious chants.

We spent the next day in the forest where the hermits
ive. It was lovely weather. The three of us—Chang, his
Chinese friend and myself—set off along the valley, which
ooked peaceful and lovely with its groves and its clearings
and the rocky streams that watered them. A path led us up
he wooded slopes of the towering, snow-capped mountain.
At the end of two hours' climbing we came to a little group of
hermitages tucked away under the trees in a place of peculiar
beauty. One of the residents invited me to his tiny log hut at
he foot of a tall pine. The living-room contained nothing
except his bunk and a recess used for storing firewood and
provisions. Next to it, and on an even smaller scale, was his
place of worship, furnished only with a stool of meditation, a
reading-desk, some bookcases and, on the walls, some
hangings and a shelf with images and butter-lamps on it.
But the man's eyes had a look of inner tranquillity; the poor,
bare cell held boundless riches.

In a nearby clearing, a group of young monks sat in a
circle in the sunlight, reading some holy work which their
master expounded to them; they were learning the technique
of meditation, and I envied the tranquillity of their existence.
What demon, I could not help asking myself, drives me
forward on my travels when I know perfectly well that inner
peace (which I, like a fool, range the whole world to find) is
here, within easy reach? But it's no good; I am quite incapable, as yet, of subduing the silly, sterile wanderlust with
which Western culture has infected me.

Further up the mountain there were other colonies of hermits; but what was the point of going up to them only to come down again? Besides, I felt in my bones that I should return one day. We turned back down the deserted path. The sun was setting in splendour, the evening air was still. It was as though nature was in league with man to invest my memories of that holy valley with perfection.

25. PRINTING AND ARCHITECTURE

WE left early the next morning with two yaks and two ponies; but my pony was such a hopeless animal that I did the whole stage on foot. We climbed up to a high pass where an icy wind met us; but walking kept me warm, and I marched bare to the waist, like the caravan-men. Our small party had been joined by a plump, jolly Tibetan lady, a very likeable person, who was making a pilgrimage to Lhasa all by herself, carrying her belongings in a bag slung over her shoulder.

We dropped down from the pass into a big, wooded valley which went on and on. As night fell we were overtaken by a violent storm and sought shelter from it in a tiny hut which luckily happened to be near at hand. It already housed, in unimaginable squalor, a family with four children, all of them black with dirt and soot and one—a baby in arms—completely naked in spite of the intense cold. A little fire of yak-dung gave out a feeble heat but filled the hut with smoke; I found, with some difficulty, room to lie down among the children, the chickens, the dogs, two calves and five kids. My bedfellows wept, barked, cackled and bleated all night long, but I, being by now accustomed to this sort of thing, slept none the worse for it.

The next day we did a short stage to Kolodong, whence our caravan went back to Dzogchen. Here the trail we had

ABOVE: *On the road to Derge*
BELOW: *Lamas at a religious service in the courtyard of the lamasery at Derge*

been following joined the direct route from Yulong, and I heard that the yaks carrying my tea were ahead of us. We were now not very far from Derge, and the country looked particularly impressive; so I set off on foot ahead of the caravan.

The landscape really was astonishing. The track wound through a deep gorge, flanked by precipices and so narrow that often the river monopolised its floor and the path was either cut out of the cliff-face or built up on wooden piles above a foaming torrent which at times enveloped one in a cloud of spume. In some places the enclosing cliffs, more than a thousand feet high, rose absolutely vertical or even overhung the river, crushing the gorge in an enormous vice and reducing the illimitable sky to a thin blue ribbon eroded by the tops of trees. There were a lot of bridges; we crossed nine in half that number of miles.

After we had been going for three hours, this cañon widened out into a valley; but this was a wild sort of place too. Presently villages began to appear; we were getting back to the world of men. We passed a big white *chörten*, then a pretty clump of willows squeezed in between the cliff and the river-bank, then a few scattered houses. We turned a corner and there, all of a sudden, was the great lamasery of Derge, fitted snugly into the mouth of a little valley which ran back into the mountain and was lost to sight.

I crossed the wooden bridge which led to the village and went straight to the Chinese magistrate's office to find out where the school was; Chang, who ran it, had asked me to stay there while I was in Derge. No one understood my few words of Chinese, but a member of the magistrate's staff who spoke Tibetan directed me to the Chinese school, where I was received with the utmost kindness by a young teacher in a disused temple at the back of the lamasery. Here I was given a room to myself, next door to an old lama who still lived in an obscure corner of the temple, surrounded by images of the most terrifying kind and

The Living Buddhas of Dzogchen gompa, with (right) the younger one's tutor

L

performing his rites without taking any notice of the alien scholastic activity which went on all round him.

Derge is a typical Tibetan township, with its houses clustering round a big lamasery like chicks clustering round a hen. The lamasery is almost a little town in itself, and its ochre buildings, vertically striped with red, white and black, as are all holy places belonging to the Sakyapa sect, looked neat and gay as they climbed in irregular tiers up the side of the valley. In front of it stood a great white *chörten* shaped, like so many others in Tibet, in the form of an inverted bell; and above that there was a courtyard surrounded by a wooden gallery full of rows of prayer-wheels. This was where merchants from Lhasa brought gorgeously coloured carpets and the rich red cloth from which the best robes are made, supple and warm as velvet. Here, too, were sold locally-made goods: the country cloth, grey or striped in red and black, knives and cutlasses, soft leather boots with brightly coloured legs, heavy woollen blankets with exotic patterns on them, birchwood eating-bowls lined with beautifully worked silver, and many other things besides.

In this forecourt a few laymen's houses and little shops were dotted about with nothing to show that they were not part of the lamasery. Further up the hill the monks' printing-press was housed in an enormous rectangular building with another big courtyard in front of it, and above this stood the handsome and very imposing castle of the kings of Derge, and the main temple. Behind them sprawled the usual architectural dog's breakfast of lamas' quarters, little shrines, one big courtyard adorned with mural paintings and a long row of *chörtens*. The monastery, with its wide terraces, its gilded roofs and its prayer-flags streaming gaily in the wind from tall poles, had, in the brilliant sunlight, a gallant aspect.

Below it, down by the river, lay the Chinese quarter, a damp, dark, drab slum, contrasting sharply with the lamasery, like a fungus growing from a healthy tree. Its little shops, the inn where the Chinese magistrate lived, the jerry-built homes of the officials—the whole place looked very dim when you compared it with the fine and ancient buildings towering over it.

The printing-press was one of my first objectives, for a subsidiary purpose of my journey was to arrange for reprints of certain Buddhist works in Tibetan. The director of the press received me with great kindness in a big room full of books and drawings. He was an elderly lama of distinguished appearance; his secretary, a large, placid man, proved astonishingly erudite. They were both delighted that a European should have come to Derge with the idea of getting books printed in Tibetan, and you could have knocked them down with a feather when I gave them a list of the titles; they had no idea that we in the West had catalogued all their sacred writings. The secretary, however, took the wind out of my sails by revealing a precise knowledge of the name, the number of chapters and the number of pages in each of the several thousand works which are to be found in the three hundred and thirty-three volumes of the *Kanjur* and the *Tanjur*. These include, between them, the whole text of the Buddhist scriptures, all the commentaries upon them and various works dealing with grammar, astrology, medicine and other related subjects.

The printing-press at Derge has no regular and continuous output; it prints, by request, whatever books are wanted by its clients. The latter, if the order is a large one, must supply their own ink and paper. The press, moreover, shuts down in the winter in deference to the cold, for its premises are not heated. Its technical methods differ markedly from those employed in Europe. Instead of metal founts, which can be readily recast, the Tibetan printers use wooden ones—long, narrow planks on which the text is carved and each of which corresponds to one complete page. (The reader can try to imagine for himself the part played by the store-room in which are kept the tens of thousands of planks required for printing all the three hundred and thirty-three volumes of the Canon, as well as the appendices to them.) Every plank in every book has its number and its place on the shelves, and the whole collection is arranged in such a way that any of its component parts can be located at a moment's notice. It is housed in a big building, several storeys high; every room and every landing is lined with shelves, and all the shelves are numbered.

The actual work of printing is done briskly. An apprentice fetches the appropriate planks and dumps them on a bench beside the printers, who work in pairs, one on each side of a big bench. Number One selects a plank and puts it down on the bench; Number Two, using a felt pad, smears it with ink. Number One then lays a sheet of paper on top of the plank, and Number Two runs off the first impression by passing a heavy leather roller over it. The sheets thus printed are collected and taken to another part of the works, where they are sorted out and checked by the lamas. The pages of a book are never stitched or bound together; they are stacked (like a pack of cards), wrapped up in a piece of silk between two small boards of wood and then put into their place on the library shelves. The boards are often decorated with carvings or paintings. The Tibetans have a tremendous respect for the written and the printed word and do not recognise the existence of anything corresponding to the waste-paper basket; if a page is smudged or printed amiss, they put it in a shrine in order not to tarnish its magic.

Though I spent a lot of time in the lamasery, I spent even more of it with the old lama in the next-door room. Several times a day he intoned his prayers in his dark, dust-laden little sanctuary, all cluttered up with images, paintings, demons' masks, thank-offering bowls and silk hangings which veiled the terrible gods. The tiny windows admitted the minimum of daylight, and the flickering butter-lamps lent the place an air of mystery. While the old man prayed,

I squatted near him in the shadows, studying the ritual gestures with which he managed the sceptre and the bell, and the way he chanted or intoned the sacred words, which were accompanied by the continuous beating of a drum, the thunder of much bigger drums and the sharp clangour of cymbals. For hours at a time we sat side by side on our cushions, facing the low altar on which butter-lamps burned in honour of the veiled image of Dodiephuwa, the tutelary diety of the Sakyapas. Sometimes the lama made me read a passage from one of the *tantras* dedicated to this god, and afterwards expounded its meaning to me and instructed me in the practice of meditation; then he would relapse once more into contemplation. I used to slip away when I felt tired, but he stayed on, hour after hour, motionless and seemingly drained of life.

These pious observances were interspersed with more mundane distractions. I was several times invited to a meal by the magistrate, whose name was Fong Chai-yuan, and was delighted to renew my acquaintance with Chinese cooking after several months of *tsampa* and buttered tea. I also spent a lot of time talking to one of the schoolmasters, an enthusiastic young man who had thrown himself heart and soul into his work. He took me to see his new school being built and I got a first-hand glimpse of Tibetan building technique.

The walls are always made of adobe, the clay being tamped down between a supporting framework of timber. This work is done entirely by women, relays of whom, bare to the waist and singing all the time, bring the clay to the site in baskets which they carry on their heads. When they have filled the wooden framework, a gang of men and youths, working shoulder to shoulder, proceed to tamp it down; they are armed with baulks of timber, which they plunge rhythmically up and down, at the same time executing what looks like a dance, so that their feet help to knead the clay into a compact mass. The dance is accompanied by a monotonous and unending song which I remember as the *leitmotif* of life in Derge.

No mortar—no water even—is used in the construction of these walls of earth, but in that dry climate they will stand for centuries: witness the ruined castles of the kings of Chala, on the road to Kantze, or those at Derge. The ground floor of a house, which is used for stables and store-rooms, is always built of this material; but in the better class of house and in the lamaseries you generally find rooms built of wood in the corners of the upper storeys. They are beautifully made, split logs being used; the rounded part of the log is on the outside, the flat part, neatly levelled off, forms the interior wall, which is often lined with panelling made of planks. The finished product is painted dark red.

The windows are square and fitted with wooden frames of an ornamental Chinese design; across the frames—also in the Chinese style—they stretch "panes" of semi-transparent paper. The flat roofs have a basis of interlaced branches or faggots, covered with a thick layer of earth tamped down in the same way that the walls are. If they are well made, these roofs are completely waterproof, and to keep them in repair it is only necessary to fill up the cracks with earth from time to time.

Temple roofs are slightly more complicated. The foundation of faggots is built up to a depth or four or five feet, and its edges, which remain visible under the eaves when the temple is finished, make an æsthetic contribution to the appearance of the building. The butt ends of the faggots, pressed tightly together and carefully levelled off, form an integral part of the outer wall; they are painted black and produce the effect of a broad bank of rough, granulated material running round the top of the smooth red walls. Along the edge of this great black stripe runs an ogee in which the round butts of rafters, projecting slightly from the rest, are picked out in white, each being in its turn surrounded by square butts, also projecting slightly. Tibetan architecture is completely unlike any other, though its classic tradition seems at times to have certain accidental affinities with the architecture of ancient Egypt.

26. AN AGONISING DILEMMA

My own affairs, meanwhile, were not making much progress. I had so far failed to sell my brick-tea, for the little town had ample stocks, and this knocked on the head a secret plan which I had worked out in collaboration with my friend Chang. The reader may recall the Tibetan woman who travelled with us on the last lap of our journey and who was begging her way to Lhasa. We had managed to persuade this enterprising lady to take me along with her; being a good pious soul, she fully understood my desire to make a pilgrimage which she herself was undertaking in spite of all the difficulties involved. The idea was that she would look after the external affairs of my expedition, do all the buying of provisions and all the talking to the people whom we met on the road. To them she would explain that I was an old lama from Mongolia who could not speak much Tibetan; with my shaven head, my face darkened by exposure and a respectable patina of dirt, and a secondhand lama's robe which I had picked up locally, this would not be a difficult role to sustain.

But this plan would only work if we travelled on foot, like very poor people, with our belongings on our backs. If I could have sold my tea, it would have been easy to take the proceeds with me, hidden somewhere on my person, and the money would have made it much easier to buy provisions. It would, on the other hand, have been out of the question to set out with ten yak-loads of brick-tea; so considerable a caravan would not only have been incompatible with our humble status, but would have meant employing two or three men—inevitably talkative and indiscreet—to look after it. I could not, however, jettison the tea, for it represented my entire capital, without which I could make no further progress.

It was an agonising dilemma. I did my utmost to retain the good lady's services for as long as I could, hoping somehow to get rid of the pestilential tea; but in the end she got bored with the whole thing and disappeared one day without a word of warning. Afterwards I often used to think of her, striding sturdily westward through fair weather and foul, immune from all the mundane worries that bogged me down.

I had lost one chance of reaching Lhasa, and this made me all the more determined to find another.

PART SIX

My Initiation

27. THE BARRIER OF THE YANGTSE

On the 10th of June, escorted by a large party of my friends, I crossed the bridge that leads out of Derge. Everybody had been extraordinarily generous. The lamas at the printing-press gave me a sack of *tsampa* and a basketful of fried cakes to which they knew I was extremely partial; a sick man whom I had been looking after produced a huge lump of butter, the school-teachers a supply of vegetables from their garden, and the Chinese magistrate several packets of English cigarettes. Everyone wished me a prosperous journey and a speedy return.

My caravan comprised two ponies—one of them for Elie —and six yaks carrying my luggage and the tea. I had an escort consisting of one Chinese soldier, whom the magistrate insisted on placing at my disposal although conditions in that part of the country were fairly peaceful; this warrior was armed with a Tibetan dagger, a gigantic broadsword and a long Chinese pipe. He was a splendid fellow, entirely devoted to my interests, but there was nothing very military about his get-up; this consisted of a pair of faded blue trousers, an old, patched sheepskin *shuba*, and an astonishing hat, round, black and hard like a bowler and decorated with an enormous pink cockade which this fop had cut out of the lid of a tin of cigarettes going under the improbable name of 'Pink Bean Cigarettes.'

Quite early in the day we reached the little inn at Kolodong, where I found an old Tibetan lady dressing her daughter's hair in a most interesting way. In Tibet the women wear their hair in a wide range of styles. In Lhasa and the provinces round it the fashion is extremely elaborate. At Kangting it is relatively simple—long plaits, with a lash of red wool on the end of each, wound round the head like a turban. The ladies of Derge, however, aimed rather higher than this.

To begin with, their hair, in order to give it gloss and lustre, gets a good going-over with butter; this phase of the operation has the incidental advantage of evicting a small but worthwhile proportion of the lice normally to be found in these well-stocked coverts. The hair is then, after being parted down the middle, carefully piled up in two close-fitting caps on top of the head. Each of these is subdivided into long, narrow plaits, all originating at the same level, which are bound round the two glossy central buns of hair. A lady can have up to fifty plaits on each side of her skull (the height of fashion is to have a total of a hundred and eight, or the same number as the beads on your rosary), and it is no easy task to build up this double circumvallation of long tresses, which in this part of Tibet are made even longer by tassels or streamers of black wool.

When a lady lets her hair down, the plaits form a lissom, revealing veil round her head and shoulders; it looks odd at first, but is very becoming. The ends of every pair of plaits in this black cascade are linked by a coloured ribbon, and this ribbon is tied to the lady's girdle. The results are very fetching, and Tibetan girls, standing on the flat roofs of their houses with their *shubas* draped closely about them and their faces framed in the gracefully parted curtains of their plaits, look like princesses in a fairy-tale.

Next day we went on retracing our steps up the valley which led back to Dzogchen Gompa. After four hours we reached an important crossroads, with a lot of nomads' tents dotted round it. Here we turned north towards Marong up a grassy valley where many beasts were grazing; they were guarded by savage, or anyhow temperamental, mastiffs. We halted for the night in the middle of a torrential rain-storm.

It was still raining when we set off again next morning; the weather seemed to have turned against us. The valley, a narrow one, was uninhabited; the only signs of life were hares, gazelles, antelopes and fat little marmots. It began to snow and we made slow progress; the animals kept on stopping to regain their breath because of the gradient and the altitude. I walked in order to keep warm (for it really was bitterly cold), but found the going difficult because of the deep snow in which we had to trample out a path. To make things worse, I slipped on a snow-covered boulder when crossing a stream and my wet boots were soon frozen stiff.

The country, nevertheless, had a sort of bleak majesty. It was the kind of scenery I had expected to find in Tibet: a high, wild pass between bare mountains, the thin black line of yaks behind me blurred by mist, the continual cries of the half-naked men urging them up the steep ascent, the intermittent halts to take the load off a beast that showed signs of foundering. (It is however only fair to point out that the weather in Tibet—especially in winter—is generally fine and dry; it seldom snows, and the bright sunshine makes it easy to put up with the low temperatures.)

We crossed the pass just before ten o'clock; it is about fourteen thousand feet high. The valley on the other side was more sophisticated, with odd patches of cultivation, and we soon reached Marong, which consisted of a single building. While waiting for the caravan to catch us up, I had a shot at drying my boots, socks and trousers in front of a fire; but it would have taken days before this experiment succeeded. From Marong we marched on for another two hours down the valley, till we sighted Gozé Gompa, a monastery which, like the one at Derge, belongs to the Sakyapas, the most important sect in the province.

It is a small lamasery. The only interesting thing about it is the roof of the main temple. This, instead of being flat in the usual Tibetan style, is designed like the roof of a Chinese temple, but each of its corners is surmounted by the emblem of a snake, such as you find in India or Cambodia.

On the pantile, two curious dancing skeletons flank a central belfry. At either end of the roof squats, like a gargoyle, the composite sea-monster with an elephant's head known as *makara*, an emblem more commonly met with in countries —like India, Cambodia and Java—less remote from the ocean than Tibet.

One man, among the small crowd of Tibetans who watched me closely while I was recording these odd things in my notebook, had a strikingly Aryan cast of countenance; with his bronzed face and his light-coloured eyes, he could easily have passed for a Chamonix guide.

I had come now to the end of the *oula* system of requisitioning transport, for we had left the province of Derge for that of Dengko, where, incidentally, the rate for pack-animals was higher. Soon after leaving Gozé we got on to the main caravan route from Dzogchen to Jyekundo. It was a dull day's march, infused with a rather vicarious interest by the fact that we passed close to the village of Lingtsong, which may have been the actual and is certainly the legendary birthplace of the greatest hero in Tibetan history, Késar of Ling.

Késar—a name whose echoes down more recent ages must surely have been coincidental—is supposed to have reigned over a small principality in Eastern Tibet which some authorities—notable among them Madame Alexandra David-Neel—identify with the Lingtsong district. Késar reigned long before Buddhism was introduced into Tibet. He seems to have been a warrior as well as a king, and his saga consists of a long series of remarkable adventures, most of them set in China. Oddly enough, the Chinese, too, have temples dedicated to Késar, but their Késar is Chinese, not Tibetan, and would seem to have been an entirely different person, unconnected with the ruler of Ling. To make matters still more confused, both in Lhasa and in Eastern Tibet temples dedicated to the Tibetan Késar are known as "Chinese temples."

Whoever or whatever Késar really was, he is easily the most popular legendary figure in Tibet, and the wandering story-tellers who beg their way from village to village seldom omit his heroic achievements from their repertoire. Although his legend is based mainly on oral tradition, versions of it exist in manuscript and even in print. I came across several of them in the course of my travels and found them of considerable interest, not only for their archaic style, but for the light which they throw on pre-Buddhist Tibet. Késar's saga is a welter of fighting and hunting, savagery and heroism. One must assume that it does roughly interpret the life of those days; and, if it does, it brings out very strikingly the changes wrought by Buddhism. Its tenets of peace and charity and gentleness have transformed the national character without impairing the pride and the high courage on which the independent, freedom-loving outlook of the Tibetans is based. Tibet, like Mongolia, is a shining example of the beneficent effects of Buddhist philosophy; it is a thousand pities that the West has learnt so little from them.

I was riding along, thinking about Késar and his adventures, when, as I rounded a corner, the monastery of Nodzé came in sight, snugly sited in a wide, shallow corrie. When I got there they allotted me the best quarters I had had so far. My room, which was both better lit and cleaner than rooms in lamaseries are apt to be, belonged to one of the senior lamas; it was well furnished, with a painted altar, many images of unusually good quality and a great many books. From my bunk, which was covered with fine Tibetan carpets, I could look down the whole length of that wide and tranquil valley.

The route which led from Nodzé to Dengko was not easy going. The steep, stony track crossed a succession of ridges and ravines (ten times in one day, by my computation, we scrambled up and ten times slithered down). About noon on the first day's march we crossed a high pass and found ourselves looking down into a big and enticing valley. Along it flowed the Yangtsekiang, here still known as the Dru Chu (in Tibetan) or the Kinchakiang (in Chinese). We dropped down to the floor of this valley and soon reached the little town of Dengko.

Here the trading centre is not only a place of considerable importance but—and this is unusual in Tibet—it overshadows the local lamasery. This is an insignificant group of buildings, tucked away in a grove of trees. The main temple was a poor sort of place, and not well looked after. An old lama showed me round it and identified the resident gods. I noticed a bundle of old *thankas*, which are religious pictures painted on silk, rolled up and stacked in a derelict pile. I got the lama's permission to examine them, found that some were extremely interesting and asked if I could buy them. He refused, as I had expected, to sell them but insisted on presenting me with three.

"They will be useful for your own temple," he said, "when you get home."

That afternoon I went and sat on the bank of the Yangtse. On the far bank I could see a little temple, a well-defined track, and the wall of mountains into which it disappeared towards Chamdo. There lay Forbidden Tibet; the river marked its frontier.

For a long time I looked across the river towards this tantalising territory of which I had dreamed for so long and which I now beheld for the first time. Every detail of the landscape stamped itself on my mind—the trees, the rocks, the little houses, the peasants going about their work, the children playing. But it was inaccessible, as distant, as unattainable, as if an ocean and not a river lay between it and me.

Within a stone's throw yak-skin coracles were ferrying people across the Yangtse as though it was the most natural thing in the world. The passengers were all Tibetans; they would never know the envy they aroused in the white man

Lamas' quarters at Derge

ABOVE: *Building the school at Derge*
BELOW: *The building which houses the printing-press at Derge*

ho watched them, smiling, from the other bank. Some
ven invited me to make the crossing with them, but I knew
hat, if I accepted, I should soon be turned back on the other
ide. This was not the bridgehead from which to launch my
aid on Lhasa.

28. TRANSMISSION OF STRENGTH

THE next stage, to Mantzen, was a long one; we kept the
ame caravan for four days. We began by fording a big
tream, where the men were hard put to it to prevent the
nimals from being swept off their feet. The country was
ninteresting; the Yangtse flowed sluggishly, winding
ound little sandy islets covered with stunted willows and
amarisks. The track either followed the sandbanks along
he river's edge or ran, thirty feet above it, along the flat
xpanse of pasture in the bottom of the valley; it was tre-
nendously hot, and I walked ahead of the caravan, bare to
he waist and getting thoroughly burnt by the sun.

Three young lamas, cheerful and friendly people, had
acked themselves on to our small party. They seized the
pportunity of putting their belongings on my pack-animals
nd strode gaily along, carrying big black umbrellas to pro-
ect their shaven heads against the sun. After weathering a
violent rainstorm we camped for the night on a bluff two or
hree hundred feet above the river; here, thanks to the
generosity of the local farmers, I had a delicious dish of sour
nilk and some cakes made of barley-flour.

The next day something alarming and unpleasant hap-
ened. After a few hours' march down this rather boring
valley we came to a little lamasery of the Karmapa sect,
ainted white (as they always are in that sect) and standing
n a stretch of turf which ran down to the Yangtse. Soon
fter this, the terrain began to alter; the track climbed

M

steeply up a high cliff overlooking the left bank of the river
then plunged into a wild and chaotic area of broken ground
For several hours we scrambled through this fantasti
wilderness, by-passing tall spurs of rocks, scaling precipitou
ridges, plunging down into gloomy ravines with torrent
racing through them on their way to join the Yangtse whic
we could sometimes see winding like a thin blue ribbon i
the distance. The track clung dizzily to the sheer rock-fac
and at length became so difficult to negotiate that I had t
dismount and walk.

After some hours on foot I felt tired and decided to res
my legs by riding again for a few minutes. We were on
stretch where the track was more or less level but ver
narrow. All at once my saddle slipped round and I foun
myself lying underneath the pony with my right foot caugh
in the small Tibetan stirrup. The frightened animal bucke
wildly and then bolted. It looked as if I was going to b
dragged behind him over the rocks, but with a last desperat
effort I managed to get my foot free and was left lying half
stunned while the wretched pony made off into the distance
bucking and kicking in an effort to get rid of the saddl
which, with my sleeping bag and other oddments lashed o
to it, now hung under its belly.

I began to realize what a narrow escape I had had. No
only had I just missed being kicked or trampled to deatl
but, if the saddle had happened to turn clockwise instead o
anti-clockwise, I should have fallen, not on the track, but ove
the precipice, for the pony had been walking—as all horse
do on mountain trails—as close as possible to its verge. It wa
instinctive, as I recovered my composure, to examine th
almost vertical slope down which I should have fallen, to finis
up in a swiftly-flowing torrent fifteen hundred feet below.

The pony, having eventually got rid of the impediment.
dangling underneath him, quietened down and was grazing
peacefully when the men recaptured him and brought him
back to me. Elie, still pale and shaking with fright, too

pains to see that the girths were tight enough, and we set off again. But I finished the long stage on foot, although I was slightly lame and the cuts on my back were very painful.

We dropped down slowly into the valley and camped near the village of Yemba, opposite the lamasery of Dantha Gompa, which stood in forbidden territory on the other side of the river. It rained all night, and the weather next morning was vile; but we only had a short stage to do before reaching Mantzen, a small agricultural settlement on the banks of the Yangtse. On the opposite bank, in the mouth of a green and fertile valley, I could see the small lamasery of Shangu Gompa. I paid little attention to it at the time, for I was not to know that before long it would play an important part in my destinies. I spent that day in the farm where we were quartered, talking to its owners and to an old lama who lodged in one of the spare rooms.

Next day, in a wild, spectacular gorge, our path was once more barred by the Yangtse. It was about two hundred feet wide at this point and its current, constricted between rocky cliffs, was extremely swift and turbulent. We addressed ourselves to the task of crossing. This time the boats involved were not the usual round coracles, but longish rectangular ferries, with their bows and sterns built up above the level of the gunwales; they were, however, constructed, like the little coracles, of wickerwork sheathed in yak-skin.

It was quite a business making them seaworthy. First we had to patch the yak-skin hull, caulking the rents in it with butter and bunging up the holes with wads of yak-hair also soaked in butter; then we had to lash two ferries together with spars of wood to give them more stability. After that we went through the usual drill. The clumsy craft was towed upstream through the comparatively stagnant water under the bank; then we piled into it and were swept diagonally across to a point on the further bank about three hundred yards lower down. A Tibetan who took passage with us swam his pony alongside; it struggled manfully against the current, its eyes dilated with fear, and was trembling violently when it came ashore on the other side. Our own animals remained behind on the left bank, and one of the lamas went off to fetch another relay from a village nearby.

It is no good pretending that I did not get a thrill out of landing on the right bank of the Yangtse. We were now in Tibet proper, and would continue to march through it as far as Jyekundo. The route (no practicable alternative to it exists) is really a sort of right of way, established by usage; but traffic on it—as I was soon to discover for myself—is very closely supervised by the Tibetans.

The fresh pack-animals arrived while we were making tea. I had to enter into serious negotiations about the cost of their hire, for we were now in an independent country; Chinese influence cut no ice here and the *oula* system was not recognised.

When we started, the track led us up the cliff overlooking the river; the great rocky gorge through which it ran was a most impressive sight. On the far side we got a glimpse of the small lamasery of Mandzri, a white oasis in a grove of trees clinging to the side of the mountain. Before long we reached the Shangu Gompa lamasery, first sighted from Mantzen on the day before. It was romantically situated on a ledge high above the valley, with its back to the cliff. After crossing a wooden bridge and climbing up a steep path, we were welcomed by its guardian pack of watchdogs, all barking their heads off; a lama got them under control and showed me to a large room where I took up my quarters. Elie and the young lama who was travelling with us were in the room next door.

Soon afterwards the local Living Buddha came to call on me—a stout youngish man whose aristocratic nose stood out anomalously in a gentle, contemplative face. He bade me welcome and said that he had been expecting me, having heard a great deal about me; not for the first time I remarked

he speed with which news travels in a country where all
means of locomotion are extremely slow.

I had a meal of *tsampa* and butter-tea and went to inspect
he lamasery; but it was not much of a place and, apart from
he two senior lamas whose quarters were close to my own
oom, most of the monks lived in lonely cells built into the
mountainside. This is normal practice in the Karmapa sect,
o which the monastery belonged.

Yielding to a strong impulse, I visited one of these cells,
painted white and poised like an eyrie on a minor peak.
Chörtens lined the path leading to it, but the cell itself was
shut up and appeared to be deserted; I was greatly struck
by the silence and the tranquillity of that lonely place. Suddenly the door opened. A smiling lama appeared and invited me to enter. His ascetic face was framed by a short
black beard, but the thing that struck me most was his eyes,
which seemed to bore into me as though he could read the
secrets of my soul. He made me sit down in his little shrine
and told me that he too had been expecting my arrival, a
lama from Dzogchen Gompa having given him news of my
approach. He interrogated me at length about my know-
edge of Buddhism, the methods I used in meditation and
my religious experiences. He made me read out various
passages from a sacred text and expounded them to me in a
most lucid and instructive way.

I did not notice how quickly the time was passing until I
realised that night had fallen. The lama shared his frugal
meal with me and then showed me into a tiny cell tucked in
at the back of the hermitage where I was astonished to find
my sleeping-bag; they had brought it up there without
saying a word to me.

From then on I gave up being astonished by anything
that happened at Shangu. Events seemed to be occurring
without my having any part in them, and I felt that I was in
the grip of a secret and compelling force which had brought
me to this little monastery in the back of beyond where

everything seemed to have been prepared for me in advance and where everything conspired to keep me an uncomplaining captive. The next morning my little caravan set off for Jyekundo as though it was the most natural thing in the world for it to leave me behind; and I, in an equally matter-of-fact way, stayed in the isolated cell on the side of the mountain, alone with my teacher.

The days passed as they pass in a dream; I still do not know how many I spent there. I hardly ever left the shrine and spent much of the time sitting beside my master, gazing at the magnificent view down the valley, reading or meditating. It seemed as though the lama had found out on that first day all that he needed to know about me; for he asked me no more questions, but answered, briefly, any that I put to him. We were linked by a current of intuitive understanding, and I learnt far more during this short period of retreat than I had from years of intensive study in Europe.

One morning we sat down side by side in front of the little altar. The lama arranged in front of us a magic circle of intricate design; on a stool were placed the sacred sceptre and bell, a ritual drum, a bowl for libations made from a skull-cap mounted on a copper stand, a round box containing consecrated pills, and another bowl filled with grains of barley. Two ritual jugs, their stoppers having the shape of a mystic jewel and being decorated with a peacock-feather design, were filled with lustral water.

While my master administered to me the elementary rites which qualify the candidate to profit by the telling of his beads, another lama entered the shrine and squatted down beside us without a word. Then began the long ceremony of initiation. Its intricate ritual lasted for an hour; at the end of it I had become a member of the Karmapa sect and powers had been bestowed on me which would enable me to progress further down the mystical path to which I was committed.

This particular ceremony is not really what is generally

understood by an initiation, though that is how its Tibetan name (*angkur*) is generally translated; the literal meaning of the word is "transmission of strength;" which conveys exactly the inner purpose of the rites. It is not, at any rate in these early stages, a question of initiating the disciple into a secret doctrine, but rather of investing him with certain powers residing in his master or in the occult forces of which the latter has gained control. The disciple's role is not a merely passive one; it is up to him to grasp and to get the most out of the psychic emanations which surround him during the ceremony. As the disciple progresses further into the realms of spirituality, he submits himself to fresh rites of the same kind which qualify him to penetrate still deeper into the mysteries of Lamaism.

The most vital part of the ceremony is the intoning by the master of a special service of consecration; my lama reverently extracted his copy of this service from a little cupboard where it was carefully preserved in wrappings of silk. Parts of this service took the form of a duologue in which I had to read certain passages of the text, repeating them three times after the lama. Our chanting had the usual accompaniment of music and mime: bells were rung, the drum was beaten, intricate gestures were performed with the sceptre, grains of barley were thrown—by master and disciple alternately—on to the magic circle and towards the five corners of the universe. Some gestures were unmistakably linked to the purpose of consecration, and openly symbolised the transmission of powers from the lama to me: for instance, he touched my head, my breast and the nape of my neck with the sceptre and with the sacred bowls. Then I was washed with the purifying water, drank some of it and swallowed the consecrated pills; there were other rites besides these. When all were done, the lama bade me repeat the "Triple Refuge" to mark my entry into the Buddhist Church, and bestowed on me the name by which I should be known to the members of my new religion.

These details will seem ridiculous to those European readers who are accustomed to dismiss as mere superstition everything which cannot be fitted into the pattern of their own religious practices. It should however be noted that Christian sacraments—confirmation, for instance—are based on much the same conceptions as those of Buddhism, and the rites of ordination into the Christian Church do not differ in essentials from those which celebrate the consecration of a lama.

I had been living for months on the frontiers of mysticism and now, in a lonely cell on a lonely mountain, I had crossed them. I was stirred to the depths of my being, dazzled by the glimpse I had had of the new and illimitable world which stretched before me. I had done my utmost, ever since entering Tibet, not to play the tourist, not to treat Lamaism as so much exotic camera-fodder, not to study a great religion as an ethnologist might study a quaint tribal custom. I wanted to immerse myself, as far as a European could, in something which dominates the life of Tibet.

Before coming here, I had studied Buddhism for years. I had visited its temples in Cambodia and Ceylon, in China and Mongolia, living with the monks, attending their services, sharing their meditations. Today, at last, I realised that a man would need to spend not one but several lives in the tantalising twilight of Tibet to unveil all its mysteries, to make any significant advance down the spiritual road which leads out of its desolate mountains towards a goal which I could never attain.

I knew that the time had not yet come for me to take that road, that the quest I had undertaken was not at an end; and in due course I set off again for Jyekundo with Gelu, the young lama who had been travelling with us and who, well aware of my reasons for staying so long at Shangu, had waited there to keep me company on the road.

After an hour's march, we reached the little village of Kaya, where the local authorities proved mildly obstructive.

We had been in Tibetan territory since crossing the Yangtse, and it is only by courtesy that the Tibetans allow travellers to take the short cut to Jyekundo, which lies astride their frontier with China. Gelu explained to the headman that I was only going there in order to continue my journey to Kokonor, in Chinese Tibet; nobody had any objection to that, and I was permitted to proceed. This small *contretemps* brought home to me the need for elaborate precautions if I ventured into territory more definitively forbidden.

Beyond Kaya, through a narrow, wooded valley, the track brought us up to the pass to Showu. It was not so much a pass as the entrance to a high corrie surrounded by bare, jagged hills. A wide expanse of prairie covered the bottom of the corrie. Thousands of ponies, sheep, goats and yaks were at pasture here. We broke our march at a big tent where a very pretty Tibetan girl served us with sour milk and refused all payment for it.

Later in the morning we climbed gently out of this corrie into another one, about twelve thousand feet above sea-level and no less thickly peopled with flocks and herds. We were marching at a good steady pace, but the absence of any form of landmark gave me the impression that we were making no progress at all. Although spring was far advanced, an icy wind was blowing; winter on these uplands must be hell.

Here and there, sheltered from the wind in the mouth of a re-entrant, you saw a cluster of tents; and at last, after making a long detour round a rocky spur, the village of Panchen came in sight. Over it towered a gleaming white lamasery, offering a marked contrast to the dingy quarters of the Chinese magistrate, who lived in a poor dwelling surrounded by refuse-heaps and mud. We got ourselves lodgings in a nondescript hovel, but the headman, fortunately, came and moved us to a spotlessly clean room in his own house.

Next day we left Panchen and its grasslands, and, after

passing another little monastery on the way, reached the lamasery of Tangu at about eleven o'clock; white as Christmas cake, it was built on top of a grassy knoll in the mouth of a small valley. We crossed the river by a wooden bridge and soon found ourselves in the broad valley leading to Jyekundo. Thenceforward we followed a proper high road, dusty and crowded with traffic. We passed a lot of Tibetans going home from market; they were all extremely picturesque, the only unexpected thing about them being that they were almost all equipped with enormous umbrellas which they carried slung across their backs as they cantered along on their spirited ponies. Some of them were also armed with Tibetan muskets, elongated and fantasticated with the forked rest which projects beyond the muzzle and which, in an often treeless country, materially increases a marksman's accuracy by giving him some support for his heavy and not always very reliable weapon. But the musketeers carried umbrellas as well, and this combination of lethal weapons with an accessory which both Prudhomme and Chamberlain tried to make emblematic of peace lent a touch of comedy to their appearance. For my part, I attributed this craze for umbrellas to the commercial acumen of the Chinese merchants in Jyekundo.

A little further on, a road branched off to the left, to disappear quickly in the mountains; it was the road to Lhasa. There was nothing very special about it. No barricades, no pillboxes guarded it; it looked exactly like all the other tracks I had jogged or plodded along for months past. But for me this dusty, pockmarked ribbon of trampled earth epitomised the hopes and aspirations of my whole life; it was a window opening on the all-but-unattainable.

I believe Gelu knew what I was thinking; I caught his eye at that moment and he gave me a friendly, understanding grin. We had been together for a long time at Shangu and had travelled a fairish way in company since then; we had come to like and trust each other, and I had no misgivings about telling him what was in my mind. He had no duties which would keep him long in Jyekundo and he volunteered, with touching spontaneity, to come with me if I tried to go to Lhasa. He well knew that I had no ulterior motive for the journey, that my purposes, like his, were pious; and to his simple integrity the idea of acquiring merit by helping a fellow-Buddhist to complete the most important pilgrimage of all made a strong appeal. We concerted our plans in some detail, then parted, cheerful and full of optimism, at the gates of Jyekundo. I had no difficulty in finding Elie, who had got me a nice room, lighter and cleaner than most, in a house belonging to a friendly Tibetan family. The prospect of a few days of relative comfort did not come amiss.

29. CAPTAIN MA

JYEKUNDO is in the Chinese province of Chinghai (literally "Blue Sea," a reference to the great lake of Kokonor which is situated in the north of this territory). The town is easily the most important trading centre in north-east Tibet. It derives this importance from the network of caravan routes which converge on it—from Sikang and Kangting in the south, from Lhasa in the west, from the Tsaidam and Mongolia in the north and from the provincial capitals of Sining and Lanchow in the north-east. Of these, the southerly routes carry by far the greatest volume of trade; traffic in the other directions is a trickle by comparison. A lot of pilgrims, singly or in little groups, set out from Jyekundo for Lhasa, but there are only two big trading caravans in that direction every year. These go the whole way across Tibet and bring back cigarettes from India and high-quality cloth from Lhasa, finally travelling east into China with wool and hides from the rich breeding-grounds around Jyekundo. The route to Sining, on the other hand, runs through empty grasslands where banditry is rife, so that only very well-found caravans can travel that way with a reasonable chance of reaching their destination unmolested.

The valley in which Jyekundo stands is so wide that you almost have the impression of being on a plateau. It is fertile land; in spite of the altitude—about twelve thousand feet—barley, beans and various vegetable crops do very well in the short-lived summer. But the real wealth of the region resides in its grasslands. They carry an enormous quantity of stock, tended by nomads whose black tents are to be seen in every sheltered fold of the ground; in summer the herds graze right up to the high ground, which at other seasons is deserted. The principal occupation of the women of Jyekundo is spinning wool, which they then weave, using primitive looms, into an admirable coarse cloth, either grey in colour or striped with black and red.

The city—the most important, after Kangting, in Eastern Tibet—has one long, straight main street from which a number of lesser thoroughfares debouch; they are flanked by the usual little shops kept by Chinese or Tibetans. I spent a good deal of time poking about among their wares, among which you could sometimes find things of considerable ethnographic or artistic interest; mixed up with the meretricious modern images and statuettes there was always a chance of finding a piece of really good bronze, an old painting or a bundle of rare Buddhist texts.

Jyekundo was full of inns, accommodating both transient caravans and more permanent residents in the persons of prosperous merchants who dealt in tea, cloth or hides. From nomad encampments outside the city many wild men came in to sell sour milk in little wooden churns, yak-meat, wool and skins; they were easily the most picturesque element in the community, with their bulky sheepskin *shubas*, their long black hair and their look of hawk-like independ-

nce. You could see that they were slightly disconcerted
by the mad whirl of city life, and they kept a little apart from
the crowd, squatting down in the less-frequented side-
streets with their goods spread out in front of them and
waiting placidly for customers to appear. I used to buy sour
milk from them; I was very fond of the stuff, especially
when it was mixed with sugar, and it had become, with
tsampa and butter-tea, one of the basic components of my
diet. The town was, it is hardly necessary to say, dominated
by a massive and well-populated lamasery built on twin hills
rising from the floor of the valley.

The day after I arrived there, I went to see the commander of the Chinese garrison, a Moslem called (as so
many Chinese Moslems are) Ma; he held the rank of
captain and was directly responsible to the provincial
governor of Chinghai. I took with me the Chinese schoolmaster whom I had met at Kangting and who spoke fairly
good English. Captain Ma received me with the utmost
affability, offered to give me any assistance I might need and
undertook to be responsible for my safety if by any chance I
was thinking of going to Lhasa.

I knew too much both about the Chinese and about conditions in Eastern Tibet to fall into the rather elementary
trap which he had set for me. I was by now a conspicuous
and well-known figure in this part of the world and I had had
plenty of evidence that both my movements and my intentions were being closely watched. If I had shown the
slightest disposition to accept Captain Ma's highly irregular
offer, the Tibetan authorities would have been immediately
informed of my plans and would have nipped them in the
bud. I knew, in any case, that this officer's writ did not run
over Tibetan territory, and that his offer of a safe-conduct to
Lhasa had only been made for reasons of face.

I therefore replied, without batting an eyelid, that I had
not the slightest intention of going to Lhasa, the journey
was far too difficult, and besides, having had everything I

possessed stolen by bandits, I lacked the material means t
undertake it. All I wanted to do was to have a good, lon
rest in Jyekundo, carry on with my researches in the loca
monasteries and then proceed to Sining. One of the tw
annual caravans was due to leave in two months' time fo
the Kokonor, and I asked Captain Ma if—since it belonge
to his commanding general in the provincial capital—h
could arrange for me to travel with it. He promised t
look into the matter, and I hoped that this ruse would alla
his suspicions about my real intentions.

In order to see what he would say, I then asked him hov
far westward his authority extended and where the pro
vincial frontier actually ran (I knew perfectly well that i
ran round the outskirts of the town, and that his authorit
did not extend a yard further). The Chinese do not like t
appear embarrassed, and he gave me a rather non-committa
reply; he had, he said, been only a short time in Chingha
and was on the very point of making a detailed study of thi
problem with his staff.

A few days later, meeting him again, I asked whether h
had yet found out the answer. He did not reply to my ques
tion but indicated with great delicacy that he personally di
not regard this topic of conversation as possessing very much
intrinsic interest.

Apart, however, from one or two little skirmishes of thi
kind, Captain Ma was extremely helpful. To begin with, h
offered to buy all my tea at a very fair price (he owned a larg
store in Jyekundo); I accepted with all the more alacrit
since he was prepared to pay me in silver dollars, which wer
legal tender throughout Tibet and which would be of the
greatest help in my attempt on Lhasa. Then he invited me tc
a banquet which was attended by all the principal dignitaries
of the place and at which were served, among other things,
the largest eggs I have ever seen. They were the eggs of wild
geese, which are plentiful on the lakes to the northward, and
the only trouble about them was that you had to broach four

or five before you found one whose state of decomposition was not too far advanced for edibility.

On the following day the captain sent me a sack of *tsampa*, another of flour, a large hunk of butter and a live sheep. Apart from the sheep, which I found a slightly embarrassing acquisition, I was delighted with these presents; the *tsampa* and the butter would prove invaluable on the road, and I gave the flour to my landlady in exchange for two rather good Tibetan paintings.

Elie had gone back to Kangting; his services were no longer of much use to me, and he was far too talkative to be entrusted with the secret of my intentions; all I told him was that I would soon be leaving for Sining and that I could not take him with me, as it would involve him in too long a return journey when he wanted to go home. We were both moved at parting, and when the moment came for him to leave, Elie burst into tears. Our relationship had gone deeper than the ordinary bonds between master and servant; in spite of his taste for drink and his general rascality, the long journey had drawn us very close together.

30. MIDSUMMER FESTIVAL

UP at the lamasery the midsummer festival had been in full swing for several days. Most of the lamas had left their quarters in the monastery and pitched a great camp in the pastureland which ran down to the Yangtse. Their white tents, edged with black, were adorned with huge Chinese and Tibetan characters and religious symbols. One vast, richly-dight tent was used as a place of worship, and to this everything that was needful had been brought. The canvas walls were covered with silk hangings; at the far end stood an altar, tall images, libation-bowls, sacrificial cakes and butter-lamps. The floor was spread with carpets and hassocks. Sceptres, bells, drums, thrones and all that appertained to the rites had been brought down from the lamasery.

The main ceremony went on all day, for midsummer has great significance in Tibet. Outside the large tent a fire of herbs was burning, exhaling scents which are pleasing to the gods. A large crowd surged round this canvas temple; it was a touching sight to watch the dear old Tibetan ladies, their bones stiffened by age, prostrating themselves before the tent in which the young Living Buddha presided over the ritual.

But the religious festival had its secular counterpart. Tibetans of all ages, all classes and both sexes have a passion for camping, and the entire population of Jyekundo and the surrounding villages was assembled in the plain outside the city, each family with its own tent. The best were splendid affairs, the poorest were made of yak's hair. These people are at all times prepared to seize any excuse for pitching a tent and having a picnic; both are pleasures which they find wholly irresistible.

No one could accuse them of travelling light on these occasions. Many of their tents are prodigious affairs, made of coarse white canvas from China, decorated with generous designs cut out of black or dark blue cloth and stitched on to the canvas; the tent-poles, eight or ten feet long, are massive enough to stand up to any stress, and the guy-ropes, which look like ship's cables made of wool or yak's hair, are fixed to the ground by broad, heavy pegs. The interior of the tent is full of mattresses covered with gaily coloured blankets, mats, sheepskins, carpets, cushions, chests and brightly painted wooden altars. Next door is the kitchen, with fire-places made of large stones, capacious cooking-pots and tremendous saucepans for brewing tea; whole sheep, haunches of yak, sacks of *tsampa* and skinfuls of butter hang from the tent-poles nearby. Nowhere else in the world can a public holiday produce a more remarkable spectacle.

The Author's retreat near Shangu gompa

I strolled through the barbaric encampment, past tents of all shapes and sizes. All their occupants greeted me with a smile and asked me to step inside to drink tea, to eat cakes, to smoke a cigarette. I went back through the part of the camp where the monks were and saw an old lama bearing down on me. He invited me into a small, neat tent, and I suddenly found myself in the presence of the chief Living Buddha of the lamasery.

A boy of about nine years old, with an alert, intelligent face, was sitting on a pile of cushions beside his teacher and looking as solemn as a little god. It was the first time in his life he had set eyes on a white man; he was fascinated (and perhaps rather frightened too) by my extraordinary face and indeed by almost everything about me. He began by being overawed but soon got used to me, especially when he discovered that I spoke his language, and we were soon firm friends.

By this time he had descended from his throne of cushions, being transformed in the process into a small boy, full of curiosity and mischief, who would have liked nothing better than to be playing with urchins of his own age. He studied with absorption everything that I showed him, but what interested him most was my camera; when I offered to take a photograph of him, he was tickled to death. We all went outside and erected a new throne on the grass, placing the ritual emblems on a stool beside it; by now servants had dressed the little boy up in his finest ceremonial robes, and I set about taking photographs of him. His teacher was a man not yet in middle age, with a clever, kindly face; he seemed much interested in my religious education and asked me to go and see him in the lamasery when the festival was over, so that we could talk about these matters without being disturbed.

Next day I had an invitation from the lamasery and was taken straight to the imposing building in which its chief dignitaries lived. I was received by a young lama of twenty-

Jyekundo. *The town stretches between two hills crowned by lamaseries*

five, the second of the three Living Buddhas in the monastery. He was busily engaged in mending an old gramo-
phone, a task in which I joined him; he had an elaborate
collection of tools and seemed much more interested in
fiddling about with them than in the metaphysics of
Buddhism. We repaired the machine, and settled down to
enjoy a concert. He had a wide selection of English records
—all dance music or military marches—as well as recordings
of Tibetan religious songs made in Lhasa; I could see that
he only played the latter in order to please me, and that he
far preferred Western dance-bands to hymns which he heard
every day.

That afternoon they held a race-meeting. It began with a
parade of all the competitors, each carrying a long spear
decorated with silk ribbons of different colours; their mettle-
some ponies were richly accoutred and in the bright sunlight the cavalcade made a gallant spectacle. A track was
soon cleared, the officials, the monks and the populace form-
ing a dense crowd on either side of it. The main events were
exhibitions of *haute école*, ordinary races, trick-riding (made
more difficult by the long Tibetan muskets which the riders
carried), shooting from horseback and various feats of skill
such as tilting at the ring. One particularly popular display,
carried out at full gallop, required the horseman to lean over
sideways and, retaining his grip on the saddle with one leg,
to pick up a small object off the ground.

After the gymkhana a dance brought the day's events to a
close. It was executed by men dressed in a great deal of
finery, wearing curious headgear rather like our top hats
from which, as from a maypole, streamers of ribbon hung
down on every side. The remarkable thing about these
junketings was that they all—even the country dances—had
a basically religious character; I saw none of the loose behaviour and bad manners which are a feature of most public
holidays in the West.

Every day I went up to the lamasery, where my presence

was required by my young friend the Living Buddha; our interviews had a certain atmosphere of fantasy. He was an intelligent and receptive youth, anxious to educate himself and to increase his knowledge of the world. He owned an English Bible and insisted on my teaching him the alphabet; he picked it up in no time and took immense pride in reading out sentences which I translated into Tibetan for him. His ambition in life was to visit the West, though he had a rather imprecise idea of the difference between Europe and America. He assured me that, if only his duties did not make it impossible, he would have asked me to take him there.

He had an ancient kodak, some old and no longer serviceable films, some bromide paper and various other items of photographic equipment, but he had no idea how to use it all. I put a film in the camera and showed him how to take photographs, then I taught him how to develop and print the results. Our great difficulty was to find a dark-room; we solved it by fitting one up under the altar in the main temple. We improvised a red light and used ceremonial silver bowls to soak the film in, then we crawled on all fours underneath an enormous image of Buddha. Two lamas put back the panel which we had removed in order to do this and then stood in front of the altar, spreading out their robes so as to block out the light from the chinks in its wooden framework. Altogether it was an unusual scene, but the operation was successful and despite its age the film did not come out too badly. We repeated the whole process in order to print the negative, and the Living Buddha's delight knew no bounds when he had a picture taken, developed and printed by himself on which he could feast his eyes and invite his friends to feast theirs.

In spite of all these mundane activities, I found time for several religious discussions with the teacher of the boy-lama, but I never quite recaptured the deep inner tranquillity which I had known at Shangu. Time was passing and I was

impatient to make a start; but it was important that peopl
should get used to seeing me about the place and that
should not leave Jyekundo in too much of a hurry, for an
appearance of haste might have aroused suspicion. Gelu
whom I saw from time to time, was also getting impatien
he had found me a ragged lama's robe—just the thing a poo
pilgrim would wear—a little wooden frame, like a basket, i
which pious travellers carry their few possessions on thei
backs, and a big sheepskin rug which would give us som
shelter against the rain and under which we could sleep a
night. Everything was ready; it only remained for me to fi
the day of our departure.

31. DANCE OF THE LAMAS

I HAD received an invitation from Captain Ma and th
religious authorities to the annual festival at the lamasery
although by accepting I automatically postponed the start o
my journey, I was very keen to see the famous lama dances o
which I had heard so much. Besides, I should have mad
myself dangerously conspicuous by refusing an official in
vitation of this kind. When the day came the party of guest
set out in great style and, mounted on a good pony which M
had lent me, I thoroughly enjoyed the three-mile ride to th
lamasery.

At its gates we were received with considerable pomp b
a group of monks, who led us ceremoniously to a stand over
looking the forecourt of the main temple; opposite wa
another stand reserved for the principal persons of th
monastery. In the centre of the forecourt stood a sort o
couch covered with a very fine tiger-skin; on it were arrangec
vessels of silver and large, brightly coloured sacrificial cakes
Round the edges a cheerful, noisy crowd was packed tightl
together, the spectators jostling each other to get a bette

view; eve ryone had put on his best clothes and his richest
jewellery.

Presently the lamas emerged from the temple and advanced into the forecourt in a slow, solemn procession. At
their head walked the chief dignitaries, wearing over their
monastic robes rich vestments embroidered with gold thread
and silk; these gravely took their places under the great
awning opposite us, the senior abbot being seated on a
raised throne under a canopy of yellow silk. In the rear
came monks carrying huge silver censers hanging from gilt
chains, and others with banners of vividly coloured silk. All
the lamas took their places in orderly ranks on either side of
the official stand, with the musicians squatting in front of it.
The dances were about to begin.

The dances of the lamas have been interpreted—or mis-
interpreted—in a number of ways. The dancers generally
wear masks identifying them with personages belonging
either to the Buddhist pantheon or to the history, legend and
folklore of Tibet; most travellers, knowing next to nothing
about Buddhism or Tibetan mythology, generally refer to
the dances as "demon dances." This justifiably annoys the
Tibetans, for in fact the dances are a form of religious
expression comparable in some ways to mediæval mystery
plays. Their themes are always either religious or historical
—the temptation of Buddha by the legions of Mara, the
triumph of Buddhism over the sorcerers, the miracles of
Padma Sambhava and his struggle with the demons, the
battle between the beneficent gods and the King of Hell,
or the murder of the Tibetan monarch Langdarma, who
persecuted Buddhism in the ninth century.

Certain characters appear in almost all the dances, and
are especially popular—the King of Hell and his minions,
whose masks Tibetan artists are at great pains to make as
malignant and terrifying as possible: various mythical
monsters, like the *makara*, which has an armadillo's body
and an elephant's head, or the *garanda*, the bird on which

Vishnu normally rides: Mara, who personifies physical desire: gods with stags' heads or yaks' heads: and the Citipatis, dancing skeletons with pieces of red stuff fastened to their legs to represent the flames of hell and who, being small and agile, are always played by boys.

There are also a few traditional comic characters—the *wa-wa*, a fat, clumsy, foolish baby; the grotesque Chinaman and his wife: the cruel Moslem. Finally, there is the master of ceremonies, generally dressed as a tiger and equipped with a cudgel made of plush with which he belabours any spectators who encroach upon the stage.

The first group of about twenty dancers now entered the forecourt. They were dressed in fine robes of embroidered silk with wide and whirling skirts; on their heads they wore elaborate silk headdresses with veils which concealed their faces. Round their waists a sort of apron of human bones hung in long loops like necklaces. In their left hand they held the ritual bell and in their right a little drum, made of the cranial cavities of two children with a covering of human skin. To the music of conches and cymbals they began a slow dance, finishing up in a single rank before the abbot's throne.

After them a party of young novices, all about ten years old, did a much livelier and more complicated dance, prostrated themselves before the cakes on the tiger-skin couch and embarked on another dance. When that came to an end, they scampered off at top speed and their place was taken by lamas dressed as sorcerers with black hats.

The dances went on and on. Each was watched by the spectators with rapt and silent attention, but it would be tedious to describe them all. They were long dances, and the lamas who performed them, burdened by heavy robes, masks and colossal hats, were in a state bordering on collapse when they had finished. Their choreography was most intricate, necessitating much posturing and gesticulation in an almost static position before the dancer suddenly launched himself into a whirlwind of rapid movement; I had noticed the same pattern of contrasting tempos in religious dances in Japan.

The slow passages are generally followed by everyone spinning round on one leg; this movement—when fifty dancers do it at the same time, all dressed in flowing robes of harmoniously matched silk—is extraordinarily effective. I was greatly struck by the beauty of the costumes. All brand-new, they were made of embroidered silk from China. Their colours were brilliant but chosen with a sure taste; since every new set of dancers was dressed differently, the whole of their wardrobe must have been worth a fortune.

All the dancers were lamas, but most of them showed a virtuosity worthy of professionals. The complicated and stylised figures of each dance were carried out without the slightest uncertainty, with an easy precision which denoted long and intensive training. Quite apart from its religious significance, the whole thing represented a major æsthetic achievement.

In the last dance of all we saw the King of Hell and his followers. It was an astonishing display of extravagant costumes. Some of the dancers wore silk tunics of white, royal blue, mauve or dark red on which terrifying demons were painted. The demons' faces on their huge masks—each one different from the others and all wearing a chaplet of human skulls—were alarmingly lifelike. They flung themselves into a frenzied dance, whirling great broadswords round their heads, leaping high in the air, then crouching low and springing forward like panthers. Their exit was carefully stage-managed, each dancer detaching himself from the main body and putting all his skill and remaining energy into a *pas seul* before suddenly whisking out of sight behind the crowd.

When the last demon had disappeared, the audience dispersed in an orderly way, deep in discussion about the performance. Six lamas presented us with the gifts traditionally bestowed on guests at these festivals—furs, silk scarves, brick-tea, sacks of *tsampa*, and slabs of butter, each gift being suitably adjusted to the social standing of its recipient and accompanied—in rather the same way that a Christmas present is accompanied by a Christmas card—with the ceremonial scarf of white silk. (Failure to present this scarf is a grave breach of etiquette and renders any gift valueless.) We had an excellent dinner in Captain Ma's sumptuously appointed tent, and I seized this opportunity to bid formal farewells to the gallant officer and to the other notabilities, telling them that I hoped shortly to leave for Bambi Gompa and other monasteries situated along the road to Sechu; this would have been a perfectly normal route for me to take, and ran in a direction diametrically opposite to that which I proposed to follow. Everyone hoped that the journey would prove beneficial to my religious studies. I referred, also, to my intention of travelling on to Sining with the big caravan which was to leave Jyekundo for the provincial capital at a date not yet determined. That, I reckoned, ought to allay still further any possible suspicions about my real objective.

The next day I went to see Gelu, who was waiting for me impatiently. He had everything ready, including enough tea, butter and *tsampa* to last us for at least a week. Our few belongings were already packed into the sort of wooden rucksacks that pilgrims use, and we arranged a rendezvous for the following night at a point on the Lhasa road which we had already reconnoitred and where we knew we should be in dead ground behind a spur of rock. Then I left him and went back to my lodging, feeling very optimistic.

I could take almost nothing with me on this journey. My notes, films and books had already gone back to Kangting with Elie. My remaining possessions were of small value; their loss—for I should have to leave them behind—was a casualty which I was well prepared to accept on the threshold of an enterprise in which success would mean so much. I

said good-bye to my landlady and her husband early in the
evening, excusing myself on the grounds—very normal ones
in Tibet—that I needed a good sleep before an early start.
They wished me a prosperous journey and a speedy return,
and I withdrew to my room to put the finishing touches to
the preparations for my escapade.

PART SEVEN

The Attempt on Lhasa

32. TO BE A PILGRIM

I put a match to the wick of my butter-lamp; it was three o'clock in the morning. I had had a short night's rest, disturbed by nightmares. Judging by the complete silence, everyone else in the house was asleep. I dressed as quietly as I could so as not to wake them.

I had the minimum of equipment and impedimenta to carry. My Tibetan boots, which had brought me all the way from Kangting, were down at heel and worn smooth by contact with snow, mud, rocks and the sweaty flanks of ponies and yaks. My jacket and trousers were made of the local cloth, and over them I wore the old lama's robe which Gelu had given me; this had, perhaps, more distinction than any other item in my wardrobe, for it had been made—many years ago—in Lhasa. The vagaries of the Tibetan climate had left their mark on this garment; it had acquired, during previous tenancies, an interesting and comprehensive integument of grease-spots by reason of the butter, mutton-fat and other nutritive substances which it had accidentally absorbed; its folds were enriched by patches of every conceivable shade of red; and the colonies of lice and nits which had installed themselves long ago in its lining supplied some at least of those intimate, personal contacts which a traveller so often misses on a long and lonely journey. I hope I have given some impression of a garment whose colour, and whose smell, always seemed to me to defy definition. My disguise as a poor, ragged lama on a pilgrimage was completed by a monk's bonnet, very old and very dirty, which I had bought secondhand in Kantze and which I now crammed firmly down on my shaven head.

I had left my pilgrim's pack with Gelu so as not to arouse comment by being seen with a form of equipment rarely used by Europeans. Thrusting a bag of *tsampa* and a packet of butter into the folds of my *shuba*, I climbed with immense caution down the ladder from my room, tiptoed across the courtyard, slipped through the main gate (which I had been careful to leave ajar when I came in the night before) and dived into the dark labyrinth of little streets outside.

Everything was quiet; Jyekundo was fast asleep. Dogs barked, here and there, as I passed; but dogs always do bark at night in Tibet and nobody—in the towns at any rate— pays the slightest attention. I reached the bridge which leads over the Yangtse into Tibet without meeting a living soul. Dawn was still a long way off and it was very dark; but I knew every foot of the way and had no difficulty in following the road to the lamasery as far as the place where that other road forked off from it and led to Lhasa.

Dawn was breaking when I reached our rendezvous; it was a place where the track went round a little hill, a sheltered spot where herdsmen had once built themselves a hut. Gelu was there already. He was squatting over a little fire which he had lit to keep himself warm. He had had, up to now, a much more arduous journey than I had, for he had been carrying both our packs, a big bag of *tsampa*, two bricks of tea, the cooking-pot and our heavy sheepskin rug. On top of all this he had brought me a little sleeveless jacket lined with sheepskin, very old and very tattered, of the kind that lamas wear; and with it a patched cloak to complete my disguise.

We redistributed the loads after fitting the carrying-packs on to our shoulders. These consisted of two curved pieces of wood held in place by yak-skin thongs; they form a sort of rack into which your luggage can be piled. There had, of course, never been any question of taking a tent or a sleeping-bag or even a raincoat; obviously foreign equipment of this kind would have stuck out like a sore thumb and made us fatally conspicuous. We would have to sleep under the tars, with only our sheepskin intervening. We were pilgrims from now on.

We drank some tea, swallowed a wad of *tsampa* and started off. Each of us was equipped with the long staff surmounted by a trident which pilgrims have carried for centuries. We soon came to the end of the valley, and the track began to zigzag through a labyrinth of grass-covered hills; every time we thought we had crossed a pass, another pass loomed up ahead of us. The whole day passed thus, and night fell just as we reached the ridge which did in fact mark the water-shed. A fold in the ground offered us some sort of protection against the bitter wind which had begun to blow from the east. We spread out the sheepskin rug and lay down, utterly exhausted. It was too much trouble to have anything to eat.

It was a wild night. At first light we made a fire of twigs and brewed tea. The track went on winding through the hills until, plunging steeply down, it brought us on to a wide, undulating plateau where sheep, yaks and ponies were grazing in their thousands.

We were now in the great grasslands of North-East Tibet, perhaps the richest pastures in all Asia. Here and there we could see the black tents of the herdsmen, but they were mostly some way away from the track and—so far—represented no particular danger from my point of view. Their occupants were, in any case, accustomed to the sight of pilgrims trudging past in the middle distance; why should they take any notice of us?

That night we settled down to sleep in the lee of some rocks; but hardly had we done so when a violent storm broke over us. Huddled together under our sheepskin quilt beside a moribund camp-fire, Gelu and I waited patiently for our ordeal to end. There are always storms in midsummer in this part of Tibet, and torrential downpours of rain, generally heralded by a minor hurricane, were of almost daily occurrence throughout our journey.

Next morning we dropped down into a narrow valley forded the stream at the bottom of it and followed the track up a gorge down which one of its tributaries flowed.

It was a fine, hot day. The little stream ran gaily down its rocky bed, and it was not long before we reached its source just below the high watershed which we had to cross. On the far side of this we dropped steeply down to yet another stream, on whose banks a little grassy ledge offered an idyllic camping-site. Unfortunately, the usual heavy storm drove us off it to seek shelter under some nearby rocks.

We made an early start next day, meaning to get across the next pass, which, according to my map, ought to have been the last major pass of this side of the Dze Chu valley. When we reached the top of it, however, we got a nasty shock; yet another valley and yet another pass lay ahead of us. We were getting tired of this switchback progress.

We scrambled down over grass and screes into the bottom of the valley and halted to make tea. The track after this sloped gently upwards for a few hundred yards, then struck diagonally along a steep hillside. Night overtook us just before we reached the crest. The weather had turned cold again, there was not so much as a twig to make a fire with and we shivered as we lay huddled together under the stiff and sodden sheepskin.

At first light, eager to get warm, we started off again. The sun came out as we reached the neck of the pass, where the ground was covered with huge flat slabs of rock; after making sure that there were no other human beings in sight, we took off our clothes and spread them out on these to dry.

This time we really were on the last pass, which is called Pumo La. Below us stretched the long, narrow valley of the Dze Chu, an important tributary of the Mekong, which rises in an outcrop of mountains on whose peaks, far away in the distance, we could see patches of unmelted snow gleaming in the sunlight. Feeling very cheerful, we marched down

ABOVE: *The young Living Buddha of Jyekundo.*   BELOW: *Tangu gompa, The Sorcerer in an apron made of human bones* and *Kantze, the Citipatis, dancing skeletons.*

ABOVE: *Country dance at Jyekundo*
BELOW: *Religious dance at Tangu gompa. The Minions of the King of H*

a long grassy slope, crossed a stream and found ourselves in a sheltered little ravine. From now on we should have to be extremely cautious, for the valley was full of nomads. I tucked myself away behind a rock while Gelu went off to a group of tents in the middle distance where he hoped to replenish our supplies of butter. He came back with the moderately encouraging news that no one had noticed us coming down from the pass; but we thought it prudent to wait until night fell before crossing the floor of the valley, where the nomad population was densest.

A few hours later we reached the Dze Chu. Gelu had enquired about fords and, after hunting for a long time up and down the rocky bank, we found the one they had told him about. Here and there in the darkness watchdogs barked fiercely, but the only human being we met was an old Tibetan lady. We bumped into her unexpectedly at a bend in the track; she had been drawing water and was on her way back to her tent. Recognising us as lamas, she prostrated herself, asked for our blessing and insisted that we should spend the rest of the night in her tent.

We could hardly have refused, and in any case the idea of warmth and shelter made a strong appeal to us, for it had begun to rain again. No great risk was involved as far as I was concerned, for, as usual in Tibet, the only light in the tent came from the fire in the middle of the floor. The old woman's husband was already asleep on a pile of sheepskins, and to avoid being asked any questions I told my beads assiduously, intoning a succession of *Om ma-ni pad-mé hums* in the whining tone always adopted by beggars, which I could by now mimic to perfection. The good old soul spread out some skins for us next to the fire, and soon everyone was fast asleep while the wind and the rain beat savagely on the walls of the tent.

33. ROUGH GOING

At dawn, refreshed by sour milk and hot tea, we left our luxurious lodging. My face, half-hidden by my beard and by a thick layer of dirt and rancid butter, burnt almost black by sun and wind, can have borne little resemblance to a European's. Gelu explained to our hosts that I was an old Mongol lama from the Tsaidam, thus accounting—apparently to their complete satisfaction—for my imperfect command of Tibetan. We bestowed our blessing on these kindly folk and went on our way.

For two days we continued down the interminable valley of the Dze Chu, generally on the left bank but sometimes on the right; there were several smallish tributaries to cross. Everywhere we saw herds of yaks and the tents of their guardians, but these had for the most part been pitched at some distance from the track, usually in the mouth of a little valley which gave them shelter from the wind. We had, nevertheless, several nerve-wracking encounters with both pilgrims and nomads, but my shambling, exhausted appearance, my seedy garments and my mumbled pieties proved an adequate disguise, and no one paid much attention to me. Gelu was an immense help in these contingencies; leaving me, as it were, out of the picture, he engaged the Tibetans in animated conversation and thus prevented them from taking too much interest in me.

The broad and beautiful valley was flanked by big hills whose reddish soil contrasted sharply with the flower-studded grasslands below them. Its floor was so sheltered that we suffered badly from the heat in the middle of the day; our thick woollen robes did not improve matters, nor did the heavy packs whose straps chafed our shoulders painfully. As soon as the sun set, on the other hand, the valley —which is over twelve thousand feet above sea-level—became bitterly cold.

On the evening of the second day we rounded a big spur of rock and found ourselves on the threshold of a deep gorge at the far end of which was the high pass which we should have to cross next day. In spite of a fire made of twigs, we slept badly. It froze hard, and by dawn all the little streams had been turned to ice; even the Dze Chu was all but frozen over. We began the ascent of the Dze La pass, which is the highest in Eastern Tibet and rises to some sixteen thousand feet. A light mist imposed a wintry pallor on the rays of the early sun.

It was midday when we emerged from the gorge and saw the neck of the pass above us, not very far away. We climbed slowly towards it, plodding painfully upwards over turf dotted with boulders and pockets of unmelted snow. We kept on having to stop to get our breath back. At last there was only a saddle of snow ahead of us; beyond it the narrow pass was outlined against the bright blue sky like the hindsight of a rifle. This last lap of the climb was terribly hard going, for our heavy Tibetan boots, worn smooth and thin by many long marches, would not grip the frozen surface. But at three o'clock we reached the pass and, subsiding on a dry boulder for a long rest, ate some wads of *tsampa* which we had prepared before beginning the climb.

Meanwhile the east wind got up and chilled us to the bone; we were forced to retrace our steps to find shelter in the lee of the pass. Night was falling when we halted on a stony ledge, a place of unimaginable desolation. There were a few stunted shrubs there, so we were able to make a fire; but its heat was not enough to make us warm again.

Next morning we crossed the pass once more and began a descent which seemed interminable. Moving down the bottom of a wild and gloomy gorge in which, since the sun never shone there, snow and ice had a depressing air of permanence, we had the feeling of being trapped. About noon, however, we struck an important tributary of the Mekong;

it is called the Purdong Chu and is really not so much a
tributary as a source. The valley through which—at an
altitude of some fourteen thousand feet—it ran was deep and
narrow. We decided to ford it as early as possible on the
following morning, while the night-frost still immobilised
some of the water which, when the sun reached the snows
above us, would increase the difficulties of a passage.

The fording of this vehement and icy torrent was, I suspect, the most actively unpleasant experience which befell
me in the course of a long journey. We were in poor shape
when we embarked on it, for the night had been bitterly
cold. We had no difficulty in finding the ford normally
used by caravans, and, although the width of the stream
was about fifteen yards, its depth was nowhere much greater
than two feet. But how we envied the lucky travellers who
crossed it on yaks or ponies!

We had to take off our boots and our trousers, hitch our
robes up round our waists and then plunge, reluctantly, into
the icy water. The current was terribly strong, and we had
to cling to each other to avoid being swept away. It was
lucky for us that at this point the bed of the stream was
reasonably level and not obstructed by rocks; for it was
difficult enough, supported though we were by our pilgrims' staves, to keep our balance on the sandy bottom.
Gelu muttered his prayers throughout the crossing, and
when we reached the other side it was not only the cold that
was making us tremble.

We had, however, reached the other side; and on we went.
An hour's march brought us to the foot of yet another pass,
the Purdong La, the last we should have to cross before
striking the upper reaches of the Mekong.

Unlike the Dze La, this pass lay at the end, not of a
narrow gorge, but of a steep slope largely covered with
screes. It took us three hours to climb it, and we arrived at
the top dead-beat, to be greeted by a cutting wind. We
gulped down a lump of *tsampa*, sucked a fistful of snow

cooped out from a cranny in the rocks and forthwith started
scrambling down the far side of the pass over a steep and
boulder-strewn face. This gave place to gentler grassy
slopes and after that to a jumble of bare foothills. We
plodded on until night fell and then collapsed in a state of
exhaustion on a piece of flat ground which was sheltered
from the wind. Gelu still had enough stamina to light a
fire and make some buttered tea; this beverage can seldom
have been more badly needed or tasted more delicious.

We were drawing steadily nearer one of the worst danger-
spots on our route to Lhasa. This was the big lamasery of
Trashi Gompa. From a religious and indeed from every
point of view it is an important centre for the nomads of
these parts, and we ran a big risk of unwelcome and dangerous encounters; so we decided to try and slip through the
place at dusk. We got a little sleep and then moved on,
without hurrying, through the grass-covered hills towards
our stiffest fence so far.

At midday we made tea beside a little stream, then
followed it until it joined the Mekong. Although we were
not far from the source of this river, it was already showing
its mettle, being nearly a hundred yards across, with a swift,
clear and powerful current.

We were now almost within sight of Trashi Gompa. I
accordingly took cover behind some rocks while Gelu once
more went forward on reconnaissance. He came back after
an hour and reported that we ought to be able to pass the
place without serious risk. The lamasery was built high up
on the mountainside, well away from the river; there were
no houses or tents close to the track; and, since pilgrims were
constantly passing that way, we should not be at all conspicuous.

Twilight was beginning to fill the valley when we drew
level with the lamasery. Caught in the rays of the setting
sun, its buildings were an unforgettable sight. Poised far
above us like an eyrie, backed by the cliffs of a narrow ravine

which plunged vertically down to the torrent below, it
white walls stood out sharply against the reddish backgroun
of the rocks behind them, and the golden roofs of it
temples dispensed a lustre which put the dying sun t
shame.

As though to help us slip past without being seen, a ligh
mist was rising from the surface of the river, caused by th
sudden drop in temperature which always occurred at dusk
We strode on along the wide, well-defined track; there coul
as yet be no question of bivouacking for the night. Presentl
the valley began to open out, and more nomad tents ap
peared. It was essential that we should get through thi
dangerous area as quickly as possible.

After an hour's march the track crossed the river by
cantilever bridge. Night had now fallen, but camp-fires an
the barking of dogs warned us that the pastures ahead of u
were populated. As we set foot on the bridge, two Tibetar
women and a boy emerged from the darkness; they wer
bringing a small flock of sheep back from the far bank. Th
bridge was narrow; any evasive action would have looked
highly suspicious.

The two women, garrulous and sociable as all Tibetar
women are, bombarded us with stock questions—Where
were we from? Where were we going? and so on. They had
recognised us as lamas on pilgrimage and were insistent
that we should spend the night in their tent.

Gelu adopted his usual tactics of keeping them interested
with a flood of words, while I hung about in the background,
telling my beads and playing the idiot boy. Unfortunately
the lad with them seemed to be intrigued by the pious but
taciturn monk who took no part in the conversation; but it
was a dark night and his scrutiny of my person could hardly
(I hoped) lead to my exposure. Gelu explained that we had
a long stage to do next day and were anxious to catch up
with some other pilgrims who were waiting for us further
along the road. At this the ladies ceased their importunities

and advised us to seek shelter for the night at a group of tents further up the valley—a useful bit of advice, for it warned us of the need to by-pass our potential hosts.

On the far side of the bridge the track became very bad, edging its way along a narrow shelf between the river and a sheer face of rock. Owing to the darkness we were in some danger of falling over the edge into the fierce torrent, and it was not long before we halted under the lee of a big boulder, having decided to go no further until it got light.

The night was not only cold but very damp as well, because of the proximity of the river. We started off again as soon as dawn began to break, eager for the exertions which would make us warm again. The valley got narrower and narrower, and the going worse and worse; the ill-defined path hugged the river's edge, sometimes taking us over broken masses of rock beneath which the current swirled and eddied with an air of menace. Presently we sighted the tents which the women had told us about; but they stood some way away from the track in a little side-valley and did not worry us unduly.

Further on a big tributary joined the Dze Chu on the opposite side, and we made a short halt above the point of confluence, on a slope where a few dwarf willows grew. These produced plenty of firewood, and we made tea and warmed ourselves; we were not afraid of attracting attention in a place like this.

Up here the Mekong had dwindled to a comparatively narrow stream plunging down the bottom of a narrow ravine which led up to the pass of Dzanag; we hoped to reach the pass that evening. Below it rises the more westerly of the Mekong's two sources; comparing the flow of water in our stream with that which we had seen yesterday coming down from the other—the northern—source, I had the impression that the latter was the more important of the two. It would have been interesting to investigate both sources and establish which has the better claim to its title; but we were travelling under conditions which ruled out the possibility of any such digression.

The climb up the gorge got steeper and steeper. The path was now no more than a mule-track which zigzagged up-wards, crossing and recrossing the steadily shrinking river. The sun blazed down on us out of a cloudless sky against which snow-mountains outlined themselves to the north-ward; in spite of an altitude of more than fifteen thousand feet it was intensely hot. Even so, the stream, when it ran through parts of the gorge which were always in shadow, was covered by a thick layer of ice, for the nights were particularly cold on slopes, such as this one, which the sun left early in the afternoon.

34. THE LONG ARM OF THE LAW

It was at this point that I began to notice that Gelu kept on turning round and staring back down the valley behind us; he looked worried, which was very unusual for him, and would not give a proper answer when I asked him what was up. I looked back too, but could see nothing whatever; only rocks, and patches of snow, and more rocks; so I naturally put my companion's behaviour down to the fact that he was tired and wanted an excuse to stop every so often.

A little later, however, I made out two dark specks moving rapidly along the track a very long way behind us; I could tell from their rate of advance that they must be horsemen, and their presence on this deserted route struck me as ominous in the extreme.

Gelu liked it no better than I did. His keen hillman's eyes had picked out the riders when I could still see nothing but rocks, and he had been aware of the danger long before I had. He did his best, in his kindly way, to reassure me, saying that they were probably only merchants bound for

Lhasa; but he did not himself seem very convinced by this explanation.

Meanwhile the ponies were coming on fast and we could see the men on their backs quite clearly; both carried muskets slung across their backs. There was no point in our trying to hide, for they had certainly seen us; the only sensible thing was to sit down and wait for them, eating some *tsampa* converted into paste with the help of the Mekong.

They were soon within hailing distance and greeted us with a friendly "*Ka le ja*," the normal salutation given by a traveller who is still marching to one who has already halted; it means, roughly, "Sit in tranquillity." We supplied, not less cordially, the appropriate riposte ("Are you tired?"), and Gelu said it as they say it in Eastern Tibet, thus showing them that we were from the province of Khams.

They dismounted, came and sat down beside us and began gossiping cheerfully, as Tibetans always do when they meet on the road. I was playing my usual supernumerary and almost inarticulate part for all I was worth, but the newcomers seemed particularly interested in me and bombarded me with questions about my native village, my relations, the lamasery to which I belonged, the purpose of my pilgrimage and so on.

I knew that the principal object of these questions was to make me talk, but to have left them unanswered would have been the height of discourtesy. I realised that the game was up and that, despite my knowledge of Tibetan, my conversational powers were inadequate to sustain the imposture; a few sentences would be enough to show that I was a foreigner, and no amount of dirt and sunburn could conceal —at such very close range—the fact that my face was not exactly the sort of face you would expect to find on the Roof of the World.

I could hear the two horsemen discussing me. The elder of them was certain that I was a foreigner, and it was clearly pointless to go on trying to pretend that I was not. The rigmarole about my being a Mongol lama might, at a pinch, have deceived ignorant nomads, but it cut no ice with these men, both of whom were intelligent and one of whom had been in Mongolia and (unlike me) knew a little of the language.

So I proceeded to tell them the plain truth. I was, I said, a foreigner who had lived in Tibet for some time; I was a Buddhist of the Karmapa sect: and the sole purpose of my journey to Lhasa was to visit its sacred places.

They seemed impressed by my frankness and my piety, and said that if I had a passport authorising me to go to Lhasa they would be happy to help me get there. Unfortunately I had no papers legalising even my presence on Tibetan territory, and the two men—who were in fact frontier-guards attached to the force which watches the Lhasa road—could not take the responsibility of letting me go on without any documents authorising me to do so. They asked me to follow them, but held out some hope that their commanding officer at Trashi Gompa might be able to produce the necessary permit.

So off we went, all four of us, back towards the lamasery which I had fondly hoped never to set eyes on again. We spent the night in the very tents which we had been so careful to avoid and reached the monastery next day. We went first, not to the monastery proper, but to a large building abutting on it; this was the residence of the _pömpo_, the chief civil authority in the district. He received me with the greatest courtesy and entertained me with delicious butter-tea, _tsampa_ mixed with particles of dried milk, a big bowl of yoghourt, slices of dried meat, brown sugar, and a kind of sweet pancake to which I was strongly addicted. It was a long time since I had had a meal of anything approaching this calibre. The conversation rambled, as it always does in the East, far away from anything remotely connected with the business in hand; but at last, with a certain amount of diffidence, the subject of my journey was broached.

I realised at once that there was no question of resuming my journey to Lhasa. The *pömpo*, himself not only a devout Buddhist but a member of the sect to which I had been admitted, could not have been more sympathetic; but it was impossible for him to disobey the stringent orders which he had only lately received. (I learned later that a minor but fairly serious political upheaval had just taken place in Lhasa. All access to the city, either for Chinese or Tibetans, had been forbidden. However much further I had got, or from whatever other point I had started, my enterprise—at that time—was doomed from the outset to failure.) The *pömpo* offered to put me up while he waited for a reply to the application which he undertook to forward on my behalf to Lhasa, but I realised that this plan, evolved solely in order to lessen my disappointment, would in practice get me no-where. It would take several months to get a reply, even if one came, and the state of my finances was not sound enough to allow me to spin out my journey to this extent; for if—as was only too probable—my application was refused, I should still need money for the long journey from Jyekundo to Sining. So I thanked the sympathetic official warmly and explained the reasons which more or less obliged me to abandon my project and go back to Jyekundo. He was obviously much relieved by my decision and said it was a wise one, for he admitted that he himself had very little hope of my application being granted. I also discovered that it was the two Tibetan ladies whom we had met on the little bridge whose idle gossip had drawn attention to us and led —quite involuntarily, I am sure, as far as they were concerned—to my arrest.

35. ENFORCED RETREAT

So now, after striving so hard to get here, there was nothing for it but to go back again. Once we had crossed that last pass we should have been within a few marches of Nagchuka, where the route enters the valley in which Lhasa stands; but I knew perfectly well that I was engaged on a forlorn hope and that, even if I had got as far as Nagchuka, I should have stood very little chance of getting past it, for of all the approaches to Lhasa it is the most closely guarded. Sven Hedin, Bonvalot, Dutreuil de Rhins, Grenard, Roehrich— almost every explorer who has tried to reach Lhasa from the north has been stopped at Nagchuka. Still, I at least had the satisfaction of having reached the source of the Mekong by a route which up till now has been travelled—with certain variations—only by Dutreuil de Rhins and Grenard, in 1894.

I had gambled and lost, but the game had been worth playing; the difficulties I had faced would make the journey all the better worth remembering. There is a lot to be said for a pilgrim's life, when every march is a physical ordeal. I knew that I should never forget the long climbs up the tall, lonely passes, with the sun or the rain beating down and the straps of one's pack cutting into one's shoulders, or the grandeur of the bitter nights under a great vault of stars: the misery while one waited for the sun to come out and warm one's numbed limbs, the thrill of pressing on, step by step, into forbidden territory, the nerve-wracking suspense when one involuntarily met strangers, the perpetual fear of being unmasked.

My escapade had given me, as well as a lot of exotic experiences, the rather primitive pleasure which you get from facing dangers and overcoming difficulties; and this helped to console me for my failure to reach Lhasa.

After a comfortable night in the *pömpo*'s house, I set about the preparations for my journey after bidding a sorrowful farewell to Gelu, who was just as upset as I was. He set off again for Lhasa, scarcely aware how lucky he was to be doing so, and for a long time I watched his slender figure getting smaller and smaller as he strode away down the track which, only a few days ago, we had travelled together, full of hope.

The excellent *pömpo* would not hear of my making the dangerous journey back to Jyekundo alone, and he gave me a pony and a man who would escort me to the outskirts of the city. After regaling me with an enormous meal, he filled the ponies' leather saddle-bags with provisions; his final act of generosity was to lend me a magnificent sheep-skin *shuba* to protect me against the rain and keep me warm at night. To receive all this kindness from a man whose official position would have justified him in treating me as an enemy touched me deeply. Buddhist charity is a very real thing.

For several days I travelled back over the well-remembered road along which Gelu and I had struggled, reliving the emotions we had felt, the comic or disastrous incidents that had happened. But this time it was an easy journey. The crossing of the Purdong Chu, which we had made such heavy weather of, now presented no difficulties; we did not even get our feet wet. The fact of the matter was that we were riding strong, well-trained ponies and my guide was clever enough to find a much easier place to ford the river than the one that Gelu and I had selected.

Stage followed stage without incident, though on the high passes we often had to dismount and lead the ponies because of the bad going. Nevertheless, we made much better time than I had on the way out, and I had forgotten what it was like to travel so comfortably. The *shuba* kept some of the cold off at nights and, not having to worry about secrecy, we always slept in a nomad's tent. We had plenty of provisions, and we stopped to make tea as often as we felt like it.

On the evening of the eighth day after leaving Trashi

Gompa we reached the last big pass before Jyekundo, having done the journey in four days less than the outward march had taken. My companion was anxious to go home and had no wish to meet the Chinese authorities in Jyekundo, whom, like all Tibetans, he detested. I was only too pleased to further his desires, for my appearance in Jyekundo escorted by a soldier from Trashi Gompa would be certain to excite comment and would knock the bottom out of the alibi with which I hoped to explain my absence. So I told the man that I could easily get to Jyekundo by myself next day and that there was no point in his wasting two more days by coming with me. He was delighted with this arrangement and next morning, after an exchange of cordial farewells, we went our respective ways.

The kind Tibetans with whom I had been lodging welcomed me with open arms, gave me a meal and showed me to my room where my possessions had been scrupulously looked after. I soon met all my friends again—the lamas, the Chinese magistrate, the schoolmaster. With immense plausibility I told them all about my sojourn in the lamaseries where—theoretically—I had been spending the past few weeks. No one doubted (or anyhow no one showed any signs of doubting) the veracity of my account; and my face was saved.

PART EIGHT

A Cross Marks the Spot

36. HOMAGE TO A HERO

JYEKUNDO was a hive of activity. The sleepy little town had suddenly come to life, and I soon found out why: the big caravan for Tangar and the Kokonor was on the point of starting. Many parties of travellers had already left for its assembly area at Juchieh Gompa; others were in a fever of anxiety to be off. All, as the saying is, was bustle and confusion, with ponies, yaks, armed men and Tibetan women carrying luggage already packed for the journey jostling each other in the streets.

The start of the caravan was a major event which only happened twice a year. The caravans carry the local products north—ponies for the Chinese army, raw wool, cloth woven in the villages and untanned hides—after bringing to Jyekundo goods from India and Central Tibet—fine cloth woven in Lhasa, English cigarettes and, above all, dark blue cotton cloth from Bengal, which is much in demand on the Chinese market. In addition, the big merchants use the caravans to convey their chests of silver dollars to Sining, where the rate of exchange is much better than it is in Sikang.

The route followed covers over six hundred miles through one of the least populated territories in Asia. On the three weeks' march from Juchieh Gompa to Sharakoto there is not a village, a lamasery, a tent or even a tree to be seen; this is the Great Desert of Grass, as Madame David-Neel has called it, an illimitable wilderness of green hills peopled only by wild animals. It forms an extension to the eastward of the Changtang Plateau which occupies the whole of Northern Tibet from the Kuenlun Mountains to Kokonor.

The empty spaces are not completely uninhabited. The Ngolog tribe, who live further east in a bend of the Yellow

River, sometimes use the caravan trail on their way to get salt from the great lakes called Ngoringcho and Kyaringcho. They are some of the toughest customers in Asia, and it was they who—some way to the south of this region—attacked the expedition of Guibaud and Liotard in 1940. Any caravan which is not well able to defend itself is unlikely to escape their attentions. This is why there are so few caravans. They not only have to carry provisions for a whole month, but they must have enough firepower to deter, or if necessary beat off, an attack. The one which was now preparing to take the road (and which I immediately decided to join) was unusually strong, comprising a thousand yaks, four hundred ponies (more than half of them in herd—that is, running loose without riders), about a hundred horsemen and a number of well-armed caravan-men.

It was a wonderful and unexpected slice of luck to have got back to Jyekundo just in time to catch this caravan; I had, as the reader will remember, known about it before I set out for Lhasa, but I expected to find it already gone. What was more, General Ma Pu-fang, the Governor of Chinghai, who owned most of the caravan, had given orders that I was to be furnished with any animals I wanted; I thanked him for his kindness when I reached Sining.

A caravan of these dimensions cannot travel all in one piece, for it would be impossible to control and traffic blocks would occur in narrow defiles; it must be split up into sub-units, each of about fifty animals with enough men to look after them, which follow each other at convenient intervals. When halted, the whole outfit covers a very big area of ground, and that was why a general rendezvous had been fixed at Juchieh Gompa, four days' march from Jyekundo and the last inhabited place on the edge of the Grass Desert, where there was enough grazing to permit the concentration of our great army of men, animals and tents.

But I wanted, before starting, to carry out a plan formulated many years earlier.

In 1894 the French explorers Dutreuil de Rhins and
Grenard made a journey through Tibet which, by the
standards of those days, was an outstanding feat. After
crossing the bitter uplands of North-West Tibet they were
arrested at Nagchuka and failed to reach Lhasa. They then
came on to Jyekundo, following the same route that I had
used and exploring for the first time the sources of the
Mekong. From Jyekundo they set out for the Kokonor; but
after two days' march, at the little village of Tongbudmo,
they were attacked by Tibetans after a trivial squabble
about a pony of which they had not realised the serious
implications. Dutreuil de Rhins and two of his men were
killed. Grenard with a few others managed to escape,
leaving almost all the scientific material they had collected
in the hands of their assailants.

Grenard made northwards and reached the Kokonor after
an agonising journey in the course of which their scanty
provisions ran out completely. Part of their written material
was recovered later, thanks to the intervention of the Tibetan
Government, but Dutreuil de Rhins' body was never found.

Since that tragedy of June 5th, 1894, very few travellers—
and to the best of my belief no Frenchmen—have been
through Tongbudmo; and I was most anxious to stop there
and pay, however belatedly, homage to the memory of a
fellow-countryman whose status in the annals of French
exploration in Central Asia is comparable only to that of
Bonvalot and Prince Henry of Orleans. I explained my
project to Captain Ma, who was most sympathetic and even
offered to provide me with an escort. Tongbudmo was not
on the direct route to Juchieh Gompa, but to go there involved a detour of only two or three days' march and it
would be easy to reach the rendezvous before the caravan
left.

I packed my things and next day, early in the afternoon,
left Jyekundo accompanied by a Chinese soldier who was to
act as my guide and personal servant.

After two pretty frightful days' march in pouring rain, through seas of mud and swollen streams, we reached Tongbudmo, a miserable hamlet where, rather to my surprise, the yaks with my luggage had already arrived. The village lay at the junction of two narrow valleys; the high ridge of rock which separated them tapered away suddenly into a long, low spur, and Tongbudmo was on the top of this spur, at the point of confluence of two streams. It looks rather like a fortress, admirably sited to guard the entrance to both valleys. In that grey, unpleasant weather the place had a sinister air and looked ideal for an ambush.

I was able to pick out all the topographical details shown on Grenard's sketch-map and it was easy to reconstruct the tragedy.

The travellers had arrived, towards dusk, by the path which I had followed. They were churlishly received, but decided to stop the night there in spite of the latent hostility in the atmosphere. Next morning one of their ponies had disappeared. They demanded its return in forthright terms and, gravely misjudging the Tibetan character, took possession of one of the local ponies in the belief that this would overawe the villagers; they would not give it back, they said, until the stolen pony had been handed over.

Needless to say, this high-handed action did not produce the desired result, and the explorers finally withdrew, taking the pony they had confiscated with them as a hostage.

They had reached the confluence of the two streams when a withering volley was directed at them from the village. There was no cover—I could see that for myself. The narrow path runs between the stream and a smooth wall of rock devoid of projections or irregularities; it was a death-trap. Some way further on a left-handed turn takes the path into dead ground out of sight from the village, but Dutreuil de Rhins and two of his men were shot down before they could reach this point. Grenard and the rest did reach it and got away.

Nothing had changed from that day, more than fifty years ago, to this—except the attitude of the villagers, who received me in a very friendly manner and seemed perfectly inoffensive; I tried to question them, but they appeared never to have heard of these old, unhappy, far-off things. I had brought with me from Jyekundo a plain wooden cross made by the local carpenter, on which I had carved the name of Dutreuil de Rhins and the date of his death. A little shelf of sand and pebbles, on the spit of land between the two streams, looked to be as near as one could get to the exact spot at which the brave Frenchman met his death; and there I fixed his cross, helped by the Chinese soldier and by (in all probability) the descendants of his murderers, who built a protective pedestal of stones round its base.

I explained to them the purpose of this ceremony; they understood perfectly and promised to look after the cross, which roughly corresponded in their eyes to a *chörten* erected over the remains of a particularly holy lama. The sun had broken momentarily through the clouds. I took some photographs, laid a bunch of wild flowers at the foot of the cross and, after standing for a moment in silence before it, mounted and rode northwards with my little caravan.

37. RENDEZVOUS FOR KOKONOR

ON our way down the valley we passed a lamasery, probably the one in which Grenard sought asylum after the murder. An hour later we debouched once more into the great valley of the Yangtse, near a village perched on top of a high bluff. At this stage in its course the river is known as the Tungtien Ho; it is very wide and its waters at this time of year are yellow and turbid, quite different from the lovely clear stream which I had crossed in Yunnan. The track followed its right bank, sometimes running along the sandy foreshore, sometimes clinging to the rocks which overhung it; but the river was so high that it often covered the path, and subsidiary tracks zigzagged up the hillside and by-passed the inundations.

I soon reached one of these by-passes and took the upper path with my Chinese soldier; the lower one was completely submerged for about forty yards. The yaks were a little way behind us and, supposing that they would follow our example, I paid no particular attention to them. All at once, looking back from the crest of the ridge, I saw with horror that the idle caravan-men, rather than face a stiffish climb, had calmly carried on along the flooded track. From my coign of vantage I could see the two yaks, with the current up to their bellies, slaking their thirst, while my luggage was quietly absorbing the muddy waters of the Yangtse. I hurled stones at them to try and move them on, but they took not the slightest notice; they went on drinking imperturbably, then ambled forward with great deliberation until they were on dry ground again. The water began to trickle slowly out of my sodden packs.

At three o'clock we reached the place where we had to cross the river, opposite a bluff with two big *chörtens* standing at its foot. We were ferried across in the usual yak-skin coracles and were caught by a violent storm just as we reached the further bank. We took shelter in a little inn, and when the rain abated I went to have a look at the nearest of the two *chörtens*, concerning which my Chinese soldier had told me a curious story.

The village is called Tanda and, according to legend, it was here that the famous Chinese pilgrim Hsuan-tsang crossed the Yangtse on his way back from India in A.D. 641. In the course of the crossing the precious Sanskrit manuscripts which he was bringing back from the cradle of Buddhism fell into the water, and Hsuan-tsang had to wait several days at Tanda for them to dry.

There were certainly two *chörtens* there. One of them was a typical square, white, modern erection; the other, much older, was supposed to have been built to commemorate the passage of Hsuan-tsang. Although it is clearly not old enough for that, and although the legend may have no basis in historical fact, this *chörten* is of an unusual design which I saw nowhere else in Tibet. It looks like a sort of sawn-off pyramid, made of four layers of neatly carved stone, each smaller than the one below it. These four layers are alternately square and circular. The lowest of them rests on a foundation of loose stones fitted securely together and pock-marked with deep cavities, like pigeon-holes, full of little earthenware images. The whole structure, which is fairly dilapidated, was decorated in the usual way with prayer-flags, but another feature which emphasised its singularity was a slab of black marble, let into the base of the monument and inscribed with the name of the immortal pilgrim.

When the storm drew off, we resumed our march with a relay of fresh animals and struck up the valley of a tributary which joins the Yangtse just above Tanda. The land here was fertile, settled and well cultivated, the crops of barley being noticeably good. We passed a Sakyapa monastery and after that a big walled village set on a rocky spur which dominated the valley at its narrowest part. This stronghold looked most impressive and was built of huge granite blocks, an unusual thing in Tibet. At seven o'clock we reached Labung Gompa and stopped there for the night.

Next morning, after retracing our steps for a mile or so, we took a poorly defined path up a gorge with a stream in it which led us out of the valley. This gradually widened out, but the gradient got steeper and steeper, and before we reached the crest our ponies—although we had led them for most of the climb—were exhausted and had to stop every twenty yards to recover their breath. Once more I noticed how much more ponies, even Tibetan ponies, feel the height than their masters do. At ten o'clock we crossed the pass at an altitude of fifteen thousand feet.

The weather had improved and we got a splendid view of the Yangtse valley and the mountains enclosing it. At first the track followed the side of the mountain through wide pastures profusely decked with flowers—big yellow gentians, Martagon lilies, edelweiss and sweet-smelling cyclamens. This fairyland did not last long, however, and soon we were scrambling down a steep face covered with screes where the ponies had a rough time of it; this brought us to a gentler valley, where herdsmen watched their far-flung flocks grazing high on the slopes above them. After passing a small hamlet and a big lamasery, we came at noon to Tsiamdo, a fair-sized village on the direct route from Jyekundo to Juchieh Gompa.

Here, I learnt to my disgust, we should have to wait for two or three days, for the governor of the province had ordered more horses to be requisitioned for the Chinese Army and added to the caravan. All day long Tibetans kept arriving with their ponies, which, after being closely scrutinised by a board of officers, were branded with a red-hot iron and turned into a big corral until it was time to start.

I checked the contents of my luggage when the yaks came in, for I was worried about the effects of their partial immersion in the Yangtse. Everything that had been packed in the bottom of the loads had come off badly—shirts, papers, maps, Tibetan books and paintings. Luckily my films had escaped damage. Next morning I settled down to dry everything out on the flat roof of the inn.

This establishment, with nomads and their ponies converging on it from every direction, was crowded with an exotic mixture of wild faces, long black tresses and outlandish clothes. Tibetan women were spinning in the courtyard while their men packed up great bundles of hides and raw wool.

At last we got off; but the night before I had had an

agonising attack of lumbago, which made the long hours in the saddle a severe ordeal. The weather, however, was perfect; our route took us down a long valley where women, naked to the waist, were reaping barley. Thence we climbed gently upwards to a wide, grass-covered pass giving access to a high plateau where thousands of sheep and yaks were grazing. Up here the ground was covered in places with large black caterpillars with red heads and two yellow spots on their backs; they were remarkably pretty, but it was almost impossible to move without squashing some of them, a bad thing from the Buddhist point of view. On this plateau I also renewed my acquaintance with the disarming little rodents which had been so plentiful at Yulong; and there were large colonies of marmots and a few antelope. All these animals were quite tame, hardly troubling to move out of our way as we rode past.

Presently the track left the plateau and we switchbacked slowly over a succession of ridges. At noon, reaching an insignificant little pass, we suddenly came in sight of Juchieh Gompa, the rendezvous for the Kokonor caravan. The monastery, isolated in a plain which stretched as far as the eye could see, looked like a toy. Its environs were pimpled with a rash of white tents with yak-loads stacked all round them. The animals were scattered over the nearby grasslands; the whole thing looked like a gigantic travelling circus.

We soon reached the lamasery, where I was given a delightful room with a balcony looking out over the plain. The place belongs to an obscure sub-sect called Drugong, which is—unless I am mistaken—an offshoot of the Sakyapas, who also own Trashi Gompa.

We were here for two days, and I spent most of my time with the monks, who were extremely kind to me. We were on the edge of the Grass Desert, beyond which lay China and her pagodas; Juchieh Gompa was the last Tibetan lamasery I should see for a long time. For the rest, I either wandered about the enormous camp or sat and read on the banks of the Yalung, which was the only quiet place to be found among the prevailing bustle. I noticed that the advance-parties had already begun to leave while fresh groups of travellers were still coming in to the rendezvous, and I wondered how much longer this sort of thing was going to continue.

38. THE GREAT GRASS DESERT

THE main body took the road on August the 9th. Hubbub had reigned throughout the camp since midnight. Dogs barked. Animals were loaded while the drivers intoned their prayers. Fires sprang into life all over the place and tea was brewed.

At half-past four they came to fetch my luggage, to which I stuck as closely as I could, in case it got sent off with the wrong party. Ponies were saddled and at five o'clock we rode off into the darkness. My little soldier had gone back to Jyekundo and I was now alone; the sub-unit of the caravan to which I was attached consisted of thirty yaks with three Tibetans in charge of them. As for ponies, I could have had any one of the three hundred odd who were being taken riderless to Sining.

A bitter wind scourged the plain and all the streams were frozen; we were still twelve thousand feet up and autumn was already setting in. The wide, straight track—almost an arterial road by Tibetan standards—followed the right bank of the Yalung as it flowed between low, grass-covered hills. At eleven o'clock we halted and made camp at the foot of a jagged-looking pass. In a few minutes a whole township of tents had sprung up; they were of all shapes and sizes, but the most conspicuous were the Chinese tents made of white canvas, edged with broad strips of black cloth, which gave them a look of being in mourning. Yaks and ponies were all over the place; it felt more than ever like a travelling circus. Tea and *tsampa*: a nap: then a louse-hunt (today's bag was seventy, almost all nits).

The afternoon sun was scorching, but the moment it disappeared behind a cloud it was as though you had been plunged into a cold bath. This is typical of the continental climate, and we were after all in the very heart of Asia, thousands of miles from the sea.

My little tent looked like a doll's house compared with its imposing neighbours, but, small though it was, it was far more comfortable—especially in bad weather—than the huge Chinese tents, to which wind, rain and snow found easy access. It was of the type called "Isotherm."

Two days later there was a bit of a crisis when we started. The men had saddled my pony while it was still dark, but at four o'clock, when I went to mount, I found that the brute had disappeared; no one knew what had happened—whether he had run away, or had joined up with another party, or what.

This was a major disaster for me, for he carried on his back my tent, sleeping-bag, warm clothes and a saddle-bag containing maps, notebooks, camera and films. Several horsemen dashed off to look for the truant, and I sat down philosophically to await developments.

One by one all the detachments of the caravan moved off, leaving me behind in the middle of the empty plain, alone save for one of the Tibetans belonging to my party whom I had luckily got hold of in the darkness.

Time passed, no one appeared, and at last we decided to set off on foot, otherwise we might never catch up with the caravan. Dawn broke, wan and chill, and we trudged slowly onward across a huge, flat, desolate steppe covered with fresh snow which hid the track. Our only landmarks were some distant snow-mountains half-veiled by mist. My companion did not seem any too confident in his powers of navigation, but without him I should have been hopelessly lost, and it would have been a demoralising experience to cross those empty wastes alone.

We passed close to two big wild asses or onagers (the Tibetans call them *kyang*); they gazed at us with mild curiosity and moved away with a leisurely and dignified gait. At last, after plodding along rather desperately for two hours, we saw in the far distance a rider coming towards us through the mist. It proved to be one of our own party, and he was leading my pony. I jumped on its back, my companion rode pillion on the other pony behind his mate and we cantered after the caravan.

We overhauled our detachment as they were about to cross the Changu La, a pass which, although it is nothing much to look at, is over fifteen thousand feet above sea-level. It offered access to a plateau across which the detachments of our caravan were strung out as far as the eye could see. It was colder than ever on this bare expanse, and sleet drove like buckshot into our faces and hands. At the end of the plateau we had an awkward descent over broken ground whose interstices were full of boggy potholes. The ice that covered them was not strong enough to bear the weight of a man, let alone a pony. The poor beasts picked their way cautiously but kept on stumbling through the ice, so that the track was spattered with bloodstains from the cuts and grazes on their legs.

At last, at about eleven o'clock, this ordeal ended and we made camp on a particularly inhospitable bit of ground. For the rest of that day snowstorms alternated with bright intervals, during which the sun's heat was scorching. On the hillside nearby we could see herds of wild yaks; they seemed to be mildly intrigued by our tame ones, who however did not return their interest but went on grazing with their usual impassivity.

It was always a mystery to me when the caravan-men got any sleep. That night, after singing until three o'clock in

the morning, they were up at half-past four and away by five.
Once more we butted our way through wind and sleet; the
sleet stuck to our clothes and to the yaks' coats, giving them
the slightly ridiculous air of large plush toys. The weather
gradually improved, and after a bit we struck the River
Cha, which is shown on the maps as a tributary of the
Yalung and appears in fact to be its eastern, and more
important, source. Although the western source also figures
on the maps as the Dza, which is the Tibetan name for the
Yalung, it has never been explored. Fording it without
difficulty, we found ourselves on a fine, wide track, the
remains, probably, of the famous *Autobahn* from Kangting to
Sining via Jyekundo.

I was surprised to find, guarding the foot of a pass, a
little Chinese military outpost consisting of two tents
housing a small detachment of soldiers; they were Chinese
Moslems, or Tungans, and looked more like Turkis than
Chinese. I noticed, not for the first time, how Moslems
seem to acquire physical characteristics which submerge or
standardise their racial characteristics; whether they are
natives of China, India or Central Asia, they all have a look
of belonging to the same family.

The men at this post lived in the most complete isolation, and I could not help wondering what useful purpose
they were supposed to be serving on this deserted track; they
were the first human beings we had seen since Juchieh
Gompa, and the last we were to see before Tahoba, which
is several days' march from Tangar.

Early next day we crossed a pass which, though not particularly imposing, has considerable geographical importance. The Tibetans call it Cha La, English maps call it the
Cha-Yakow Pass and it appears on Grenard's sketch-map as
Padhong La. Whatever its correct name may be, it marks
the watershed between the two great river-basins which—in
effect—between them water the whole of China; for it
separates the Yangtse from the Yellow River.

We camped at the foot of this pass on the banks of a little stream. It was a bitterly cold but wonderfully beautiful night, with a full moon and a cloudless sky. Dawn, when it came, was even lovelier—so lovely that for some reason I felt impelled to get away from the caravan and rode off across the empty plain on which man had left no trace. Far away in the distance, snow-capped mountains stood out against the sky; here and there, upon the great irregular plain, little blue lakes shone like jewels in the rays of the rising sun.

But the next two marches were as dull as ditchwater. I beguiled them as best I could by riding round the other detachments of the caravan, thoughout which I was by now a well-known figure.

The most interesting feature of the whole circus was the herd of three hundred riderless ponies. They ran loose, without even head-stalls on them, and were herded by a dozen mounted Tibetans who, whooping wildly, took them along at full gallop. At this gait they naturally outstripped the caravan. Having established a biggish lead, they stopped to let the ponies graze and the caravan overhaul them; when it had passed they put on their act again, thundering past and obviously enjoying the whole thing like mad.

These outriders were all young men with a great air of pride and self-confidence. Everything they wore, from their boots to their hats, was made of sheepskin. They carried muskets with forked rests slung across their backs, broadswords thrust into their belts and daggers dangling at their thighs. Many of them also had lances with wooden shafts and iron heads, and a leg of mutton or a haunch of yak often hung at their saddle-bows, acquiring—by reason of the sun, the frost and the pony's sweat—a dark, rich patina. They rode extremely well, with leathers as short as the jockeys' in England. Their bearing, their accoutrements and their outlandish appearance would have become the horsemen of Attila or Genghis Khan.

We crossed the river and reached the Ngoring Cho, one

of the two biggest lakes in the country south of the Kokonor;
the other, the Kyaring Cho, lies to the west of the caravan
route. The Ngolog tribe come all the way from their home
territory on the banks of the Yellow River to collect salt
from the shores of these lakes. We saw none of these people.
Even if there had been any about, the strength of our caravan would have deterred them from attacking it, or even
from showing themselves; they are, among other things, not
particularly keen on making contact with Chinese soldiers,
who have a number of old scores to settle with them.

There was a tremendous lot of wild life in this region,
which is in effect a sort of sanctuary undisturbed by man.
Herds of yaks, wild asses and gazelles were all quite easy
to get near, and geese and various kinds of wildfowl
abounded on the shores of the lakes.

39. CHINA ONCE MORE

On August 18th the yaks got under way at three o'clock in
the morning. I started an hour later, on foot. The track,
after following the water's edge, climbed a low pass beyond
which lay a valley along whose sandy floor an upper reach
of the Yellow River meandered tortuously. It was about
fifty yards wide, with an average depth of eighteen inches.

For some days the whole caravan had been talking about
Tahoba, where we were due shortly. It is the first village
on the far side of the Grass Desert, and everyone spoke of it
as a place offering the rarest delights. Estimates of the
number of days it would take us to get there remained rather
imprecise and elastic, and on the 19th we certainly made very
little progress towards it.

We moved off down the valley at five o'clock in fine, clear
weather, with a high wall of mountains in front of us. I was
delighted by the prospect of a good, steady day's march

under ideal conditions, but at half-past seven everyone suddenly halted and made camp. I was furious at our failure to push on while the going was so good, but forced myself to admit that my chronic impatience was a regrettable by-product of my Western upbringing. Instead of continually hurrying to a destination where I immediately found something else to go chasing madly after, I should have done far better to follow the example of the caravan-men and enjoy each passing hour for what it brought, without bothering about what I had wanted it to bring.

It took us three more days to reach Tahoba, but they were interesting, eventful days and the weather was lovely. We left the valley of the Tharadi River for that of the Sora, a much more spectacular place. The river flowed through a deep gorge cut like a cañon out of the rocky cliff, and so narrow that its high walls formed the actual banks of the stream.

We climbed out of this valley while it was still dark on the morning of the third day and set off across a series of steppes towards Tahoba. The well-defined track skirted a low range of hills, and I rode on, alone, a longish way ahead of the caravan. On either side empty gorges cut into the hills leading to an unknown world, a world whose solitudes and mysteries attracted me far more than noisy, overcrowded China, to whose borders every stage brought me inexorably nearer.

Dawn was breaking, and in the uncertain light I stopped at the mouth of a little gorge to savour the silence and the peace of those great waste-lands. Suddenly both were shattered by strange noises which seemed to come out of the shadowy recesses of the gorge. They were like nothing that I had ever heard before—groans, strangled shrieks, wails of agony. These cries were certainly not made by the wind, nor by animals, nor—least of all—by human beings; it was impossible to attribute them to any natural cause, and my blood froze as I listened to them.

My pony was terrified too. He stopped grazing, pricked his ears and pawed the ground; I had dismounted, and if I had not kept hold of his reins he would have bolted. All at once, the ghastly sounds ceased as suddenly as they had started; all was quiet again, and the pony began to crop the grass. Presently the caravan came in sight and its familiar sounds dissipated the atmosphere of mystery; but the mystery itself remained. It is still with me today, part of a whole gamut of strange experiences undergone in a land where things happen that happen nowhere else on earth.

At noon we halted on the plateau of Tahoba. We were on the edge of a world which we had almost forgotten existed, for all round us were tents and nomads and their herds. They brought us fresh butter, fresh milk, yoghourt and *shura*. I found it, however, difficult to believe that these were the luxuries of which there had been so much talk on the road when anyone mentioned Tahoba; and eventually I gathered that there did exist, a little further on, a small village where a few Chinese merchants and officials lived. But I knew too much about these little trading-posts to be tempted by the crude form of civilisation which they represent, and I decided to stay where I was, among the nomads.

August 30th was a day of rest for the body but of anguish for the mind. On the evening before, the caravan-men— probably expecting me to be delighted by the news— announced that we were going to stay here for ten days or more. I was shattered by this unexpected development. Next morning, however, the headman explained that, although the main body was indeed going to lie up for a fortnight, to let the animals rest and put on condition, it would be possible for me to start rather earlier with a small advance party.

I settled down to make the best of this enforced delay; but in the afternoon the Chinese magistrate from Tahoba came to call. He described the place to me, and I thanked my stars that I had not gone on there, for it consisted (he

Q

said) only of three small officials' houses. When he said good-bye, he mentioned casually that he was dispatching a small caravan to Tangar on the following day and would put at my disposal a couple of yaks and a pony.

I thanked him warmly and set feverishly about my preparations. I slept very badly, expecting to be woken up and told to start at any moment; but the sun rose and still nobody appeared. The Tibetans whom I questioned said that they knew absolutely nothing about my famous caravan, and I was beginning to wonder whether the magistrate had not meant the whole thing as a joke when, at ten o'clock, I saw a party of horsemen and yaks approaching. This really was my caravan. My things were loaded on to the yaks and I sprang into the saddle, delighted to be on the move again; but we had ridden for only a quarter of an hour when we halted at the mouth of a little valley leading to the Paka La.

Towards evening a long caravan of camels, with the usual little donkey at their head, passed quite close to us; it was the first camel-caravan that I had seen and came as a reminder that Mongolia was not far away.

At five o'clock in the morning, after an undisturbed night, we finally left the Tahoba plateau. It was wonderful to be no longer surrounded by the bustle and noise of a big caravan. Our party consisted of four men, three ponies, one mule and about fifteen yaks; the old Chinese in charge of it disapproved of night marches, and from now on we did leisurely stages, starting at a reasonable hour, loading the animals without hurry and always finding time for tea and *tsampa* before we moved off. The weather was mild and for the first time since Jyekundo I found that I could dispense with my *shuba*. After riding for an hour, we crossed the pretty little Paka La, beyond which lay a wide valley dotted with tents and herds; we had done, at last, with the Grass Desert and its empty solitudes.

The Panaka nomads are noticeably different from the Tibetans of Sikang, being in general rather taller and having a more Mongoloid cast of countenance. They wear odd-looking felt hats tilted slightly to one side; these hats have flat brims and high conical crowns, often culminating in a little platform. The women wear their hair in a hundred and eight slender plaits—a style fairly common in Jyekundo; but they also wear, over their *shuba*, a curious adornment found only in the territory round the Kokonor and on the borders of Kansu. It consists of a wide strip of grey or red cloth, something like a chasuble, hanging down the back and fastened round the neck by a cord. It is sometimes so wide that it covers the whole back and reaches right down the skirts of the *shuba*; sometimes, on the other hand, it is composed of two parallel strips. But the striking thing about it is the silver-work. The yoke and the dependent strips are adorned with huge cabochons of chiselled silver, shaped like bowls turned upside down and often eight inches across by four inches high. These empty cabochons are sewn on to the strips of cloth in long rows, gradually getting smaller as you look down the strip. Occasionally their place is taken by big round lumps of amber or coral, but this is exceptional, for the amber, which comes from the country round Lake Baikal in Siberia, is worth roughly ten times its own weight in silver. The whole piece of finery is immensely heavy and it was a mystery to me how these women could lug round so considerable a burden, which often represented the whole of their fortune. It was not a *de luxe* accessory, trotted out to make an impression on special occasions; the Panaka women even wore it when working in the fields and herding their beasts, and it was extraordinary to see the indifference with which, when they squatted or stooped, they let the great silver gauds trail in the mud and the dung.

Next day a narrow gorge brought us to a settlement consisting of a few adobe houses and a large building in which I was surprised to find a flour-mill worked by the stream; the handful of Chinese employed there wore the masks of white which disguise millers all over the world.

The mill was an unexpected phenomenon, but scarcely less puzzling was the sight of a huge dump of timber stacked in tall piles. How on earth had all this wood been conjured out of that treeless landscape? For whom, in that deserted land, was the flour being ground? I tried in vain to get these mysteries explained, but the dialect here was different from that of Sikang and I made little headway.

We did not, in any case, stay there long; the men loaded the spare yaks with timber and we pushed on. The track took us across a wide desert of white sand, on which grew sparse tufts of stiff, desiccated grass, as high as a man. There were few signs of life; only a few camels cropped the scanty grazing. We made camp near a muddy water-hole. It was overpoweringly hot, without a square inch of shade or a breath of wind; the glare of the sun on the sand was very irksome.

Next day we passed two big inns where Chinese travellers stay. They consisted of huge rectangular courtyards surrounded by a wall with a single narrow gateway in it. Inside were a few houses of adobe or of wood, some chickens, various nondescript objects and—oddest of all—a large cartwheel leaning up against a wall. This phenomenon, which would have been unremarkable anywhere else, made a sharp impact on me; it was concrete evidence that I had travelled out of one world into another. Since leaving Kangting six months ago, I had not set eyes on a wheeled vehicle; the complete absence of a form of transport universal throughout the rest of the world is one of the distinguishing characteristics of Tibet. I accepted the fact that I was now in China.

The empty plateau we were crossing sloped gradually down into a wide basin with a biggish lake, called Gunganor, in the centre of it. The track dropped down to its shores through a narrow sandy corridor, a pretty little lane running between high bluffs like fortifications. This brought us to the soggy green ground in the bottom of the basin, which offered a marked contrast to the arid plateau we had left. Here we found a lot of tents and animals and, in particular, some calves which were obviously not bred from yaks, for they looked like European calves and mooed instead of grunting as yaks do.

It took us an hour to cross this oasis of verdure, from which another sandy lane, the exact counterpart of the first, brought us out on to another plateau. Soon after this we struck the Obe Chu, a tributary of the Yellow River, and followed its left bank. The hills gradually got lower, and we had a long, hard march through dunes. The change in the landscape was very marked: behind us, mountains and hills, storms and rain and mist: ahead of us, sand, drought, blue skies. About noon we came on a tiny settlement in the heart of the dunes; a few tents and huts, and some plots of barley which the Tibetans were harvesting. There was even a tiny field of beans; they were beautifully ripe, and I could not resist the temptation of munching a few. It was so long since I had eaten fresh vegetables that these raw beans seemed to me food for the gods. We camped near a muddy stream in which the yaks and ponies wallowed gratefully.

At five o'clock in the morning we set off again along the little river which brought us into fairly densely populated country; there were tents, and adobe huts, and cave-dwellings scooped out of cliffs of loess, and fields where Chinese peasants were working in their little round skull-caps and dark blue jackets. After that came more sandy desert, sparsely tufted with coarse grass. It was an intensely desolate place, devoid of all life except for a few camels which watched us pass with their air of remote and contemptuous hauteur.

I felt as if our march across this desert would never end; there was nothing to break the monotony, it was fearfully hot and I was exhausted. But all of a sudden the plateau came to an end and plunged down into another basin; and there, as if by a miracle, was a real village! Houses, barley-fields, green pastures, a stream and, standing a little way off, an enormous house built of stone—a proper house, painted grey, with balconies and pillars. In front of it were trees—

real trees—such as I had not seen since Derge. Chinese peasants were bringing in the harvest on little grey donkeys. This was Charatong.

We camped on the lip of the plateau overlooking the village, and I pitched my tent in the lee of a fine *chörten* of white stone. We had done a tough stage of almost ten hours and I was glad of a rest. The men went to the village and came back with some wonderfully sweet water. This was a real treat. For several days we had been drinking brackish, muddy water and our tea had been a sort of warm, discoloured slime which was far from appetising.

Next day, for the first time, we moved off while it was still dark and floundered through a succession of streams, the animals making slow progress. By dawn we were out of the basin and climbing up a crevasse cut, as though by the stroke of a sword, in the high loess cliff beyond it. We crossed a plateau seamed with ravines and came to an imposing highway, along which ran a telephone line.

This was civilisation with a vengeance. We met Chinese travellers, strings of coolies and little hamlets where you could buy cakes and bean-curd. For two days we rode eastward along this great road. We crossed the Lisago La, a biggish pass, and reached the village of Totango. At this place I had my first proper Chinese meal for a long time, finishing it off with the delicious little apples that they grow in Tangar.

In the afternoon I walked up to the pass. On it stands a granite monument with three Chinese characters carved on it: Jih-yueh-shan, meaning the Mountain of the Moon and the Sun. I was now in territory which had been adequately explored, and I recalled the names of some of the travellers who had crossed this pass, from Rockhill in 1892 to Pereira in 1921 and Ilya Tolstoy in 1943. Some ten thousand feet high, it used to mark the frontier of Kansu before the province of Chinghai was formed, and—in practice if not on paper—it separates China from Tibet.

We were now less than thirty miles from Tangar. When I got back to camp I explained to the men that I was desperately anxious to have a look at the Kokonor, which was not far away to the westward, instead of continuing north to Tangar. For years I had dreamed of this inland sea, which can fairly be called the heart of Central Asia, and I was determined not to miss an opportunity which might never recur. The old Chinese was reluctant to make a detour because he was responsible for the caravan, but one of the Tibetans agreed to go with me in return for a sizeable reward.

40. THE BLUE LAKE

I LEFT my luggage with the caravan, taking only my tent and sleeping bag on the pony; my companion had a bag of *tsampa*, some tea and some butter. Leaving Sharakoto on our right, we took a track running westwards. In the sparsely populated valley the Chinese element soon petered out and we found ourselves back among the black tents of the nomads. We were no longer slowed down by the yaks and made good going, camping at the point where the stream we were following joined another coming from the south. Two little ruined forts stood on the hill-tops overlooking this place.

Next day the valley flattened out slowly. There was any amount of good grazing, and we saw many big flocks of sheep. It was a grey sort of day, dank scarves of mist hung in the hollows and in this drab light the countryside seemed dull and lifeless. Towards dusk it became possible to make out, far ahead of us, a sort of vast, pale plain across which the wind was driving patches of mist; this was the Kokonor. In a short time I was pitching my tent on its shores.

The weather was better next morning, but the sky was still

overcast and the grey waters of the lake merged into it on the horizon. I was sadly disappointed; the sparkling blue lake on which I had hoped to feast my eyes presented itself as a drab, illimitable expanse of water and gave one no idea of its size, enormous though one knew this to be.

The Kokonor, though not on the same scale as the great lakes of Siberia, is the largest in Tibet and among the largest in Asia. Lying at an altitude of just under ten thousand feet above sea-level, it is roughly seventy miles long by forty miles across. Kokonor, the name by which it is generally known in the West, is Mongol for "Blue Lake," and the Chinese and Tibetan names for it both mean the same thing.

While Lozon, my Tibetan guide, was starting a fire of yak-dung, I went to draw water for our tea. The water was less salt than it had been in the lakes further south; the animals drank it freely, and it was really just about the right flavour for making Tibetan tea. The degree of salinity in the waters of these lakes varies according to the season, being modified by the increment of fresh water from the streams that flow into them; now, at the end of the rainy season, it must have been at its lowest.

I would have liked to have a bathe, but there were some herdsmen's tents nearby whose occupants would have been horrified to see anyone swimming in waters which they regarded as sacred. For the same sort of reason no form of boat is allowed on the lake, for its shadow would offend the gods who live in a city far beneath its surface. Only one boat, belonging to a Russian expedition long ago, risked ignoring this embargo; it was caught by a sudden and extremely violent storm and only just managed to regain the shore.

When we had finished our *tsampa*, I left my tent in charge of Lozon and rode off along the edge of the lake. Nomads' tents were pitched here and there in the lee of the hills. They were mostly Tibetan tents, square or polygonal, made of coarse black cloth woven from yaks' hair and stretched out like spiders' webs round one, or sometimes two, tall poles. In one little valley, by way of contrast, I found a cluster of Mongol yurts, which were very different affairs and much more comfortable. Based on a circular framework of light wood with vertical walls, they were covered with thick, solid-looking brown felt. The entrance could be closed by a door, also made of felt, and a hole in the centre of the roof let the smoke out. Inside, the arrangements were much the same as in Tibetan tents. In the middle of the floor there was a fireplace made of clay; along the sides of the tent were stored painted wooden chests and leather bags for flour and *tsampa*; and the far end was occupied by a little altar, some images, a painting on silk and some prayer-books on a shelf.

The amalgam of Tibetans and Mongols in the territories round the Kokonor is of comparatively recent origin. According to Chinese historians these grazing-grounds were an exclusively Mongol preserve between the sixteenth and the eighteenth centuries. In those days the Tibetans lived further to the south, on the other side of the mountains which enclose the Kokonor basin. Gradually, under pressure from the Ngolog tribe in the Yellow River valley, the Tibetans shifted northward by a process of peaceful infiltration, first settling on the southern shores of the lake and then working round to the wide grazing-grounds which lie to the north of it.

These particular Tibetans belonged to eight tribes called Na, and they soon became known by the composite name of Panaka, which means "The Eight Tribes Called Na." The Mongols call them Tanguts or Kara-Tanguts, meaning "Black Tibetans." Both communities are on excellent terms, being united both by the ties of religion and by their fear of the Ngologs, whose forays sometimes extend as far as the south shore of the lake.

The weather showed no signs of improving and I gave up all hope of seeing the famous island in the middle of the

Kokonor, on which a community of lamas lives for most of the year (since there are no boats) in complete isolation; supplies only reach them in winter, when the lake is frozen. It was a cold day, with a damp, bitter wind blowing, and I was glad to get back to the shelter of my little tent. Lozon had got hold of some fresh sour milk and cooked a huge dish of wild roots, something like small potatoes with a slightly sweet flavour. There were a lot of them around here.

Early next day we left the lake, which was still looking surly and inhospitable, and headed for Tangar. The ill-defined track ran north-east across the undulating, rather boggy steppes at the east end of the Kokonor. About noon we started climbing a range of low, sandy hills and at four we reached the top of it and made camp on the edge of a big plateau which separates the Kokonor basin from the valley of the Hsi Ho which leads to Tangar. It was a desolate expanse, with nothing growing on it except a few tough, knobbly-looking plants.

Next day we crossed this plateau and dropped down into the valley whose grassy floor was dotted with Mongol and Tibetan tents. After spending the night in the lamasery of Sewa Gompa about twenty miles from our destination, we rode into Tangar in the afternoon of September 12th.

PART NINE

Across Inner Mongolia

TANGAR is quite an interesting little town, but I only stayed there two days. Charmingly situated on the side of a mountain, overlooking a wide, green valley, it is, like so many Chinese towns, surrounded by a massive wall. With its steep streets, its flights of steps, its terraces and its houses built in tiers, it reminded me of an Alpine village. The main street—the only one with any claim to being horizontal —runs right through it, from one of the main gates to the other; the gates are still quite an imposing sight with their overhanging roofs of wood and their curved arches.

This street is a high road for the caravans setting out from China for the Kokonor and the Tsaidam; it was crowded with camels and yaks and big grey mules from Sining. It is also a business thoroughfare, flanked by Chinese shops dealing in all the various things that a caravan needs; the little market-square is a rendezvous for Tibetans, Mongols, Turkis, travellers and merchants—a microcosm pervaded by the atmosphere of Central Asia. Beyond it is the administrative centre, with barracks, schools and municipal offices.

In the past months I had got so completely de-urbanised that I spent hours wandering up and down, staring at the shops and wearing (I suspect) the same dazed and slightly apprehensive air which I noticed on the dark faces of the nomads in their *shubas* and high boots. When I got tired of sight-seeing I sought asylum in the shady, overgrown grounds of a deserted Confucian temple; here I found the divinities I knew so well and would henceforward meet no longer in the strange, compelling atmosphere of Tibet.

It was in the course of these wanderings that I met Dimitri. At first I took him for a Chinese, but he was in fact a White Russian who had left his country during the

Revolution and had finished up—after various fantastic adventures—in Tangar, where he was married to a Chinese woman and got his livelihood from a little business which dealt in tea and paper. His main languages were Russian and Chinese, but he had a smattering of English and Tibetan and we managed to understand each other. He took me to see his family, and it was through his good offices that I got a place on a cart which was expected to leave shortly for Sining.

I had found the men with my caravan installed in one of the numerous inns in the lower part of the town where most of the trading is done. They brought my luggage to my lodging, and I made them a present of my old boots, my saddle, bridle and other tack which henceforth would be of much more use to them than to me. Parting from them was in effect saying good-bye to Tibet—the tranquil monasteries, the hermits' cells tucked away in the mountains, the care-free life of the caravans, the great empty lands. I loved it all, and already I felt homesick for it. But I knew in my heart that my return to civilisation could only be an inter-lude, that the long pilgrimage to which my life was dedicated would one day bring me back to the Roof of the World.

On September 14th I left Tangar on a big cart drawn by two ponies and crammed with merchandise on top of which I perched in company with a dozen Chinese passengers. It is only twenty-five miles from Tangar to Sining and at six o'clock on the same day we entered the capital of Chinghai province. We all alighted, and the carter took me round to the Catholic Mission. It was more than six months since I had eaten European food, or sat on a chair at a table with a cloth on it, or used a knife and fork; I suddenly found it quite an effort to restrain myself from using my fingers.

The Fathers at the Sining Mission almost all came from Central Europe; there were Germans, Austrians, Dutch, Hungarians and a few Poles, and in this cosmopolitan society we talked French, English and German in turn. The talk was a welcome relaxation, and so were the hours I spent browsing in their library. One of the Fathers came with me when I called on General Ma Pu-fang, the military governor of the province, to whom I was indebted for his good offices in the matter of the caravan from Jyekundo. He received me with great courtesy and tried to insist that I should stay in the best hotel as his guest. I was able to decline this generous offer without offending him.

General Ma was the best type of Chinese Moslem, an administrator as well as a soldier. He was the undisputed overlord of Chinghai, a province carved in 1929, for political reasons, half out of Kansu and half out of Tibet. For centuries Sining has been the centre of a big Moslem community, scattered through the territories on China's north-western frontier; nobody knows much about its origins.

These Moslems, who have strongly marked ethnic characteristics, have jealously preserved their religion and its customs, and form an individualistic and only half-assimilated enclave in the Chinese race; they are known as Tungans. In the past they have fought bitter wars with the pure Chinese, and in those days the Moslem government at Sining, though nominally subordinate to the provincial government of Kansu, was for practical purposes independent. In China a provincial governor's importance depends basically on the strength of the army he controls, and the Tungans make splendid soldiers. In order to put an end to their recurrent intransigence, the Chinese Government, most judiciously, legitimised a situation which they were powerless to alter and promoted the Moslem commissioner at Sining to be governor of the brand-new province of Chinghai.

Sining is very much like most other Chinese towns. The two main streets, running at right angles to each other, lead to the four gates (North, South, East and West); and a huge wall, from which watch-towers sprout at intervals, surrounds the town. What is singular about the place is the Moslem quarter, which is insulated from the rest of the city by another wall with a big gate in it; this internal municipal boundary dates from the bloody Moslem revolt of 1895, which claimed thousands of victims. The principal trade is in furs and hides. Craftsmen work the raw skins brought in from Tibet, and whole streets are devoted to their activities; they look very picturesque, with thousands of fur robes and *shubas* flapping in the wind outside the shops.

The famous lamasery of Kumbum (the name means "One Hundred Thousand Pictures") is not far from Sining. It is the most important in this part of Tibet and has a complement of three thousand monks. It stands upon a commanding site and is immensely rich; and, besides its lovely temples, its gilded roofs, its paintings and its images, it has the additional interest of being an important centre of pilgrimage, for it marks the birthplace of Tsongkhapa, who founded the Gelupa sect.

Its innermost shrine is supposed to contain the miraculous tree whose leaves are marked with the sacred formula *Om ma-ni pad-mé hum*. In fact the original tree is sepulchred in a *chörten* somewhere inside the temple; the existing tree, which you can see in one of the courtyards, was grown from a cutting of the old one and, personally, I could make out no lettering of any kind on its leaves.

A gallery with a wooden floor runs round the front of the main temple, and generations of pilgrims have worn smooth, shallow ruts in it with their hands as they prostrated themselves. Although Kumbum is a fine and lovely place, I liked it less than the truly Tibetan lamaseries; its style of architecture was Chinese, and most of the buildings were comparatively new, the old monastery having been burnt down some time ago. Nor did I rediscover there that atmosphere of isolation and spirituality which so powerfully attracted me to the simpler holy places of Tibet.

In Sining it appeared that my journey eastwards to Lan-

ABOVE: *Motoring in North China.*   *On the road to Paotou*
BELOW: *The lamasery of Kumbum*

chow presented difficulties. All lorries had been requisitioned
for military operations against the Communists and the
regular passenger services had been suspended. I managed to get a seat on a convoy of horse-drawn carts, but it
was a long, slow journey and for days afterwards I stank
of untanned leather, for it was on bundles of this commodity
that I reclined in transit. The carts took eight days to do the
two hundred miles from Sining to Lanchow—eight interminable, exasperating days, interrupted by endless delays in god-
forsaken villages, false starts, heated wrangles with inn-
keepers—the whole gamut, in fact, of the pleasures which
await the traveller in the interior of China.

42. LORRIES AND QUAGMIRES

LANCHOW is an important city with half a million inhabitants,
set picturesquely enough among the bare mountains which
surround it. It is a busy place, with several wide avenues
lined with shops and offices, but there is—except for the
perpetually fascinating spectacle of a Chinese crowd—
nothing particularly interesting about it. You can, however,
tell that you are in a frontier-town. You see a good many
non-Chinese types—Tibetans, Mongols and Tungans from
the Tsaidam, and one quarter in the city is occupied by
Turkis from Sinkiang, who sell carpets and dried grapes
from Hami, a pale, sweet and delicious fruit. I was struck,
too, by the number of White Russians, all—like their compatriots in Shanghai and Tientsin—leading the sad life of
exiles, far from a motherland for which they are still homesick and whither many long to return.

A telegram from the French Consul-General at Peking
informed me that it was still possible to travel there by way of
Ninghsia, Ordos, Paotou and the railway which runs from
the latter place to Peking; since, moreover, the direct route

Image of Tsongkhapa at Kumbum
R

via Sian was in Communist-controlled territory, this longish detour represented my only hope of reaching the coast. The consul also mentioned that some friends of his would be glad to put me up in Peking. Everything seemed to be going rather well.

By a tremendous stroke of good luck I was able to leave Lanchow on October 1st in a brand-new American lorry carrying merchandise and a dozen Chinese passengers. On this occasion I had the unprecedented privilege of sitting in front beside the driver. He was an extremely nice young Estonian called Liepa, and he had with him an endearing Scotch terrier pup which he looked after as if it had been a child and which travelled the whole way curled up on my knees. It is practically unknown in China to take passage in a lorry which is in first-class order, has new tyres and is driven by someone who does not behave as if he were being hotly pursued by all the fiends in hell.

To begin with the road ran through picturesque mountain country before crossing the Yellow River, about a hundred miles from Lanchow, on an extremely primitive ferry. It poured with rain, everything was soaked through and, as usual, innumerable *contretemps* delayed us. First of all, a bridge having been destroyed, we had to ford a tributary of the Yellow River, a biggish river slap in the middle of which the lorry stuck fast. The driver remained at the wheel while the passengers jumped overboard into water up to their knees and waded ashore after tying a strong rope to the front of the vehicle. We then proceeded to haul on this rope, but our combined efforts produced no result. After a great deal of talk we managed to persuade some coolies who were working on the road to lend a hand and at last, with much difficulty, we got the lorry out on to *terra firma*. Exactly the same thing happened again a little further on, and finally, while the lorry was stationary in the main street of Ningling-ting, the surface of the road gave way under one of its wheels and it subsided into a drain. We had to unload everything and work hard for several hours before we got it back on an even keel again.

Eventually the road debouched on to a wide, empty plain where herds of camels were at pasture and rejoined the Yellow River about two hundred miles from Ninghsia. At this point the river flows through a deep, rocky gorge, but this is a sort of geological freak, and it soon resumes its leisurely meandering across the boundless plain. We crossed it, and for the rest of the way to Ninghsia travelled through a region of marshes and paddy-fields, dominated by the distant, cloud-wreathed peak of Alashan.

In Ninghsia I met two journalists of whom I had heard much talk in Sining and who had just travelled down the Yellow River by raft from Lanchow. One of them, a German called von Briessen, had been in Peking since the beginning of the war; the other, Tichy, was Austrian and also lived in Peking. They were great travellers, especially Tichy, who had already done a journey from Vienna to Calcutta by motor-bicycle, using much the same route that I had followed, on an ordinary bicycle, in 1939. He had crossed India and, entering Tibet, had got as far as Kailasa, the sacred mountain in the south. We got on well together, as travellers generally do. Von Briessen and Tichy had had worse luck than I had. They had set out from Peking meaning to enter Eastern Tibet by the route I had followed in the reverse direction, but they had been unable to get permission to travel further than Sining, where they had spent two fruitless months trying to soften the hearts of the authorities.

We wanted to take advantage of our stay in Ninghsia to spend a few days at Alashan, which is an important centre of the far-flung Mongol community; but the Chinese officials refused to allow this because of the uncertain military situation. The prevailing bad weather took the edge off our disappointment; it simply poured with rain, and the streets of the little town became quagmires. As a result of these

conditions, no lorries had arrived at Ninghsia for the last
two days, and the Chinese drivers who were already in town
refused to leave, saying that the road was impassable. Liepa
took no notice of this defeatist talk and staked his prestige
as a European on making a journey which the Asiatics had
no stomach for. His attitude, and ours, emboldened several
Chinese to face the risks involved, and we left Ninghsia
with the best part of thirty passengers.

After following the left bank of the Yellow River, we
crossed it soon after passing a big village called Shintsuishan.
On the far bank we found ourselves once more in Mongol
territory, and on the ferry going across there were some
young Mongol girls with very arresting coiffures. Their
hair was braided in two enormous, but very short, plaits,
which were fantastically enlarged by two swags of black
wool; the huge pear-shaped pendants were decorated with
coral ornaments.

The province of Ninghsia is one of the four provinces—
the others are Suiyuan, Chahar and Jehol—which make up
Inner Mongolia, or that part of Mongolia which is under
Chinese control. It boasts only a narrow zone of fertile land,
which extends along both banks of the Yellow River and is
almost entirely inhabited by Chinese; on either side of this
lie the two great deserts of Alashan and Ordos, both populated—though sparsely—by Mongols.

We now had to cross the Ordos country. It looked forbidding—an immense plain without a tree or any other kind
of landmark to catch the eye, except for some indistinct hills
on the horizon. But the thing that I found the most disconcerting was the fact that Mongolia, which I had always
understood to consist entirely of a dry and waterless desert of
sand, did in fact consist of a vast sea of mud; it took us five
days, and an immense amount of back-breaking work, to get
across the Ordos.

It was the drabbest of landscapes—rain, mist, marshes
and the ubiquitous yellow mud. For several miles we would

make slow and difficult progress, skidding, side-slipping and
zigzagging along the dirt track; then the lorry would stick
fast in a lagoon of mud. Everyone got down—men, women
and children—and we all pulled and pushed according to our
varying abilities until we managed to shift the lorry out of
this quagmire.

The third day, virtually the whole of which was devoted
to operations of this kind, was the worst. The lorry got
bogged every hundred yards or so. I have no idea how many
times we had to get down and push, but I do remember that
in one particularly frightful place the combined efforts of
thirty passengers failed to budge the lorry and we had to
supplement them with three camels requisitioned from a
group of tents nearby. The whole thing made a really rather
remarkable *tableau vivant*—an American lorry, embedded up
to the axles, being pushed by a horde of Chinese and three
Europeans, all floundering wildly in the mud, and towed by
three camels, whose grotesque silhouettes, blurred by the
mist, stood out with an air of the monstrous against the dun,
displeasing immensities of that nightmare landscape.

At the end of that day's stage we were plastered with mud
and had covered less than twenty miles, but I could not—
once more—help admiring the Chinese for their patience
and their cheerfulness. Every time we stuck, they jumped
down into the mud without showing a trace of irritation and
set about shoving with all their might, all the time chattering,
laughing and cracking jokes with unruffled good humour.

There were, thank goodness, some comparatively dry
stretches of road through regions where herds of camels
were grazing and you could buy cheese and milk from the
yurts of the nomads. Very occasionally we passed a lamasery,
but, apart from a rather imposing one at Laopi Chao, they
were mean places, badly built and housing only a small
complement of monks—mere shadows of the great Tibetan
lamaseries.

On October 9th we set off from the little village where we

had spent the night, and found ourselves confronted by what really amounted to a lake astride the road; there was no question of going any further. We did however struggle experimentally along a side-road which seemed to have been less drastically affected by the inundations; but after a hundred yards we stuck fast and were reluctantly compelled to admit that there was no future in pushing on over going that got progressively worse.

We managed to extricate the lorry, turned it round and drove back to the village. Someone found an ox-cart which could carry our luggage. The passengers shouldered their personal belongings, rolled up their trousers and strode boldly forward into the lake, whose muddy waters came up to our knees. After we had waded thus for about three miles, the road improved (there was room for improvement), and we covered the remaining five miles to Wuyuan in the highest of spirits.

At Wuyuan, a place of some local importance in the province of Suiyuan, we had a day's well-earned rest. There had been a marked improvement in the weather; the sun shone fiercely, but it was cold at night. I passed the time agreeably enough, strolling round the town, eating Chinese sweetmeats and talking to a young Chinese Father from the Catholic Mission who spoke quite good English. A lorry from the University of Fujen had just arrived from the opposite direction, bound for Ninghsia and Lanchow; the driver decided to take his passengers as far as the inundations, so that they could wade through and take our original lorry on to Ninghsia; he, meanwhile, would convey us to Paotou.

The Chinese Father had a well-warmed *k'ang* and we spent a most comfortable night at the Mission. The *k'ang* is an ingenious combination of a bed with a radiator, in universal use throughout the inns of North China and Mongolia. It consists of a hollow platform made of clay with a network of pipes or air-chambers built into it. The heat and warm smoke from a fireplace (which may be either in the same room or outside it) are drawn into these pipes, finding their way out up a chimney at the far end of the *k'ang*. As a result, the platform retains the heat for a long time, for clay, once heated, is slow to cool. There is little firewood in Mongolia, so fires are generally made with dry grass or dung and do not burn for long if they are not stoked; but a good brisk blaze which lasts only for an hour or two will keep the *k'ang* pleasantly warm all night long.

The road by which we left Wuyuan on October 12th turned out to be in poor shape and it was not until the evening of the 13th that we reached Paotou. Rather surprisingly, however, the journey of a hundred and twenty-five miles had been—by local standards—uneventful.

Reservations had been made for us on the train to Peking. There was a dining-car, there were sleepers; I had forgotten what luxury was like. Thirty-six hours later we reached our destination. A car from the Consulate was there to meet me, and in no time at all it delivered me at the house of an old friend who is one of the foremost authorities in France upon the Chinese and Tibetan languages.

PART TEN

Captured by the Communists

43. EXCURSION TO THE TOMBS

Of all the cities that I have visited Peking is—for me—incomparably the most attractive. In autumn the climate is wonderful. I meant to spend a couple of weeks there, but I stayed for three months. These were the things I especially enjoyed:

Wandering round the poorer parts of the city, surrounded by people less noisy, more orderly and more dignified than their counterparts elsewhere in China. Unforgettable evenings at the theatres, where Chinese classical drama was being played. Rummaging about in the antique shops and the stalls in the markets, where I found rare Chinese books which Orientalists in Paris would have given their eyes for. Visits—tranquil interludes in a mundane *va-et-vient*—to temples and palaces, classically designed and nobly erected, whose glazed tiles blended beautifully with the blue of a cloudless sky. Long walks to the Western Hills, in whose pretty little valleys shrines and pagodas are sited with the inspired precision which underlies the highest tradition of landscape gardening.

But the civil war was closing in on Peking, and before long the city was invested by the Communists. Their troops, obedient to the classical dictates of Chinese strategy, did not surround the city completely; two slender lines of communication still remained in Nationalist hands—the railway to Paotou, leading to Mongolia, and the railway to Tientsin, leading to the sea. Communist forces lay on the flanks of both railways; they could easily have cut them but they did not want a million and a half of their compatriots to starve.

Peking became an island. Outwardly its inhabitants were calm and apathetic; but embers were smouldering under the surface. Anyone who was in touch with the younger generation knew that the secret flame of revolt burnt fiercer every day. Thoughtful people, people who believed themselves to be in touch with reality, had nothing but hatred and contempt for the Kuomintang, with its seedy politicians, its time-serving officials, its army of deserters, its drug-peddling generals, its secret and inexorable police.

For a long time there had been revolts against the tyranny of the Kuomintang. The universities had staged demonstrations; many students were in prison or had disappeared mysteriously. Intellectuals, teachers, business-men, Army officers—hardly any of them Communists—made no bones about voicing, and voicing quite openly, their disgust at the régime in power; they were well prepared to throw in their lot with a new Government, for they knew—or thought they knew—that it could not be worse than the old one. When, a few months later, the Communist High Command decided to occupy Peking, its troops met the minimum of resistance and its officials found plenty of collaborators.

Some time before this happened, however, I embarked once more on the Peking–Paotou Railway. I spent a day round the Nankow Pass, where the Great Wall of China is to be seen at its best; there is something very moving about this immemorial monument to the Chinese capacity for sheer, uncomplaining hard work. Thence I travelled on to Tatung and visited the astonishing caves of Yunkang. There, in the living rock, were the amazing Buddhist carvings whose lovely intricacy I had so often admired in photographs and drawings. Nowhere have I seen better expressed the detachment, the serenity and the mystical fervour—based on a wisdom not wholly of this world—which are the distinguishing marks of Buddhism.

But the caves, which should have been a sacred and inviolable place, offered sad evidence of the indifference to spiritual matters of the Government of the day. They were uncared for, most of the carvings had been mutilated, and everything movable had migrated to the antique shops in Peking.

I had always wanted to visit the Ming Tombs, about sixty miles north of Peking. I mentioned this project to my friends and acquaintances, none of whom suggested that it was rash, ill-advised or untimely (the foreign community in Peking were, not for the first time, only rather remotely in touch with the political and military situation in North China). Madame Marguerite Wu-Morey, a professor in one of the universities who was married to a Chinese and spoke the language like a native, had never seen the tombs and was anxious to come with me; so on December 2nd, 1947, we caught the train at the South Station, taking little more than tooth-brushes with us and telling everybody that we should be back on the following evening.

The railway journey to Nankow, the little station where you alight if you are visiting the tombs, is a short one. It took us, nevertheless, the best part of a day to cover the fifty-odd miles, shivering with cold in a huge cattle-truck, its walls seamed with chinks and its windows devoid of glass. There were sixteen degrees of frost, and the draught-ridden truck was chock-full of hold-alls, chests, household utensils, baskets full of pimentos, crates of ducks and chickens; on top of these sprawled soldiers who smoked, shouted, argued and spat on to the floor the husks of sunflower-seeds or the chewed pips of water-melons.

We were still a long way from Nankow when night fell. There was no light in the truck, and the darkness made the cold seem worse; when the train finally drew in to the station, we were numb with cold.

We had been told that there was a comfortable guest-house near the station. We asked the way to it, only to find that it was occupied by troops and guarded by a sentry with a heart of stone. The whole village, at that late hour, was fast asleep, and it was only after wandering endlessly through narrow alley-ways, getting lost in sinister-looking compounds, tripping over dung-heaps, and beating off attacks by horrible mangy dogs, that we eventually found an old man who took pity on us and with a princely air flung open the door of a draughty shack designated, according to the sign hanging up outside, the Inn of Peace and Prosperity. There were few visible signs of prosperity, but there was, to our great joy, a large *k'ang*. The kind old man quickly got the fire going and we spent quite a reasonable night, roasted on one side, frozen on the other, and more or less asphyxiated by the smoke pouring out of cracks in the *k'ang*, which was as ancient and dilapidated as its proprietor.

We were only five miles from Changpingshao. This is the starting-point of the Sacred Way which leads, for five more miles, to the Ming Tombs, a group of thirteen temples disposed in a green amphitheatre on the side of a hill. Everything was normal in the village, the peasants were going about their work, a few Nationalist soldiers lounged about the streets or sat round big braziers playing cards; they did not seem at all surprised to see us and nobody made any comment when we set off in the direction of the tombs. No guard was being mounted, there were no trenches or barricades: only the odd sentries that you find round every military post. It seemed clear that we were a long way from the front, in a quiet sector where there was nothing to worry about.

The great gates of white marble and red sandstone through which we entered the long avenue leading to the tombs were decorated with very fine bas-reliefs. Beyond them the approach was flanked by enormous statues of beasts and warriors, a worthy bodyguard for the great emperors who were borne along this ceremonial way to their last resting-place in the sacred hills. The place was deserted; the only living souls we saw were two countrywomen carrying big baskets of fruit.

When the double rank of stone animals ended, the Sacred Way ran in a series of capricious zigzags, the idea being to baffle any evil spirits who might be planning to disturb the peace of the Imperial souls. Streams were crossed by little hump-backed bridges, beautifully worked in marble. We were getting close to the hill on which the tombs stand, and already we could see the great flight of steps which leads up to the most important mausoleum. The place had an austere beauty. The slopes were covered with tall cedars and yews whose foliage looked almost black, and the great tombs of grey stone stood out against this funerary background. There was not a sound to be heard, not even the cry of a bird or the buzzing of an insect. Clouds hid the sun. It was as though all the forces of nature were in league to create an atmosphere of mystery, a tranquillity not of this world.

44. LED AWAY CAPTIVE

THE silence oppressed us; it seemed to hold a hint of menace. My companion had not spoken for a long time; it was almost with reluctance that she advanced towards the entrance of the first tomb. I was so acutely aware of her uneasiness that I suggested that we should turn round and take a short cut which would bring us quickly back to the station. But she, not wanting to upset my plans, would have none of this. I must admit that, as far as I was concerned, I was rather attracted by the atmosphere of mystery and hidden danger, so I did not press the point and we went on. Soon, after climbing the great flight of steps, we stood before the entrance to the mausoleum called Changling.

Its high portals gave into a huge, dark chamber, its roof supported by tall lacquered columns. Beyond this we found ourselves in an inner courtyard, a fascinating place where we lingered for some time. The walls were panelled with marble bas-reliefs, and in the centre stood an elegant pavilion of pinkish stone, covered with moss and creepers whose leaves, nipped by the early frosts, were turning gold. Further on, a pair of marble gates led to another pavilion with scarlet pillars.

I was busily engaged in taking photographs when a sudden harsh cry made us both jump. The sound was exaggerated by the silence which had enveloped us for the last hour or two, and it seemed somehow to bring to a head the misgivings which we had both been feeling.

A few seconds later a dozen armed men appeared, framed in the entrance to the tomb, with their sub-machine-guns at the ready. One of them gave a brusque command.

Marguerite understood it and screamed "Put your hands up!" I did so with alacrity, for the posture seemed to me a very reasonable one to adopt when you find yourself, armed only with a Leica and a lady's handbag, looking down the muzzle of a gun. Thereupon the soldiers dashed forward, tore off the haversacks we were carrying and emptied my pockets in a wonderfully expeditious way.

Although it was almost a year since I had been attacked and robbed on the road from Ya-an to Kangting, I now felt that I knew the form pretty well. Assuming that this was another case of banditry, I got ready to remove my clothes in order to spare my assailants the trouble of undressing me. However, to my great surprise, they did not seem to be thinking along these lines and I was able to keep my clothes on—a concession which the presence of a lady, to say nothing of the extreme cold, made me disinclined to underrate.

Better still, after a quick scrutiny had revealed that they included no weapons, all our belongings were returned to us intact, with smiling apologies for the brusque manner in which we had been searched. We realised by now that we were in the hands, not of bandits, but of the Communist Army; and when Marguerite explained to them how my misadventure of a year ago had caused me to draw the wrong conclusions about their status, they all roared with laughter. Then they escorted us out of the tomb and along

ABOVE: *The Great Wall of China*
BELOW: *Chinese roofs in the lamasery of Kumbum*

a little path to a nearby village tucked away in the woodland which covered the sacred hill.

We were taken to a poor-looking house, where a young officer plied us with tea and cigarettes and cheerful conversation. He explained that his unit was part of the Eighth Route Army, the oldest and most renowned of the Communist field formations, among whose exploits was the Long March which ended at Yenan. The village of Changpinshao, where we had spent the night, was in actual fact, despite its garrison's weakness and lack of vigilance, the most advanced Nationalist outpost in this sector. It was almost inconceivable that, during active operations, the sentries guarding such an exposed position should have allowed two foreigners to wander off towards the enemy's lines; but the whole thing was typical of the apathy and indifference prevailing among the Nationalist forces.

When we had exchanged the preliminary courtesies, our host began to interrogate us closely about our reasons for crossing the lines and entering a zone held by the Communists. We explained to him exactly what had happened. He was obviously well disposed and quite prepared to believe us; but, being used to the strict discipline enforced throughout the Red Armies, he simply could not understand how the Kuomintang troops had let us go off into no-man's-land without either stopping us or at least warning us what we might be in for. All the same, I had the impression that the young captain believed in our innocence and would have been quite ready to let us go; but he was under orders from higher authority and said that he would have to send us back to Army Headquarters, which was several days' march away.

When he had finished questioning us the officer suggested that we should return with him to the tombs and complete the tour of them which his men had interrupted. So we went back to Changling, with two heavily armed soldiers as escort. Captain Chang was an intelligent young man, a

A raft of inflated sheepskins, used on the Yellow River

graduate of Peking University and a passionate admirer of his country's artistic heritage; so he made a most instructive guide.

Nevertheless, when we came to the inner courtyard of the tomb, it did cross my mind that all might not be for the best. Stories, true or false, of Communist atrocities—they were always given great prominence in the Nationalist Press—came into my mind. We were, after all, in a sinister and lonely place, completely at the mercy of armed men who had adequate excuse for believing us to be spies, and I could not help wondering rather anxiously whether our excursion to the tombs might not be the prelude to a summary execution. But nothing in the least untoward happened, I was allowed to take as many photographs as I liked and at the end of it all we went back to the village on the best of terms with our captors.

A *k'ang* had been heated for us in a peasant's house, where we slept in a room with a clean earthen floor, looked after by the old lady to whom the place belonged and who slept in an adjoining room. When I went outside I saw that no sentry had been posted to keep an eye on us, and I wondered whether it might not be worth making a bolt for it; we could easily find our way back to the Nationalist lines. We probably stood a fairly good chance of success, but there was always the risk that we should bump into a sentry on the outskirts of the village or that the dogs would start barking and give the show away. Besides, Captain Chang had seemed a decent, straightforward man; he had assured us that we should be released as soon as we had made our explanations to headquarters and we had no reason to distrust him.

I must also admit that I was looking forward with lively curiosity to this new adventure. I had always wanted to get a first-hand impression of conditions in Communist territory, about which nobody seemed to have any reliable information; having got this unique chance of seeing something of Red China for myself, it seemed silly not to make the most of it, even if there might be some risk involved. Next morning, observing the high wall which ran all round the village, the heavily guarded gates and the ubiquitous sentries, we thanked our stars that we had not tried to escape.

The preparations for our journey were complete. The soldiers had found a little donkey for Marguerite to ride; they apologised for their inability to produce a mount for me, but said it would be easy to pick one up further on. We set off along a path which followed the bottom of a ravine. In spite of our optimism we could not help wondering whether all the Communists were going to be as agreeable and considerate as the ones we had met so far.

The hills looked lovely in the clear sunlight of a Chinese winter. Marguerite, unfortunately, was not used to riding and found her donkey something of an ordeal; it was a tough journey for her. Moreover, her knowledge of Chinese made the comments of passers-by only too easy to understand, and they were not at all cheering comments; she was considerate enough not to pass them on to me, so I strode forward full of confidence, delighted to be back in rural surroundings. Our escorts were charming men; they paid very little attention to us and kept on stopping to talk to the peasants, so that if we had not waited for them every so often by the roadside we might have lost them altogether.

The countryside seemed to be perfectly normal. The peasants were working in the fields and appeared to be on good terms with the Communist troops who were quartered in the larger villages. The soldiers, oddly enough, were not playing their usual purely parasitic role, but were helping with the work on the farms as far as their duties allowed; we often passed one pushing a wheelbarrow or wielding a spade. At certain isolated farms, however, our escorts' appearance undoubtedly caused alarm. Women, when they saw us coming, rushed into their houses, yelling to their children and ramming home the heavy bolts on the doors. The age-old distrust of the Chinese peasant for the soldier, whatever colour his uniform or his politics may be, is based on centuries of bitter experience. However, most of the peasants in this part of the country seemed to have come to the conclusion that there really was something different about this new army.

45. LIFE IN RED CHINA

WE spent the nights in little villages, where the best room, the warmest *k'ang*, and the least insanitary quilts were always put at our disposal. After moving for two days along mountain-paths, we came at last to a cart-road, where a farm-cart was requisitioned for our use. We cheered up at the prospect of a less tiring method of progression, but our pleasure was short-lived and we soon found ourselves halted in a miserable village where we had a long wait for a fresh escort.

The atmosphere here was noticeably unsympathetic. The villagers, who took us for Americans, cast hostile glances at us. Nobody offered us a room to sit in, and we had to stay in the middle of a revoltingly dirty street, frozen to the marrow by an icy wind. I sat on a rock and looked forward philosophically to happier days; but Marguerite, who had to listen to all the remarks that were being passed about us, was at the end of her tether; I saw that she was weeping silently and shivering with cold.

At last our escort arrived and we took the road again, worn out, but thankful to be able to walk and get warm.

Without a map or a compass it was not easy to make out where we were going. I tried to keep a rough check on our course with the help of the sun and the stars in case it became necessary to try and escape, but in this mountainous country the lie of the land was so complicated that we could never have retraced our steps, especially if we had had to travel at night. Day followed day on this monotonous march and our guards could not, or would not, tell us how much further we had to go.

We had crossed the provincial frontier of Jehol, and soon we could see in the distance a railway-line which could only be that from Peking to Chengteh, the provincial capital. Occasionally we saw the smoke of a locomotive; the railway would be an invaluable landmark if we did decide to escape. We did not, it is true, feel particularly like prisoners; we were almost always alone and our chief preoccupation was not so much to elude our guards as to avoid losing them altogether, for if we had run into a patrol while wandering along by ourselves, apparently completely at liberty, an awkward situation might have developed.

After several days we found ourselves once more in a zone of active operations and slept one night in a military post in the front line. A young captain lent us field-glasses and pointed out the Nationalist positions a couple of miles away; he also explained, with a wealth of gesture, the unenviable fate which would almost certainly overtake us if we tried to slip across to the enemy lines after dark. Even without his warning, a cursory survey of the manner in which the Communist positions were guarded would have deterred us from trying anything rash. Here there was none of the couldn't-care-less atmosphere of the Kuomintang forces, the idle sentries, the officers who spent their nights drinking or playing mah-jong. Discipline among the Communists, enforced without brutality and based on understanding and good-will, was perfect; the men did their duties well because they knew what they were fighting for. These Chinese soldiers, whom everybody always thinks of as comic-opera figures, had somehow been turned into tough, conscientious men who took their work seriously and did not shirk; they had dropped the happy insouciance and the air of fantasy and caprice which make the Chinese perfectly delightful as companions and practically hopeless as soldiers. All the

Communist troops, from the private to the regimental commander, seemed to be animated by the same faith, the same ideals, the same will to win; I was amazed by the extent to which the new régime had succeeded in altering their mentality.

The soldiers led an ascetic life. No drinking, no gambling, no stealing, no looting. There was nothing to distinguish the officers from the other ranks. All wore the same grey uniform, without stripes, badges of rank or decorations. All ate the same bowls of rice, slept on the same mats, did the same hours on duty; and all drew very nearly the same pay.

Outposts, like the one we spent the night in, seemed to be in a continual state of activity, of which the main object was to raid the enemy positions for arms and ammunition. In the end, almost everything the Americans gave the Nationalists finished up in Communist hands. The Communists captured their small arms and light equipment in local actions (like these raids), while the heavy stuff—tanks and guns and lorries—generally came to hand after a pitched battle, or—even more conveniently—was sold by the Kuomintang generals.

When we explained to the friendly commander of the outpost that our long absence must be causing considerable anxiety to our friends in Peking, he immediately undertook to arrange the delivery of any letters that we cared to write to the French Consulate-General in Peking, and he even provided paper to write them on. There was in fact a regular system of communications between the embattled armies, and agents were always coming in with detailed reports about conditions behind the Nationalist front. Every day peasants drove their carts across no-man's-land with a load of supplies for the Reds, and a Communist outpost was established—in theoretical secrecy—between the two front lines. We accepted the captain's offer to arrange for the delivery of our letters and later learnt that they had arrived with the minimum of delay.

Our own progress was much less brisk, but the long marches were enlivened by incidents which broke the monotony and often shed some light on life in Communist China. One evening, after a hard and bitterly cold stage, we ended up in a god-forsaken little village. At first sight it seemed to be completely deserted, but lights were burning in the biggest of its buildings. Our guards took us there, and we found ourselves suddenly in the presence of the entire population; a meeting of the local soviet was being held.

Everybody was there. Young men, old men, women with their babies clinging to them, all packed round an improvised dais on which sat the principal persons of that place, among whom I noticed several tough and resolute characters.

The audience, tightly packed, wreathed in tobacco-smoke and dimly lit by primitive oil-lamps, presented a fascinating spectacle in a rather Hogarthian style. Our guards introduced us to the assembly in terms which must have been favourable, for everybody beamed with delight and we were given seats in the front row.

But the stir caused by our arrival was quickly forgotten, and the village returned to the discussion of its problems as if we had not been there. Fascinating though these problems were, we were dead-beat and interrupted the proceedings to ask for a place to sleep; the chairman immediately gave orders for a *k'ang* to be heated and a meal made ready in his own house. Throughout our journey we were always given the best of everything. It was not always—it could not be—very good, in a region where the people live largely on millet or salted vegetables; but at almost every halt they gave us rice (a luxury in North China), cakes made from maize or wheat, and ducks' eggs.

I remember another evening when, in a bare, cold room lit only by one smoky oil-lamp, a teacher, sitting on a mat on the floor, taught a group of illiterates how to begin to read the Chinese characters. His pupils were not little children.

The teacher, who had already done a full day's work in the local school, regularly took a night-class for the adults who were busy during the daytime—farm-workers, soldiers and young people who combined both functions.

I questioned some of these people, using Marguerite as interpreter; they were clearly delighted at the opportunity of talking to foreigners. They all said how wonderful it was no longer to slave away in order to pay the money-lender or the landlord but to work, instead, for one-self and one's family. They seemed obsessed with the idea of bettering themselves, of building a new world, which was a new and unexpected attitude to find in a race as sceptical, selfish, egotistical and materially-minded as the Chinese.

Twice we stopped for a whole day in a village and had a chance to get into closer contact with the people. We were quartered in their houses, and it was natural to mix with them and talk to them. Marguerite, who spoke idiomatic Chinese, was soon on the best of terms with everybody, especially the women, and we had only to do some small service for our hostess, or for her children, to set everybody's tongue wagging affably. We learnt a good deal in this way and formed the impression that—even allowing for the people's fear of being denounced and their indoctrination with propaganda—they were, on the whole, in favour of the new régime.

Whenever the Communists got control of a district, the first thing they did was to dispossess the larger landowners and distribute their property to the worker-peasants, on the basis of four *mou* (roughly two hectares) for every member of the family; this did not make the peasants rich, but it gave them a chance of making a livelihood. The process was, of course, unfortunate from the point of view of the landlords, but in the past their rapacity and the inhuman manner in which they had exploited their tenants had been so notorious that they got little sympathy. I met one or two of these dispossessed landlords; they had simply reverted to being ordinary peasants and were tilling the small-holding which they had been allowed to keep.

One thing that the older women did grumble about a good deal was being made to attend technical lectures, sessions of the local soviet and discussions about current affairs. Being practical, thrifty people, they deplored the waste of time involved in leaving their work and going to listen to a lot of talk about subjects which were nothing to do with them. They were also required—it is one of the immemorial inconveniences of war—to put in a certain amount of work for the army. Every woman had to turn out so many pairs of black cloth shoes every month and to knit a certain number of woollies. I often saw them doing this work, and they left me in no doubt that they would rather have done it for their children. Feeding the army, too, was a heavy burden on the peasants, even though the soldiers lightened it by helping in the fields.

This burden is in any case not a new one; there have always been armies to feed in China. The difference today, as the peasants themselves admitted, was that requisitioning was carried out with scrupulous fairness and was no longer tantamount to systematic looting on a large scale. The new ideals of honesty and fair-dealing struck us very forcibly throughout our journey. Theft, for instance, seemed to be practically unknown. It was impossible to tell whether this was due to the fear of exemplary punishment or to a change of heart; the fact remained that nobody did steal and it made a nice change. Time and again, in some little village, we left our belongings and our money in our room without anyone looking after them; nothing was ever taken, and both the peasants and the soldiers seemed to think it odd that we should even entertain the idea of losing anything in this way.

One day we came to a unit headquarters, where we were interrogated for several hours by the commanding officer. His manner to begin with was minatory and disagreeable;

but our frankness and obvious *bona fides* had a mollifying effect and we were soon the best of friends. The fact that one of us was a doctor and the other a professor gave us a certain standing among revolutionaries who were mad about science, hygiene and all forms of culture; we ranked as intellectuals, with almost as good an ideological status as peasants and artisans; the officer even assured us that if we cared to stay in Communist territory they would be delighted to have us.

Only once during our journey did we receive anything but considerate treatment. We had done a long march through the wildest sort of mountain country; the weather was overcast and bitterly cold and snow covered the ground. We were very tired, and when we came to a little village we stopped to wait for our escort to catch up. Some children who were climbing about on top of a bank took it into their dear little heads to start snowballing us, and unfortunately Marguerite, rendered irritable by exhaustion, scolded them rather harshly.

Her thoughtlessness very nearly cost us dear. The children's parents appeared, abusing us and inciting their little ones to retaliate; and before long stones as well as snowballs began to fly. A crowd gathered and was naturally hostile to these two foreigners who had appeared from nowhere. I was cut on the head by a stone; tempers were running high and things looked nasty for us. Just then, luckily, our guards arrived and explained everything, everyone burst out laughing and all agreed that it had been a delightfully ridiculous occurrence.

I knew, nevertheless, that we had been in real danger. The reactions of mobs, and especially Asiatic mobs, are violent and unpredictable. We had been alone, cut off from any help, deep in the heart of a country which is fundamentally hostile to Europeans; it would have been the easiest thing in the world for us to disappear without anyone being any the wiser.

46 SAFE IN PEKING

AFTER travelling, altogether, for twelve days we finally reached the little town in which Army Headquarters were established. It took our guards a long time to find the duty officer. Finally we had an interview with a colonel whose uniform was indistinguishable from that of a private soldier. He gave us tea, cigarettes, a meal, a towel and a cake of soap to wash with, and then installed us in a clean little house.

Two hours later he sent for us again; but by now he was fully briefed on our case and only asked us the obvious questions which everybody had asked us before. He was extremely reassuring and promised us that we should be set free next day.

Now that this crisis in our affairs was approaching we could not help feeling slightly anxious. It is true that we had been treated throughout with great kindness, that nobody had lied to us and that we had always been told that we should be freed as soon as our release was authorised by headquarters; but we were subconsciously influenced by all the anti-Communist propaganda we had heard, and this bred in us involuntary and quite unjustified misgivings. Still, our last day in captivity was both enjoyable and interesting. We wandered round the little town and, having changed our Nationalist currency for notes issued by the Communist bank of Yenan, were able to do some shopping.

Our room quickly became a popular resort of the younger generation. Many students of both sexes were attached to the staff; they talked to us cheerfully and with remarkable frankness. They were all full of enthusiasm, idealism and devotion to their cause, and once more we were struck by this contrast to the normal Chinese temperament.

Many of the students spoke quite good English and chattered away as if they had known us all their lives. They told us how much the Communist Government had already

done in the field of education; several new Universities had
been founded and most of the students—who were the sons
and daughters of poor people—paid no fees and were fed,
housed, clothed and taught entirely at the State's expense.
All these young people had a shining confidence in the
future and were working fanatically to build a new and
juster world. Their unselfishness, their idealism and their
wish to serve the community were a complete contrast to the
money-grubbing self-interest of the Kuomintang officials; it
was, in point of fact, a reversion to the early, unsullied traditions of the Kuomintang, when it, too, was a brand-new
revolutionary movement inspired by Sun Yat-sen, before it
was betrayed into reaction by Chiang Kai-shek and his
clique.

There were several foreign doctors—Germans, Russians
and even Americans—working in the Communist hospitals
as volunteers, and by good luck Marguerite came across a
friend of hers, an American surgeon who was in charge of
the hospital in Jehol. All day long there was a constant
va-et-vient in and out of our room, and in the evening
our new friends took us to dine in their mess. We were
very kindly entertained there, but their fare was as plain
as their uniforms. I was impressed by the number of women
and girls in uniform; they wore their hair short and it was
not always easy to tell them from the men. They did not all
do office work on the staff, but went on active operations
and fought alongside the men.

Early next day we were visited by the friendly staff-
officer. He told us that the authorities had withdrawn the
charge of espionage, were convinced of our innocence and
accepted all our explanations; we should be escorted to the
frontier—unless of course we wanted to stay where we were.

I explained to him the numerous reasons—domestic and
professional—which made it imperative for me to return to
Peking, much as I should have liked to gain a wider knowledge of conditions in the Communist zone. He said that he

perfectly understood and that we could start back at once. The only condition he imposed was that I should hand over the films I had taken in Communist territory, in case they fell into the hands of Kuomintang officers who might be able to learn from them something about the lay-out of the Communist positions. This seemed a reasonable request and I gave him the haversack which contained my camera, films and various odds and ends; he refused to accept it or to examine its contents, insisting that I should merely hand him the exposed films. It struck me as remarkable that throughout our detention by the Communists we were never—except when we were first arrested—searched at all. We had, as a matter of fact, made certain arrangements by which we should have known if our luggage had been gone through when we were not present; but it never was.

We had a meal and then set off with an escort of two soldiers. We were not going to retrace the interminable route by which we had come; we took a shorter way which would bring us to a place called Tangshan, on a sector of the front much closer to Army Headquarters. At the end of our second day's march we arrived after dark at a front-line outpost, where I was once more impressed by the Reds' defensive arrangements, based on a network of well-dug positions. In the command-post an atmosphere of order and discipline was humanised by a certain youthful zest. Two girls in uniform were resting on a bunk while the wireless set crackled importunately; one of them, who was engaged on liaison work, was a redoubtable walker, said to be capable of covering fifty miles in a day.

We now had to cross no-man's-land to Tangshan without being machine-gunned. Two Communist soldiers took us as far as a little village which lay between the lines and where the headman produced two peasants who guided us on until we reached some Nationalist sentries. At first these men would have nothing to do with us and adopted a rather threatening attitude; we began to wonder whether we might not have to go back to the Communist lines. But at last, after a lot of argument, the sentries decided to arrest us and take us to their command-post.

We had a chilly reception and there did not seem to be much future in talking about archæology; I formed the definite impression that we were regarded as dangerous spies. I asked the officer in charge to telegraph immediately to the French Consul-General in Peking; he did so, and we soon had a reply in which the Consul-General guaranteed our *bona fides* unreservedly.

After this we were rather more courteously treated, but it was obvious that, without the help of that telegram, we should not have been given the benefit of the doubt, as we had been by the Communists when appearances were much more against us. We should probably have been accused of spying and might well have been treated with the brutality for which the Kuomintang counter-espionage service was notorious.

As it was, we had to submit to another long interrogation and, when we came back to the room where we had left our luggage, we saw that it had been thoroughly searched and that certain papers—actually of no importance—had disappeared. The Nationalists had welcomed us home in characteristic style.

We spent the night in a big room which also housed about a dozen officers; nobody thought of giving us anywhere to rest in privacy, as the Communists invariably had. There was no question of getting any sleep, for our gallant companions talked, drank and played mah-jong all night; the pile of bank-notes and coins in front of a successful gambler would have kept one of his soldiers in comfort for a year.

About three o'clock in the morning a farcical and unexpected development occurred. There was a tremendous burst of firing outside, and we gathered that the Communists had launched an attack on the outposts. Panic

seized the officers, most of whom were drunk. Two laid
hold of a little chest containing the regimental funds, two
others carried off a bag full of documents, and the whole lot
piled into an enormous American lorry which had drawn up
outside with its bonnet pointing significantly towards Peking.

We, needless to say, were completely forgotten and were
thus able to witness the sequel. The firing soon ceased, the
crisis passed, the money and the archives were brought back
into the office and everybody went on playing mah-jong
until it got light. It was not very difficult to decide who was
going to win the war.

One cannot, of course, judge a régime on the basis of three
weeks spent in a zone of military operations. I never forgot
to make allowances for the propaganda to which we were
inevitably subjected. The authorities, knowing that we were
going to be released, were naturally anxious that we should
take away a favourable impression. I am well aware, too, of
the cruelties practised by the Reds on many of their prisoners
and of the atrocities they have committed against missionaries: though I suspect that in both cases counter-propa-
ganda may have exaggerated the heinousness of their mis-
deeds.

I am myself neither a Communist nor an anti-Communist.
I do not believe that the problems of mankind are sus-
ceptible of purely political solutions, and I am convinced
that spiritual forces are more important than ideologies.
Spiritual things should never be subordinated to temporal
things; but nor, on the other hand, should a veneer of
spirituality be used to whitewash a tyranny, as it sometimes
is. Freedom must never mean the freedom of the strong to
oppress the weak.

There is no doubt that, at the time with which my narra-
tive deals, China was the prey of a deep-seated *malaise*.
Throughout the country there existed—as there existed in
India—poverty on a scale of which those who have not seen

it can hardly form a conception. Thousands of people died every year of starvation, thousands more had to work like slaves to keep themselves precariously at subsistence level; and on all this misery a corrupt government battened and grew rich. What the mass of the people needed was the chance to live, to eat, to keep a roof over their heads. The most urgent task was to satisfy these minimum requirements; the rest would follow later.

Now I had seen, behind the Communist lines, the young people making a real effort to establish decency and justice. They really wanted desperately to improve conditions, to combat poverty, to restore his dignity to the individual, to bring the impulse of altruism into the life of the community. I saw men leading a rough, austere, ascetic life, men who did not steal or drink or gamble, men aflame with a purpose which was not directed at filling their own stomachs or their own purses.

However much people may disagree with the doctrines on which this human experiment is based, however widely they may differ about its consequences for good or evil, I, personally, saw in it an expression of the human spirit from which I found it impossible to withhold my admiration.

ENVOI

Later that day we returned to Peking by train, and shortly afterwards I set out upon my second journey to Tibet. It was, I think, no less instructive and eventful than the one I have tried to describe in this book; but the reader has already borne with me long enough, and this seems a convenient point to invoke a disyllable to whose appearance I fear he may have long been looking forward with impatience and to write—

FINIS